TALL TALE
AMERICA

*A Legendary History
of Our Humorous Heroes*

Walter Blair

Illustrated by
John Sandford

THE UNIVERSITY OF CHICAGO PRESS

Chicago & London

The University of Chicago Press, Chicago 60637
The University of Chicago Press, Ltd., London

© 1944, 1987 by Walter Blair
Illustrations © 1987 by John Sandford
All rights reserved. Published 1944
University of Chicago Press edition 1987
Printed in the United States of America

96 95 94 93 92 91 90   5 4

Library of Congress Cataloging in Publication Data

Blair, Walter, 1900–
    Tall tale America.

    1. Tall tales—United States.   2. Legends—United
States.   I. Title.
GR105.B45   1987   398.2'0973   86-14596
ISBN 0-226-05596-5 (pbk.)

CONTENTS

v

President, *1801-1809—Mike Fink Born in Pitts-
burgh—His Education on the Frontier—He Starts
Keelboating—He Battles and Becomes King of the
Keelboatmen.*

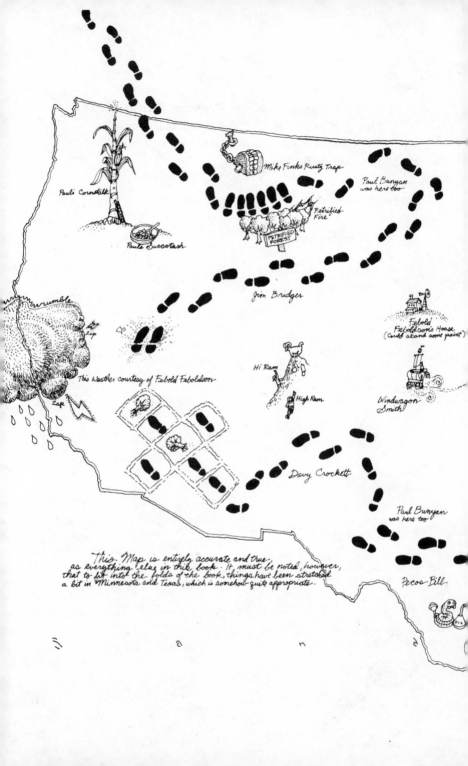

Pauls Cornstalk

Pauls Succotash

This weather courtesy of Febold Faboldson

Zip

Rumble

Zap

Mike Finks Rusty Trap

PETRIFIED FOREST

Petrified Fire

Paul Bunyan was here too

Jim Bridger

Febold Feboldson's House (could stand some paint)

Windwagon Smith

Hi Ram

High Ram

Davy Crockett

Paul Bunyan was here too

This Map is entirely accurate and true, as everything else in this book. It must be noted, however, that to fit into the folds of the book, things have been stretched a bit in Minnesota and Texas, which is somehow quite appropriate.

Pecos Bill

The Pretty Good Lakes

Faucet left on
ooops

The Great Lakes

Appleseed Again

Blair

Cayuga Ridge

Hannibal

John Take

Dan'l Boone

Mississippi River

John Henry

More Mississippi River full of keel boats, steamboats, Sawyers and catfish

Purple Mary

Joe Magarac

Young P. Bunyan

Stormalong

Slick

Appleseed

Mose

Mike Fink

Big Cheese

West Carolina

Rounds

Ocean
(makes for good shorelines; keeps the other continents from hanging on to ours)

Real estate for Yankees

Some of these guys may have moved since this map was drawn; it might be a good idea to check addresses before sending catalogues

1

Overcoming Hardships, America Gets Discovered and Settled

WHEN IT COMES TO RAISING UP HEROES, THERE'S NOTHING under the sun that's as helpful as hardships. This is because the way a man gets to be a hero is by overcoming hardships.

Well, from the beginning, we Americans have had a better stock of snarling, snorting, rock-ribbed hardships than any other country in the world. And that's one good reason why we've had so many star-spangled heroes like Old Stormalong and Davy Crockett and Paul Bunyan and others that made our high, wide and handsome history.

It's clear, then, that our country got off to a flying start when, by good luck, it had such an all-fired tough time of it, first, getting onto the map at all, and secondly, getting settled.

To get onto the map, of course, America had to get discovered, not just for the time being, but so it would last. You can see this if you think a little while about that Norseman, Leif the Lucky. Leif discovered the place all right, shipshape and aboveboard, about the year 1000. But as the fellow says, it didn't *stay* discovered. So it didn't get onto the map.

And so Christopher Columbus had to do it all over again in 1492.

Now, don't think that Christopher did this on purpose. I should say he didn't. Why, he wouldn't even own up that he'd as much as set eyes on the place until he'd been here two or three times and had found that he couldn't wiggle out of it.

There's no blinking the fact that, whatever his good points were, Christopher didn't care a snippet whether ringtailed roarers like Mike Fink and John Henry and Joe Magarac had a country to be heroes of, or not.

What Christopher wanted to do was find the other edge of India, just leaving America off the map and sailing straight through the place where he didn't want America to be. He was in a whirlwind hurry to get to India so people could ship stuff from there to Europe—spice and silver and silk and pearls and the like. And he was downright put out when America turned up there in front of India.

But three things drove him slambang and willy-nilly against our shores.

One was the kind of maps they had in those days. The mapmakers back there, not having traveled enough, had to take a flying guess at all kinds of things. And oftener than not, they guessed wrong.

Take Marco Polo, for instance. He'd traveled around as much as anybody in his day, and he had quite a name as a mapmaker. But he'd never been to Japan.

Well, when Marco tried to draw his map of the world, he drew in the countries, the sea serpents, the giants and the other things that he'd seen with his own good eyes. Mostly, he put them in the right places and got good likenesses—though at times there was a little something wrong about the mouth. But after a while, he stopped and looked at his map and said:

"Say, I haven't put in Japan."

He picked up his quill pen, rolled up his lace cuffs, and started to draw Japan. Then, before the quill got to the paper, he stood up, scratched his head, and said (in Italian, of course):

"But where in thunderation *is* Japan?"

He didn't know, naturally. And being in prison at the time, he

couldn't ask anybody. (If he had asked, he'd have found that they didn't know, either.)

So he shrugged and went ahead and drew Japan several hundred miles east of where, at the time, it really was.

Other mapmakers made mistakes just as bad, or worse. Take the way they figured out the size of the world. Nobody had been around the world yet. Matter of fact, people weren't at all sure,

3

with the sea serpents and such larruping around in the ocean, that you could get around the world.

But those mapmakers had to figure out how big the world was if they were to make maps of it. They'd scowl and add up figures and multiply them. Then they'd say:

"Well, I suppose it must be about two hundred and fifty-two thousand miles around, at least."

Or they'd say:

"I'll just bet it's not a smidgeon more than twenty thousand four hundred miles."

Then they'd draw whichever size of a world they'd decided was proper. You and I know, naturally, that the right size to show would be twenty-four thousand eight hundred and seventy-six miles. But those old mapmakers hadn't had our upbringing and education.

Well, when Christopher took maps like that and tried to steer a course by them, he had a downright good chance of going to a place he was trying his level best to ignore.

The second thing that helped force Christopher into finding our country against his will was the kind of ships he had to use. These were tubby little things called caravels, seventy feet or so long and about a third as wide. What made them go—not too fast, though— was the wind blowing against their sails.

But you couldn't sail them dead against the wind—nobody could. That meant that if the wind was against you, you had a rough old time for yourself. Because you'd have to claw off, and heave to, and jog off, and zigzag all over the ocean, and heaven knows what all, to try to get to where you wanted to go. Then, unless you were a whiz at zigzagging, or unless you were a hound dog for luck, you'd probably wind up at the wrong place.

The third thing that worked against Christopher's plans to snub this country was the kind of things admirals or captains had to do to work out their courses. Even if the wind was right at their back, they'd have oceans of trouble figuring out where they'd been, where they were, and where they'd be next.

Maybe you'll say, "Why didn't they look at the stars?" Well, they did. But you see, they had nothing but a little old-style quadrant to do it with.

What you had to do to work an old-style quadrant was harder than peeling a potato with a feather.

This quadrant was nothing but a quarter circle, sort of like a piece of pie, made out of hard wood. Along one straight edge, there were a couple of pinhole sights. You'd have to stand on the deck of a heaving ship and peek through those sights—both of them—until you saw the North Star. Then a silk cord, with a plummet tied to it, was supposed to hang down over the right marker on the arc.

Right then, on the dot, you were supposed to tell another fellow that was helping you, "All right!"

And right then, not a tenth of a second later, the other fellow was supposed to see where the cord was. But it would be dark as tar out there on the ocean, and mighty hard to see. And the little ship, at this point, would probably be doing a heave or a roll or a swoop, and this other fellow would probably be looking for something to catch hold of.

So he'd probably say, "Sorry. I didn't get it."

Then you'd have to go through all that agony again.

Well, in the end, instead of monkeying around with a quadrant, Christopher sailed by dead reckoning. That meant he'd lay down his compass course and then at dinner time he'd guess the best he could how far and how fast he'd gone that day. Now the compass Christopher used was a little off, and he wasn't too good at figuring up speed, so after he left land, he never knew within several miles of where he was.

Using careless maps of that sort, and cockleshell ships of that sort, and the happy-go-lucky way of sailing he did, first thing he knew, Christopher had bumped all three of the caravels in his fleet smack up against America. No chance to dodge it—there the *Niña,* the *Pinta* and the *Santa Maria* were, nudging up against an island off the shores of America.

Our country had overcome the hardship of getting discovered—this time for good.

That was the start of quite a boom in the discovery business. Discoverers by the dozens kept bobbing around in their tubby little boats and discovering America. Some even went ashore, had a look around, and scared the daylights out of the Indians.

After a time, the place was getting discovered every few months. It was quite the style.

And after a while, America was on every up-to-the-minute map. People all over the world, one way or another, heard about the place. And nobody would give two cents for a map that didn't have this country on it.

The people in England and Holland and France and Germany and Spain, like most people, had homes. At home, they knew where to find things. They knew the neighbors and the shopkeepers. They had families near by, to visit now and then. No wonder, then, that these people—most of them, anyhow—thought well of home as a place to live in.

But if America was to get settled, and was to raise up a mess of heroes like those this history tells about, thousands of people would have to leave their homes. What's more, they'd have to pack up everything, take long trips in those zigzagging old sailtubs, bother along the way about never knowing where they were, then, after landing, they'd have to set up housekeeping in the middle of a lonely forest full of Indians and wild animals and weather. It was a stunner of a hardship for America to overcome.

How did she do it?

For one thing, the discoverers helped. After they'd come home from their trips, of course they wrote books, the way discoverers do. And since nobody else knew enough about America to check up on them, these discoverers had plenty of room to use their fancy. What they wrote was a caution.

More than two-thirds of the lies they told weren't true at all.

They said America had the best climate in the world—not just Florida and California—but the whole country had the best climate. One old man, for instance, wrote:

"You know, back in *old* England, I had to wear two suits of heavy underwear and an overcoat all the time. But in *New* England, I go around in thin clothes even in the wintertime. Feel fine and warm, too." (This old man took a bad cold and died the winter after he wrote this, but you can bet that, in his book, he didn't say a word about *that*.)

As good a story as any in these books came out of some talk an old Spaniard named Juan Ponce de Leon had with some Indians. These Indians didn't think too highly of Juan Ponce de Leon, because he was sort of careless with his guns, and he had a dog named Berezillo who was such a fierce Indian fighter that he drew full soldier's pay and rations.

Well, the Indians told the old boy that if he'd just go to Florida (taking his dog, Berezillo, along with him) he'd find a Fountain of Youth.

"Just bathe in this fountain," they said, "and you'll drop off years at the rate of two years an hour."

So old Juan Ponce de Leon tottered over to Florida and sloshed around in every creek, spring, pond or mudpuddle he could get into, while Berezillo stood on the shore and guarded his clothes. Though he didn't have much luck, the old fellow pointed out that there were a good many ponds and such he still hadn't tried.

Therefore, the discoverers started to say in their books that there was a Fountain of Youth down in Florida.

Those writers also got into the habit of saying that in America grain and vegetables and fruit grew to be ten times as big as in the old country, and that they tasted twelve times as good. They'd go on to point out that sheep over here were as big as cows in Europe, that frogs were as big as year-old babies, and that other birds and animals were built to scale. They'd tell in their books that no one dared to go fishing over here with less than two boats, for fear he wouldn't have room for his catch.

But when they got around to writing about gold and precious stones, the discoverers really hauled off and told themselves some whoppers. Because there was more gold than copper in this country, they said, if you took a little copper along to America, you could buy yourself three times as much gold to take home.

And, "Why, man," one of them wrote, "in that country, all their dripping pans and ash cans are gold, and they put gold chains on all their prisoners. These Americans go out on holidays and gather up a bushel or two of diamonds and rubies on the seashore. Then the children hang these jewels on their coats, or stick them on their caps, or play marbles with them."

But it's likely that even these stories wouldn't have tempted many people to go into the settling business if it hadn't been for the way things were in the home countries at the time. Times were bad, and prices were high, and money was scarce, and there wasn't enough religious freedom to satisfy some people. All that—and the discoverers' books—made America look mighty good.

So people started to zigzag over here to settle—shiploads of them from England and Holland and France and Germany and Spain. And a good many of them brought along a few bushel baskets, to take to the seashore on holidays.

And pretty soon a good part of America was settled.

2
Captain Stormalong, the Revolution and Clipper Ships

EVEN AFTER THE EASTERN SEACOAST GOT PRETTY WELL settled, it was some time before America raised up any first-rate heroes. At the start, the heroes we had to make out with were fellows like old Miles Standish in New England and John Smith down in Virginia.

Miles had learned something about the hero business when he'd been a soldier in the Netherlands. But over here, when it came to popping the question to a girl name of Priscilla, the best he could do was to ask another man to do it for him and then to sneak out for a nice quiet afternoon fighting Indians. And, in a stand-up fight, Miles couldn't lick more than four Indians at a time.

Captain John Smith was a little more promising. Before coming over here to settle, he'd practiced up by serving in two or three armies. In Tartary, he'd bested a Bashaw. At the siege of Regall, simply to give the ladies watching the rumpus a little treat, he'd slain three Turkish champions.

The ladies everywhere gave the captain quite a name as a rip-snorter—Lady Callamata in Tartary, Lady Tragabigzanda in Turkey, Madam Chanoyes in France, and others elsewhere. John could hardly go for a walk without saving the life of a beautiful damsel, or having one fall heels over head in love with him. (He told all this himself, so it's known to be true.)

But he didn't pan out much better in this country than Miles did. When the Indians made John a captive, the only way he could get free of them was by doing tricks with a compass or a blunderbuss. And if he didn't have a compass or a blunderbuss on him, twenty-one medium-sized Indians could handle him handily. And once, you'll remember, when he was about to get whacked by an Indian chief named Powhatan, a little bit of an Indian girl named Pocahontas had to save John's life by draping herself across the poor fellow's neck.

The trouble with Miles and John, though they meant well enough, was that they were imported heroes. Almost always, in America, the homegrown brand has made more of a name for itself.

It wasn't until the days of the Revolution that any homebred heroes with much style to them came along. There were quite a few at that time—the Minute Men, Paul Revere, Moll Pitcher, Betsy Ross, Ethan Allen, George Washington and others. I want to tell now about one who isn't in most histories, though he was a humdinger.

This was Captain Alfred Bulltop Stormalong. He was a sea-going Down East Yankee—a sailor in the days when wooden ships and iron-muscled men, under clouds of sails, flew over the seven blue seas and made quite a splash.

The story of Stormalong proves a point that was made a while back—that when it comes to raising up heroes, there's nothing that helps so much as a mess of snarling, snorting, rock-ribbed hardships.

Where Alfred was born nobody knows for sure—some say Kittery, some say Kennebunkport, some say Nantucket. It seems fairly safe to guess that maybe he was either born in one of those places or someplace else.

Wherever it was, at that time the land there, like the land in a few other parts of New England, wasn't quite first-rate farming. The weather didn't help overmuch. Winter froze the place up from

October to June, with the snow fluffing up over the tip of the steeple of the First Congregational Church on the northeastern corner of the village commons. The summer breezes were on the brisk side, that is, they blew the pinfeathers off of the Plymouth Rock hens. And the fieldstones were middling thick, that is, the farmers found that the sheep couldn't get at the grass between the stones unless someone sharpened their noses.

What's more, the country was still sort of wild. It seems that, according to the census, there were sixteen thousand nine hundred and seven wild animals residing in the township. Foxes, weasels, muskrats and skunks had an unhandy habit of sneaking into the pens, flipping chickens or ducks over their shoulders, and streaking home for dinner. Wolves waylaid the sheep. Bears paid calls on the livestock, and after they'd gone, if you counted up the lambs and the calves, you'd find that some turned up missing. Blackbirds and crows pecked the young corn, and if they left any corn to ripen, black and gray squirrels would nip away with that.

Well, because of these hardships, a good share of the Down Easters in those parts went away to sea. Among them was Alfred.

One morning in Ogunquit, the owner of the trim schooner called the *Silver Maid* was signing up hands for a voyage. The *Maid* was going to take a cargo of furs and hides and ginseng to China and then was coming home with a cargo of silks and spices and tea, so he wanted a crew that could step lively.

The owner looked up from his desk and saw a fellow standing there, about a fathom long.

"It seems my name is Alfred Bulltop Stormalong," says the fellow, "and I sort of think I want to be a cabin boy."

"A tall fellow like you?" says the owner.

"Well, I think maybe I'm a smidgeon too big for my township. And maybe I'm a mite overgrown for my age."

"How old are you?"

"My folks say that I'm twelve, sort of going on thirteen."

"Well, that's about the right age for a cabin boy, sure enough. Are you hale and healthy?"

"Middling," Alfred told him. "I calculate that I can crack a coconut with one hand, if I can get a coconut. I can fling a salt mackerel a few feet farther than any young one in the township, they tell me. When it comes to swimming, I'm as slick as an eel in a keg full of oysters—pretty near. I'm not considered sickly, by most people, that is."

"I see. But maybe you're a farmbred boy that can't learn to tell a mast from a poop deck. Any of your folks sea-going people?"

"We-ell, a few of them—just a few. Old Adam Stormalong, they say he helped Noah build the ark and then he helped to steer it in the flood. Then there was Ulysses Stormalong, that folks claim was a master-mariner on a galley. Lief Stormalong, so I've heard tell, he was captain on a Viking ship; Antonio Stormalong was reported to be a mate on a caravel; and Lord Percy Stormalong, the family Bible says, was an admiral in His Majesty's navy. There may have been one or two others. Oh yes, there was my daddy, Luke Stormalong; he was said to be one of the first skippers to scoot a bark around Cape Horn."

"I guess your folks weren't exactly land-locked," the owner said. "You might do pretty well." And he signed him up as a cabin boy.

They started their trip with a chantey. It went like this:

> *Up aloft this yard must go,*
> *So handy, my boys, so handy!*
> *Oh, up aloft from down below,*
> *So handy, my boys, so handy!*
>
> *We'll hoist it high before we go,*
> *So handy, my boys, so handy!*
> *And when it's up, we'll leave it so,*
> *So handy, my boys, so handy!*
>
> *Stretch her leach and show her clew,*
> *So handy, my boys, so handy!*
> *A few more pulls to bring her through,*
> *So handy, my boys, so handy!*

The sails caught the wind, and the *Silver Maid* moved to sea.

That trip, Alfred learned a good share of the things he had to learn to what his initials stood for—an A.B.S.—able-bodied seaman.

He learned to take salt pork, jerked beef, lobscouse and coffee sweetened with molasses as a steady diet.

He got so that by looking at her lines and her rigging, he could tell—quicker than you could say "Davy Jones's Locker"—whether a vessel was a ship, a bark, a barkentine, a brig, a brigantine, a schooner, or a clipper.

He got the hang of swarming up to the crow's nest, holding fast to the bowsprit in a squall, and reefing a sail in a blizzard.

He found out the way to talk the seagoing lingo—not to call a forecastle a forecastle, the way landlubbers do, but a "foaksl." He got so he called a cross-jack a "cro-jick," a studdingsail a "stunsl"—things like that. He even learned to call a spritsail topgallant sail a "sprisltiglnsl"—which no one *can* do, ordinarily, unless he's got some salt water running in his veins.

He took lessons in tying sailor knots. And that led to his doing the first thing that won fame for him.

The *Silver Maid* was scudding along one day under full sail, just scudding and lurching along over the billowy waves, when all of a sudden—it stopped.

The pans in the cook's galley jerked away from their hooks and clattered in a clutter on the floor. Some Jack Tars scrubbing the deck went skidding along until they could grab a mast or a deck fitting. And three sailors that had just come off watch and started to take a snooze plunked out of their bunks.

The white sails bellied in the wind. The masts and spars creaked. But the ship stood still as a picture.

Some of the history writers who have told about this affair say that an octopus caused the trouble. Well, that's wrong. An octopus couldn't stop a schooner that way.

Everybody on board—even the cabin boy—knew what was the trouble, quick as a wink: either a Kraken had laid hold of the keel with his tentacles, or a Remora Monster had fastened onto the bottom of the vessel with his suckers. And there was no telling when the plaguy rascal would let go. Remora Monsters had been known to hold onto a vessel until everyone aboard had got powerful hungry, and Krakens had been known to hang on until everybody aboard had starved.

The captain trotted around, wringing his hands and carrying on. "What'll we do?" he moaned.

Nobody answered. But Alfred flung and kicked off his clothes, then dived into the ocean.

After he'd been under the water a minute or two, there was a big welling and swelling of waves under the ship that banged around those loose kettles and pans in the cook's galley. Then there was another, and another, up to the number of ten.

Then, after the tenth heave, the *Silver Maid* gave a jerk and started kiting along over the water again.

When they looked aft, the crew saw Alfred Stormalong bob out of the ocean, sputter, take his bearings, and start swimming after the *Maid*. He overtook her quicker than you could say "Mother Carey's Chickens," grabbed a rope, and pawed his way aboard, hand over hand. He was panting a little when he stood dripping on the poop deck.

"What was it?" the crew asked him. "How'd you handle it?"

"Well," said Stormalong, "it appeared to be a Kraken, but I guess perhaps I fixed him. I tied a different kind of a sailor knot in each of his ten tentacles—a Figure-of-Eight, a Reef Knot, a Half-hitch, a Bowline (I mean a Bo'-ln), a Sheepshank, a Black-wall Hitch, a Stunner Hitch, a Cat's Paw, a Becket Bend and a Fisherman's Bend."

"Wasn't that all-fired hard to do?" they asked him.

"I suppose it was middling hard," Stormy told them. "I had to kind of hold my breath, and there were a few sharks and whales and such that kept more or less bumping into me, and the Kraken wasn't what I'd call helpful. I tend to the notion that he may not be able to stop many ships for a while."

"How'd he take it?" the crew wanted to know. "Did he get snorting mad and rare and tear around?"

"There's a bare chance, from the way he acted," Stormalong told them, "that the fellow was just a wee bit peeved."

When this trip was over, the captain told Stormalong he could sign as an A.B.S. for the next trip, even if he was only thirteen. (He'd had a birthday off of the coast of China, you see.) But Stormalong had grown about a fathom, so he told the captain:

"Well, thanks just the same, but maybe I'm a smidgeon too big for this schooner. Cramps my style a bit, I suppose. Maybe I'd better look for one a mite bigger."

It happened that while Stormalong had been on this voyage, the Americans had started the Revolutionary War.

Patrick Henry had yelled, "Give me Liberty or give me Death!"

Paul Revere, the well-known Boston silversmith, had gone galloping through the night, howling along the way, "The British are coming! To arms!"

Ethan Allen had taken Fort Ticonderoga, which the British had hardly thought he was likely to do.

George Washington had kissed Martha good-by and had gone north to be a general.

The Liberty Bell had rung, rung for liberty.

And Paul Jones had decided you couldn't win a first-rate war without a navy.

Therefore, Paul had got together a navy of three full-rigged warships and a school of privateers, and now he was enlisting sailors. Stormalong took a look at the commodore's ship, the *Poor Richard*, figured it might be big enough, and signed up as a sailor.

When the ships put out to the sea, the sailors sang:

> *Ye Parliament of England,*
> *Ye Lords and Commons too,*
> *Consider well what you're about,*
> *What you're about to do.*
> *For you're to war with Yankees,*
> *Who know you'll rue the day,*
> *You roused the Sons of Liberty,*
> *In North Ameri-kay.*

Stormy helped Commodore Jones take the American Navy to Whitehaven and led all hands ashore to set fire to the shipping there. When he galloped around, waving a torch over his head, he scared His Royal Lordship, the Earl of Selkirk, out of his periwig, his monocle and his boot buckles.

Then the time the American fleet fought the British fleet off of Flamborough, Stormy was right helpful.

When the *Serapis*, the head ship in His Majesty's Royal Navy,

came along toward the *Poor Richard*, a nice polite voice hailed:

"What ship is that?"

And Stormy answered, just as polite, "Well, maybe if you came a little closer you might find out."

"What's your cargo?" came another yell from the *Serapis*.

"I guess we've got a cargo of round grapeshot," Stormy told them, "and maybe there's some double-headed shot somewhere aboard, likewise."

By that time, since the two ships were close enough to fire a volley, they did so. And it was with this first volley that Commodore Jones and Sailor Stormalong had a touch of bad luck. For three of the starboard guns on the *Poor Richard* burst all to smithereens at the first firing. Next thing they knew, there was a big hole in the *Poor Richard*, and the British guns kept pouring in eighteen-pound shots.

"Wouldn't be surprised if we were in for a little trouble," Stormalong told the Commodore.

Then Stormalong heard water gurgling, had a look below, and came back to report. "There's a fair-to-middling chance we're sinking," he said. "There's a hole that's middling big down there— about big enough for a whale to swim through if he's a mind to. Maybe if we could close with them and get on board the *Serapis*, we could fight a mite better."

"Good idea," Paul hollered out. "You steer her."

So Stormy steered the frigate until she ran her jib-boom between the enemy's shrouds and mizzen vane. There was a banging and splintering sound, and Stormy yelled:

"We're pretty near there!"

"Well done, lad!" Commodore Paul told him. "Now throw on board the grappling irons and get ready for boarding."

Stormy lashed the ships together, and Paul and he and the rest of the crew leaped onto the *Serapis*, swinging whatever they could lay hands on. It seems safe to guess that when the British sailors saw Stormy prancing around in the moonlight, waving and shooting off a medium-sized cannon, they were disturbed, not to say nonplused.

"We have just begun to fight," yells Paul, above the noise.

"We sort of think perhaps we'll do a snippet more of fighting," yells Stormy.

Which they did. And after a while the *Serapis* gave up, along with another enemy ship that the rest of the American fleet hadn't got around to sinking yet.

When Stormy and Paul got back home, they found that Washington and the other generals, as well as the Minute Men and the Continental Congress, had won on land just as they'd won on sea. Washington had set off for Mount Vernon to tend to his crops, and Paul and his navy had worked themselves out of a job.

"Don't worry," Paul told Stormy. "I've got an offer from Catherine the Great to be an admiral in the Russian navy. You can come along and be a captain. I'll be Paulimir Joneski and you can be Captain Stormalongovitch. What do you say?"

"Well, thanks," Stormy told him, "but I'm afraid maybe I'm a smidgeon too big for those Russian frigates." (He'd grown another fathom or two while in the navy.) "I've a notion that I may possibly build me a vessel of my own that's middling big."

Sure enough, the clipper that he built in the course of the next thirty-three months was sort of roomy. For lumber, he used hackmatack, white pine and fir from the North; yellow pine planking and live oak from the South; red pine from the Far West. There was a lumber shortage all over the country after that for two years.

The six masts were so tall that one man with good eyesight couldn't see to the top of any of them: it took five. These tops of the masts had to be hinged, so they could be bent down to let the moon and the sun go by. The whole kit and caboodle of the Boston sailmakers had to be shipped to the Sahara Desert, so they'd have room to sew the sails.

The *Albatross*—for that was old Stormy's name for her—was as pretty a clipper as any you'll see, too, for all her size. With her sharp floors, heavy drag, deep draft, low freeboard and fine lines, she made a sea-going man's mouth water just to look at her. Painted handsomely she was, too—had dark green topsides, and a red-white-and-blue band from her stem to her stern. While the seven hundred and eight painters were putting paint on her, old Stormy had a fine idea that other ships took up later on: he had the deck fittings painted white, so they could be seen at night and a body wouldn't stumble all over them.

She was the fastest sailer up to that time on the seven blue seas. She could beat champion clippers like the *Witch of the Wave,* the *Staghound,* the *Lightning,* the *Herald of the Morning* and the *Comet*—beat them singly or two at a time.

It took ten mates, a thousand hands, and three hundred and four white horses—besides old Captain Stormy—to sail the *Albatross.* They used the horses to get around the decks, and old Stormy felt that white ones were more shipshape than others. Even a horse, though, couldn't get from the forecastle to the poop deck without taking a breather. And even with horses, about eighteen sailors were likely to be late for mess every time it was served.

As a rule, it took thirty-three seamen to manage the wheel, but old Stormy, having got his full growth now, could whirl the wheel with one hand and fan off a school of flying fish—and their school-teacher, too—with the other.

Stormy used this clipper of his for a number of things. He took cargoes in her to India, China, Russia and other places. There was some trouble, though, almost every trip he took. Reason was that no harbor was big enough for the *Albatross,* and the only way he could get her unloaded was to have a fleet sent out to take her cargo ashore.

Old Stormy never took her to England but once, on account of the way she nearly got stuck in the English Channel. The minute old Stormy had a chance to size up the channel, he knew it would be a tight squeeze. Thinking fast, he yelled out:

"All hands get out there and soap her sides. Step rather lively, men, or there's a chance there may be some trouble."

So they frothed up the sides as fast as they could, in the hope that she'd be slick enough to slide through the Channel. She was, too, only she really leaned up against the black cliffs of Dover. When they got through, the men looked back, and saw that the cliffs had scraped off all the soap on the starboard side of the *Albatross*. Those cliffs were as white as a whale's belly—still are, as a matter of fact, to this day.

Well, after all this trouble with harbors and cliffs and such, and after a law had been passed that said the *Albatross* wouldn't be allowed to try to go through the straits of Gibraltar, old Stormy started to use her almost entirely for whaling.

By that time, the great days of whaling had come along. People used whales for whale oil, for perfume and for stays. The oil made lamps burn; the perfume—which came from ambergris—made a body attractive; and the stays, from the whale bone, were used in some things which were called corsets that women wore back then.

Old Stormy took to whales from the start—both right whales and sperm whales. Since a whale weighed about thirty times as much as a full-grown elephant, he figured that there was an off-chance that here was an animal that might be able to give him something of a tussle. And some whales could.

Everybody in the whaling business was glad old Stormy got into it because, in time, he figured out some new dodges in whaling that were pretty good.

In the whaling business, in other words, old Stormy showed more of this know-how stuff than he'd ever shown before, maybe because he'd finished growing up and could do some branching out. At any rate, there are plenty of signs that he really began to use his thinkpiece.

Now of course, he'd shown promise along this line from the start. He'd been clever to think up that way of handling the Kraken, for instance, back there on the *Silver Maid*. And that had been a very smart idea he'd had about tying up to the *Serapis* when the *Poor Richard* was sinking. But it was chiefly on the *Albatross* that he showed he had good sound horse sense as well as a fine brand of Maine strength.

Once, for instance, after thinking and thinking, he said:

"The reason people put out in small boats may just possibly be that big boats can't get close enough for the harpoon throwers. Now if I can throw a harpoon far enough, I reckon there's a bare chance that we may be able to get the *Albatross* close enough."

Up to that time, nobody, no matter how hard he grunted, had been able to throw a harpoon more than five fathoms. Well, old Stormy he practiced and practiced until he learned to fling one twenty-five fathoms—straight, too.

After that, the sailor in the crow's nest, on sighting a whale, would howl, the way he was supposed to:

"There she blows! Bl-o-o-ows! Bl-o-ows!"

A little later, he'd yell, "There goes flukes!"

Then, instead of lowering a boat, which was the usual thing, they'd scoot along in the *Albatross* until they were twenty-five fathoms away from the whale. Stormy would have his harpoon all ready by that time, and he'd give it a fling and hit the mark. Then, whether the whale made a run for it or not, he'd pull the beast in, just as easy as if it was a sick mackerel.

Another time, old Stormy, after a think or two, said: "Why do whalers tow the whole whale in to shore, the way they do? All they want, mostly, is the oil, the perfume, and the bones, seems to me."

This mate he was talking to looked at him sort of funny and said: "But you can't get the oil out until you get the whale to the try-works on the shore."

"Well," old Stormy said, "maybe if we had some try-works with us on the ship, we might possibly save ourselves some travel."

Before long, old Stormy had built up some try-works right there on board the *Albatross*. So instead of pulling a whale ashore every time they got one, they'd fry out the oil and stow it away in barrels. That way, they could go all the way around the world without harboring.

Though the other whalers couldn't copy that idea about throwing the harpoon so far, they could copy the one about the try-works. And first thing you knew, all the whalers had try-works aboard and were sailing around the world without harboring.

With these big try-works aboard, for the first time in his life old Stormy could have meals cooked up the way he liked them. For a starter, he'd have himself some whale and shark chowder served up in a Cape Cod boat. Then he'd have ten whale round steaks, hot off the griddle, served to him as fast as ten sailors could rush them to him in wheelbarrows. Then he'd drink a vat of Maine cider through a fire hose. After dinner, he'd pick his teeth with a marlinspike.

"Makes me feel almost healthy to live the way I'm living these days," old Stormy would be likely to say, after a meal like that. "Here on the *Albatross*, I don't feel cramped, to speak of, the way I did on the *Silver Maid* and the *Poor Richard*. And it seems to me that there's a chance that I'm getting pretty nearly enough to keep body and soul together. If I keep aboard this ship, and if I keep having that kind of grub, it's barely within reason that I may possibly, just possibly, live a fairly long time."

And as almost always, Captain Alfred Bulltop Stormalong was, in a way, just about right.

3

Jonathan Slick, Southerners, Dutchmen, and Daniel Boone

WHILE OLD STORMY WAS HELPING PAUL JONES AND GEORGE Washington win the Revolution, and while he was working up new wrinkles in whaling, people in different parts of the country—the Yankees of New England, the Quality Folks and the Poor Whites in Virginia and Carolina, the Pennyslvania Dutch, and the Frontiersmen of the Back Country—came to be as different from one another as a wooden nutmeg, a dueling pistol, a corn crib, a dumpling and a coonskin cap.

This was one of the main things Jonathan Slick found out when he climbed into his peddler's cart and went jangling and jingling all over the country. Jonathan was a Yankee like Stormalong, except that instead of going to sea, he went to see the country.

The Yankees were different partly because they were cantankerous, partly because there wasn't enough good meadow farmland to go around. In meadowland farms, the soil was as rich as anybody would want. But there were too many uplands where the stones were as big as haystacks and as thick as pebbles on the beach, and where the land was so hard that you could sow seeds in it only by shooting them into the soil with a gun. If you weren't careful, you might find that you'd used all your profits to buy gunpowder.

23

Since only part of them could farm, many Yankees went to be sailors, while others made money by being the sellingest people in the world. They could peddle anything—a ton of ice to an Eskimo or a warming pan to a South Sea Islander—at a good price, too.

So a lot of them came to be peddlers—Johnathan Slick, for instance.

Jonathan was born in Slicksville, just about the middle of Down East. Neighbor Scrooge, who owned and ran the general store, kept his eye on Jonathan from the start and soon saw that Jonathan was an up and comer.

"By the time he was seven," Scrooge told people, "he'd saved up two dollars and twelve and a half cents out of his allowance for sugar plums. At eight, he was earning fourteen cents a day for riding the horse that led the oxen in plowing, over on Deacon Goodrich's farm. At nine, he was peddling molasses candy, ginger-bread and cherry rum at country fairs—got good money for 'em, too. And at ten he was a clerk in my general store, where he could strike a better bargain than many a grown man."

By the time he got his growth, Jonathan was as lank as a leaf-less elm and as slick as a trout. He had a hawk-bill nose, a hatchet face, a mind as sharp as a razor, and he'd saved every penny he'd ever earned in his life.

So he set himself up as a peddler.

He swapped a good-luck horseshoe, a ball of twine, and a fishing pole for a pair of lean horses. Then he bought a blue and yellow peddler's cart and a peddler's stock at a bargain. The peddler's stock was what he aimed to peddle—bright colored ribbons, tops and Barlow knives for the children; calico cloth with red, green and blue flowers on it, glistening jewelry and gleaming tin pans for the women folks; and shiny knives, sparkling razors, Seth Thomas clocks and a few other things for the men folks.

Then he loaded his cart, hitched up his skinny horses, told the family good-by, and started his drive over the bumpy country roads. A piece down the pike, when Neighbor Scrooge saw him passing, Scrooge hollered after him:

"Remember, son, sharp bargains make fat purses."

Jonathan always kept that in mind. In New England, he never sold much, since he figured that Yankees were too keen for him to make the profit he could other places. Out beyond New England, though, he'd string the bells on his cart, whistle "Yankee Doodle," and keep an eye open for customers. And after a few years on the road, he could give most any man a head start and outswap him.

Take the time he came riding into a town not far from Albany, New York. He wore a bell-shaped white hat, a light green coat, yellow nankeen britches that just came down to his calves, and a pair of boots that he'd got from a bootmaker in a swap for a cobbler's awl. The sun was shining on the tin pans on his yellow and blue cart, the bells were tinkling, and Jonathan was feeling as chipper as a squirrel.

Then a fellow came running out of a house, had a look at Jonathan, and yelled at the top of his voice:

"Run for your li-ives! Here comes a Yankee!"

Jonathan pulled up and looked at the fellow. "Why do you holler a thing like that, mister?" he asked.

"We know Yankees in these parts," the man sort of growled. "They sell wooden nutmegs, mahogany hams, cloth full of sizing, and clocks that won't strike. They play Yankee tricks, and cheat a man out of his eyeteeth." Then he raised his voice and howled again:

"Run for your li-ives!"

"Well," Jonathan said to him, "some Yankees may be a little too sharp at a bargain. But a man like me that gives good values doesn't have to cheat to make a living. Now here's a razor, bright as the morning star and so sharp it'll shave the hair off of a hair. It's worth four dollars, but since you're a man that knows a bargain, you may have it for two."

"I tell you," the fellow told him, "I don't want any of your trash, so you'd better be going."

"Well, now, I declare! I'll bet you five dollars if you make me an offer for that razor, we'll have a trade yet."

The fellow squinted a little and looked sly. "Done," he said. And he put the money into the hands of a man that had come up to listen.

Jonathan put up five dollars, too, and said, "Well, make me an offer."

"Now," said the fellow, quick as a flash, smiling from one ear to the other, "I'll give you two cents for it."

"Well," Jonathan said, "you do drive a sharp bargain, I'll vow you do. But it's yours." So he handed over the razor and took the two cents—and the bet.

It wasn't until then that the fellow managed to figure out what had happened. The smile faded from his face like the breath off a razor; he looked mighty glum, and the crowd that had come to watch was laughing at him.

"Oh," said Jonathan, "don't look so sad! I calculate a joke's a joke, and if you don't want that razor, I'll trade back."

The fellow looked happier. "You're not such a bad chap after all," he told Jonathan. "Here's your razor. Give me the money."

"There it is," Jonathan said, as he took the razor and passed over the two cents. "A trade's a trade—and now you're wide awake, I'll tell you what Squire Scrooge says: 'Sharp bargains make fat purses.'"

And away he rode, with the razor and the wager, while the crowd doubled over with laughing.

After Jonathan came home from a trip, his stock gone but his pockets full of money, he'd have stories a-plenty to tell about his travels. Jonathan's father, Phineas Slick, his mother, Debby, the eleven Slick children, and some of the neighbors, would sit around the hearth fire in the kitchen to drink a mug of cider, eat a few fine winter apples, and listen to Jonathan's talk.

Soon as everybody was settled and comfortable, just to get things started, Phineas said: "Tell us again what places you went on this last trip, son."

"I went through the Middle States," Jonathan told them, "then on down into the South. At Charleston, I got a new stock that came by boat. Then I came back, a different way, to Slicksville."

The company started asking questions. First, they wanted to know what kind of people lived in the South.

Well, Jonathan said, most of the people there weren't much different from most folks in New England, except for little things, like the way they said "I reckon" instead of "I guess" or "I calculate." The slaves were just like those up North, except that there were more of them, and they did other kinds of work. But there were two kinds of folks in the South that were different.

The Quality Folks, for one, were different. They were all descended from Cavaliers, so they claimed, and they wouldn't think of letting anything but sky-blue blood flow through their veins. They lived in great white houses in the middle of whopping big farms— plantations, they called them. The trees on the lawns were all so old they appeared to have gray whiskers. A fellow that owned such a place was likely to be named Colonel Randolph Pinckney Lee, or

Byrd Izard Mumford II, or something gaudy and handsome like that.

A thousand slaves said, "Yes, massa," and took care of the crops; a coal black mammy took care of the chillun; and Mistress Lee or Mistress Mumford took care of the slaves and the coal black mammy. The grown men among the Quality Folks went to horse races, wore red coats and rode horseback to chase little foxes, danced, ate, drank, visited one another, lost their red-hot tempers, and fought duels.

"They any good at a bargain?" asked Neighbor Scrooge, from over in a dark corner of the kitchen.

"The more a thing costs, the better they like it," Jonathan answered back. "If they can't pay enough for things here, they send over to Europe for 'em."

"Hum," Neighbor Scrooge said, "Thought not."

The other kind of people that were different, Jonathan went on, were the Poor Whites—called sandhillers, hill-billies, wool-hats, conches or other names—depending on where they lived. Everywhere they stayed in log cabins or tumble-down shacks. They liked to lie in the sun; to eat hawg jowls, hominy grits, turnip greens and corn pone; and the only thing they liked less than work was more work. The men wore calico coats, jean pants, hickory shirts, and yarn suspenders. The women wore linsey-woolsey dresses shaped like potato sacks. The children wore anything left over (which wasn't much), always went barefoot, never went to school, never washed.

For the first time, Jonathan's little brother Elijah looked excited. "Sounds good to me," he said.

"Lije!" Mrs. Slick said. "Don't say such things!"

Jonathan told how he came up to a hill-billy once, sitting on a barrel in front of a rotten shanty and playing a sad tune on a fiddle. When Jonathan came along, the man didn't say hello—just sort of grunted.

"Could I get lodgings here for the night?" Jonathan asked him.

"Nope," the hill-billy said. "It'd be too much work, and we ain't got as much as a dust of corn meal to eat, and it might rain."

"Why haven't you any food?"

"Too much work."

"What difference would it make if it rained?"

"There's only one dry spot in the house, and my wife Sal and I sleep on it."

"Why don't you fix the leaks on your roof?"

"It's been raining all day."

"Why don't you fix them in dry weather?"

"Roof don't leak then."

So Jonathan left him, still playing that sad tune on the fiddle, and had a time of it getting to the next town by sunset. Jonathan said that this man was a sample of the Poor Whites, except that he seemed to have more energy than most, since he was playing a fiddle.

"How are they at a bargain?" Mr. Scrooge wanted to know.

"Haven't anything to bargain with."

"What worthless folks!" Mr. Scrooge said, and he clucked a little.

"Now tell us about those Pennsylvania Dutchmen," Jonathan's father said. "I tell you, Neighbor Spriggins and Deacon Goodrich, they're a caution."

"Well," Jonathan said, "first thing you notice is miles of pasture-land, with cows on it so round and shiny that you have to look twice to make sure they're not big pumpkins. And the barns, I'll swear, I never saw such big ones—look like churches—bigger than the houses, they are. And the outsides are all prettied up with curlicues, all painted blue and yellow like my peddler's cart."

"Do tell!" Neighbor Spriggins said. "Could I have just a touch more of that fine cider? Thank ye kindly. I hear tell the houses are made out of stones."

Jonathan said that was a fact. Instead of building stone fences and wood houses, the way Yankees did, these Dutchmen built wood fences and stone houses. Another thing, instead of having two chimneys apiece these Dutchmen's houses had one big chimney apiece. Then he went on to tell how the haus-fraus (which was what they called the women) almost drowned the floors sloshing them clean with soap and water.

"Some folks claim," he said, "that they paddle around so much that they get webbed feet, like ducks."

At that, Jonathan's sister Susan opened her eyes wide. "My stars!" she said. "Do they for a fact?"

"I dunno," Jonathan told her. "Never saw one with her shoes off."

Fat old Deacon Goodrich broke in. "Let me have another of those fine winter apples, please. Thank ye kindly. Tell us what they eat, Jonathan."

"They eat outlandish things, and that's the truth of it—sauerkraut, dumplings, scrapple, doughnuts, liverwurst, smearcase, apple fritters—truck like that you never heard tell of."

"Well, I wouldn't like that kind of vittles," Deacon Goodrich said, and he crunched his apple.

"Tell about the women's clothes," Mrs. Slick said. "Mrs. Spriggins and Mrs. Goodrich, you'll hardly believe him."

So Jonathan told about the way the women dressed—how they wore so many petticoats of linsey-woolsey that their dresses puffed out like a pincushion, how they wore these great huge pockets in their dresses. "I heard tell," he said, "that when a woman loses something in her pocket and has to empty the pocket to look for it, what she takes out fills two corn baskets to overflowing." He said the haus-fraus wore scissors and keys hung to their belts on brass chains, and these jingled about when they moved like the bells and the tin pans on a peddler's cart.

"Any good at a bargain?" Neighbor Scrooge broke in.

"Tolerable good," Jonathan let him know. "They keep track of their pennies."

"Too bad," says Neighbor Scrooge.

Everybody sat quiet for a while then, crunching their apples, sipping their cider, watching their shadows dance on the walls, and sort of mulling things over.

"Strange thing," Neighbor Spriggins finally said, "the more you hear about these people around the country, the more you see that none of them come up to Yankees. Their houses aren't so good, for one thing."

30

"Or the vittles," Deacon Goodrich said, making a sour face.
"Or their clothes," Mrs. Slick put in.

"Well, I don't know about that," Lije told them. "Take those hill-billies, why—"

"I told you not to talk that way, Lije," Mrs. Slick said.

"They don't come up to Yankees, do they, Jonathan?" Neighbor Scrooge asked him. "I mean in the way of bargaining, of course. You wouldn't swap places with any of them, would you, son?"

"None I've seen," Jonathan said. "But I haven't been to every part of the country, you know—just every part except the Far West. Come next spring, I'm going to hitch up my cart, start my bells jingling, and head straight for Kentucky."

It was then that Prudence Scrooge, Neighbor Scrooge's daughter, said the first word she'd said all evening. She'd been sitting right close to Jonathan, and taking in all his words. Now she spoke up to say: "Land's sakes! We had a notion maybe you'd seen enough, and aimed to settled down in Slicksville for a while. What makes you want to go there?"

"Is it the Indians?" asked Lije. "Want to shoot some redskins?"

"Well," Jonathan answered them, "I don't exactly know why I want to go out there. I guess maybe that it's this—that what I've heard tell of the West makes me sort of puzzled. People out there don't seem to be rich, like the Quality Folks; without get up and gumption, like the Poor Whites, or even foreign, like the Pennsylvania Dutch. Down South, there was a fellow that told me about one of them named Daniel Boone, and if the rest are like him, I can't make them out."

"What puzzles you so about this Boone fellow, son?" Jonathan's father asked.

"Far as I can figure it out," Jonathan said, "he liked to get away from everybody. But if you do that, I can't for the life of me see how you can swap or make good bargains. It's powerfully puzzling, don't you think?"

"Well, suppose you tell us about him," says Jonathan's father.

So Jonathan told what he'd heard about Daniel Boone.

Daniel had seemed to take more to hunting than to bargains from

31

the start, Jonathan said. In school, he'd got so provoked that he'd tripped up the master, "I need elbow room," he'd said. "Going to be a hunter."

"*That's* no puzzle," Lije said. "I wish——" But his mother hushed him up, and Jonathan went on.

So at an early age, there Daniel was in the woods, a long way from any other humans. And his father and mother, seeing how much talent he had for hunting, moved into the woods to live with him. "Hope nobody else comes," Daniel said, "I need elbow room."

"Didn't he even want a wife with him?" Prudence Scrooge wanted to find out.

Well, yes, in time, Jonathan told her, but it was a queer sort of a courtship. A few years later, Daniel was out hunting in the dark forest at night. Seems that it was his way, on the blackest night, to take along his torch and his gun and shoot any panther or deer or the like that came along—shoot him square between the shining eyes.

That night, he saw these two bright eyes sparkling in the torch light. "By gum, a deer!" says Daniel. But when he raised his rifle, something went wrong. His knees got all trembly, and his heart did flip-flops.

"Oh, Jonathan!" Prudence broke in, "I hope he didn't shoot!"

No, he didn't, Jonathan said. And when he got closer, he was glad, because these eyes, he saw, were the eyes of a beautiful girl. "You're pretty as a fawn," says Daniel, after they'd made themselves known to one another, "won't you marry me?"

At this point in Jonathan's story, Patience heaved an oversize sigh.

After the girl did marry Daniel, Jonathan went on, Daniel and Mrs. Boone moved away from Father and Mother Boone, moved out into the deepest and farthest part of the forest—all alone. But soon, when someone came along to settle within a mile of them, Daniel said, "Too crowded—too crowded! I want elbow room!"

So he moved again.

But people kept following. Therefore, Daniel kept making longer and longer searches for places where no one was likely to follow. He got into Kentucky once on one of these trips: he was the first white man to see that country. Wild things were behind every tree in the thick woods, and wild pigeons flew like gray clouds across the sky. Well, he liked the loneliness so much that he stayed there for several months, alone, before his wife and babies joined him.

They stayed in one place for a while out there, liking the quiet, bothered only by Indians. But it seemed that Indians weren't any bother for Daniel. If they tracked him, he'd throw them off the trail by swinging on grapevines. If they tried to shoot him, he'd wait for the flash of the powder, then dodge the bullet. If they captured him (as they did three or four times) he'd manage to escape.

So Indians weren't any trouble—or wild animals either, for that matter. But when white folks settled within a mile— "Too crowded!" Daniel would yell. "I want elbow room!"

Then he'd start another hunt for a place where he wouldn't be pestered. He went down from the Alleghenies into Tennessee, and traced the Cumberland River. He visited Ohio; he found the head-waters of four great rivers. Maybe he even went to Yellowstone Park.

In the end, when he was an old man, he said, "I want elbow room," and went into the wilds of Missouri. He died there, at a deer lick, with a gun in his hands, waiting for deer.

"A strange man," said Jonathan. "I can't understand why he never wanted anybody within a mile of him to strike bargains with. I'd like to see whether other Westerners are like him, and I guess that's why I'm going out to Kentucky—to find out."

Patience Scrooge sighed another of those big sighs, and her father said:

"I wonder whether those Westerners are any good at a swap after you once run them down. Sharp bargains make fat purses, you know."

4
Mike Fink,
King of Mississippi
Keelboatmen

THAT SPRING THAT JONATHAN SLICK PLANNED TO GO WEST, HE didn't.

It turned out that, unbeknownst to him, Patience Scrooge had set her cap for him. First thing he knew, she'd worked him around into popping the question. And when Jonathan went to ask her father for her hand, the way they did in those times, Neighbor Scrooge said it looked like a good bargain to him and offered Jonathan a partnership in the general store.

So they were married. And Jonathan did well in the store, just as you'd expect.

That was the spring, as far as I can make out, when, for the first time, a president was sworn into office in the brand-new capital named Washington, D. C.

You see, a few years after Stormy had helped win the Revolution, the people had made themselves into a new nation named the United States. First they'd elected General George Washington president, then they'd elected John Adams, Esquire, and then Mr. Long Tom Jefferson.

Meanwhile, General Washington had hauled off and heaved that dollar across the Potomac, to see where the capital ought to be, and

34

then they'd started to build it there. By 1801, it wasn't quite finished. "But," says one of the politicians, "all we need are some cellars, kitchens, houses, men, women and streets, and it'll be quite a place. Let's move the government here anyhow."

So they did. And in March, Mr. Jefferson put on one of his oldest suits of clothes, just to show he was one of the folks. Then he walked from his boarding house through the mud up the hill to the brand-new Senate chamber, took his oath of office, and started to run the country.

And though Jonathan wasn't going West that spring, plenty of Americans were. Yankees from New England, Quality Folks and Poor Whites from the South, Pennsylvania Dutchmen, people of all sorts from every part of the country, were going West. They went afoot, in covered wagons, in stagecoaches, on flatboats and keelboats—any old way so they got out there.

Going West was all the rage.

And, as they moved through the green forests, this spring of 1801, some of them were singing:

Come, all you young men, who have a mind to range,
Into the Western country, your fortune for to change;
For seeking some new pleasure we'll all together go,
And we'll settle on the banks of the pleasant Ohio.
   So it's Westward Ho,
    Away we'll go,
And we'll settle on the banks of the O-hi-o.

Come all you lovely girls, wherever you may be,
Into the Western country, where sky and air are free;
If you will card and spin, we'll plow and reap and sow,
And we'll settle on the banks of the pleasant Ohio.
   So it's Westward Ho,
    Away we'll go,
And we'll settle on the banks of the O-hi-o.

That was the spring when a well-known Ranger named Mike

Fink, who'd been settled in one spot out West longer than it pleased him, started his first trip on a keelboat down the Ohio and Mississippi Rivers.

From the start, it had been as plain as the nose on an ugly pig's face that Mike was going to be a hero. He had about as fine a mess of rock-ribbed hardships to fight as anyone you could think of. Another thing, he made it his lifelong habit, after he'd worn one batch of hardships down, to get into a line of business where there were new ones.

Mike was born in Pittsburgh, right on the edge of the Indian country. His home was a log cabin of the type then in style, so he started out life the hard way.

You may remember that being a baby is, at best, a dratted nuisance. There are these women that keep lifting you out of your cradle, and talking foolishness to you in horrible cooing voices. There are these men that keep holding you the wrong way and rubbing your tender little face with their scratchy whiskers. The grub is tiresome, too—milk, milk, milk, and nothing else—until you think that if you have to drink any more of that junk, you'll turn into a calf. Then there's the boresomeness of not having anything you can do except wave your arms and legs around, and cry, and say "Goo" and such nonsense. Well, being a baby in a log cabin, the way Mike was, was even worse, because on top of these troubles, he had others.

In the daytime, the cabin was dark because the only light was a dim gray beam that came into it through the greased paper pane in the window.

At night, the place was dark and damp and creaky and cold.

And all the time, the cabin, inside, was drafty and smoky and full of soot.

Even in his cradle, with everybody doing their best to make things pleasant, Mike wasn't what you'd call comfortable. The only mattress he had was stuffed with oak leaves and cat-tails that had been dried in the sun. Such a mattress wasn't exactly soft, and it rustled so that it'd wake him up when he wiggled around in his sleep. The bedclothes were bearskin and deerskin that scratched a body. So Mike was mighty glad, I'd guess, when he got grown up enough to spend the days and some of the nights outside the cabin.

Soon he had a real boy's clothes—tow britches and a roundabout for summer, and a linsey coat, a wool cap, mittens, and a pair of old knitted stockings with the feet cut out to pull over his shoes for the winter.

You might think that Mike's troubles were over now. Some of them were, but, as was his habit, he found some new ones. What his father and mother did was start him doing a few little chores around the clearing right away, so he could earn his keep.

First thing in the morning, he had to pull, husk and silk enough Indian corn for breakfast. Some time during the rest of the day, he had to hoe the garden, split and haul in wood for the fireplace, clean the candlesticks, fetch water from the spring, feed the stock, go to the mill, churn, and grind the corn into meal at the hand-mill.

On a rainy day, he rested; all he had to do was use his jackknife to carve ax helves or to make split-brooms and scrubs out of hickory saplings.

On top of that, besides sleeping, he had to get the kind of learning a boy needed in the backwoods.

He had to learn to tell when the ice on the rivers would hold you up—whether it meant anything serious or not when it started to make cracking noises. He had to learn to tell directions by looking at the moss on the trees, in case he might get misplaced in the forest some time.

He had to learn to make noises like every beast and bird in the woods. It was a handy thing to be able to gobble like a turkey, because that way you could bring a turkey into shooting range. Or if you could bleat like a fawn, maybe a deer might come running to see what the trouble was. Another thing that made it useful to know how animals or birds sounded was this—that Indians might use such noises to signal one another at night out under the black trees. In such a case, it paid a body to know the difference between a redskin and just a varmint.

The chores he had to do, and the things he had to learn, gave

Mike plenty of troubles, you see, until he came to the age to have a gun.

Around Pittsburgh, every boy that was old enough, and every man, whether he was old enough or not, had a rifle. A rifle in those days would be about six feet long. It would be a forty-five caliber flintlock, and it would have silver trimmings on its stock. It would be slicker than a wildcat and quicker in action.

And Mike had to learn to shoot his rifle, so he could take his turn at the loop-hole in the fort, and so he could shoot a redskin or a varmint if either of them got cantankerous. From the start, it was clear that Mike was made for a gun and a gun took to him like a cub bear takes to its mother.

At seventeen, when he'd grown as far up as he was going to but not as wide across, he saw this sign on the tavern walls:

DAVID NEAL OFFERS A FIRST-RATE BEEF, WORTH $11, TO BE SHOT FOR AT HIS FARM, AT 25c A SHOT, NEXT SUNDAY, 1 P.M.

On Sunday, Mike got out to the Neal Farm on time. They'd built a fire, and the men were holding some boards close to the blaze.

"What's that for?" Mike asked. "You're getting those boards as black as a hunk of coal in a dark cave."

"Of course we are," David Neal answered back. "When a board gets black, we put a piece of paper in the middle. We put a cross on the paper. Then the place where the lines cross is the bull's eye. Now you go home and bake johnny-cake, knit some mittens, and tend the truck patch."

These things were what little girls had to do, so Mike began to boil a bit.

"I think I'll stay," says Mike, "and I think I'll win beef with my shooting. How many prizes are there—or don't you know?"

"Everybody but a baby knows that," says David, sort of sneering. "There are six quarters, so there are six prizes, of course. Make the best shot (which you're not likely to do), and you win the hide and tallow. The second best wins one hind quarter of the beef; the third best wins the other; the fourth best wins one fore quarter; the fifth best wins the other, and the sixth best gets the lead in the tree where the targets are hung. Maybe if there were twenty prizes, you might have the luck to win one, but there are only six. So go home, baby, and tell your mamma that a nasty old hoot owl scared you in the woods."

"Thunderation!" Mike thundered. "Give me the paper and take my money, for my wrath is up and I aim to shoot! What's more, I aim to win five prizes, for I've money enough to shoot five shots."

On the paper that he grabbed from Mr. Neal, "Mike Fink," he wrote, "puts in 5 shots. $1.25." Then he reached in his pouch, gave the farmer the money, and went to the fire to char his target.

"The shots are all taken," David Neal told the men. "Now the judges can take their posts by the tree where we're going to put the targets.

"I'll pace off sixty yards to the north—so." (He took the paces.)

"Now," he went on, "I'll mark the line with a log—so." (He laid down the log.)

"And now," he ended up, "I'll call your names in the order you wrote them down. Then each of you can take as many shots as he paid for." (He started to call the names.)

Then these Pittsburgh men began to shoot. They were tip-top shots, nearly all of them. At forty paces, they could hit a nail square on the head and drive it into a tree. In the darkest night, at fifty paces, they could make the light of a candle flicker but not go out—snuff the candle, as they called it.

Now, shooting at these black targets with the pieces of paper in the center, almost every man of them said after he'd shot, "I ate paper!" That meant he'd put a bullet somewhere in that white paper dot. Some came powerful close to the bull's eye.

But Mike paid them no heed. He got his target board nice and black over the fire, then, finding he had a little time, he molded himself some bullets.

Finally Mr. Neal yelled, "Mike Fink's next! Now, do you still want to shoot, young one, or do you want to save your lead from being wasted?"

"I aim to shoot," says Mike, "and I aim to drive the center of the cross on every shot. My eye's as keen as a snake's, and when Bang-all and my shoulder get together, the Finks will get first-rate beef at low prices." (Bang-all was the name of his gun.)

This made David Neal kind of wrathy. So he said to Mike, "You couldn't hit the side of a barn if the door was swinging. See here, for each quarter of that beef I've put up that you win, I'll give you another quarter of beef free. But if you win none, you'll have to bake the johnny cake, knit the mittens and tend the truck garden on my farm for a week, since my little girl's too grown up for it. Have I called your bluff, sonny?"

"Where there's no bluff," Mike answered him back, "there's none to be called. I'll take that bet, and I'll take that beef. For Bang-all can't miss the bull's eye when I aim it, and that's gospel."

Standing over by the log, Mike loaded his rifle. He held a bullet in the cup of his hand. Then he poured powder in until the bullet was covered. After he'd wiped the powder into his charger, he dumped the charge into Bang-all.

"It's all over but the shooting," Mike said, as he toed the log. "Tell your farmhand to slaughter another beef."

Five times he shot, and everybody could see that he ate paper every time—maybe he even bit the bull's eye. And when the judges had studied all the shots, Mike's and the rest, the head judge said:

"Fry me for a crawfish! Mike's won the first five quarters!"

David Neal came up to Mike. "You won fair and square," he said, "and here's my hand on it. You rile a man with your tall talk, but you sure as shootin' can shoot."

"It was a good day for me," Mike said, shaking hands. "Every day's a good day for Mike and Bang-all, though, when they get together."

After that, he stood and thought a minute. Then he said:

"I want to say one more thing at this time. The next man that calls me baby or sonny is going to fight me, rough-and-tumble. I can outshoot and outfight any man in Pittsburgh, at any time, at the drop of a hat."

"Come on and get your beef," says David Neal, running his arm through Mike's. "Come on—Mr. Fink."

From that time on, whenever they had a shooting match in those parts, they'd give Mike first prize free, to keep him from shooting and winning *all* the prizes.

Not much later, Mike joined up with the Rangers. The Rangers were scouts that went snooping into the Indian country to find out what shenanigans the redskins had afoot.

Mike would spend days in the middle of the forest, living on whatever game he could kill and whatever berries he could pick. At night, before he went to sleep, he'd snake over to the edges of the redmen's camps so he could listen to their talk. A Ranger didn't have any place to sleep except out in the open, and as a rule it was a danger to have a fire. So when it rained, Mike got soaked, and when it snowed, he like to froze.

As is well known, this way of living is very good for a person— if it doesn't kill him. And to improve his health even more, now and then Mike would join some other Rangers in fighting a tribe of Indians, fists, guns, hunting knives and tomahawks.

Well, by 1801, Mike was in such good shape that he could start to work on a keelboat, where there were even more hardships than there were in the Ranger business.

Understand me, everybody that got out West those days had to be tough. You couldn't get West, let alone live out in the forest and lick Indians and varmints and other hardships, unless you were tough. But some were tough, some were tougher, and some were toughest.

The toughest would be the keelboatmen.

You see, everybody was in a hurry, those days, to get into the wild country out past Pittsburgh. One good way to get there was by going down the Ohio and Mississippi Rivers.

To do that, maybe you could go on a flatboat—a big old lumbering affair like a great big box that didn't have to do much of anything but drift along with the current. That was easy enough, of course. People that took the trip that way would loll around, taking things easy, and first thing they knew, they'd be in Kentucky or Tennessee, or wherever they'd planned to go.

All they had to do was follow these few simple rules:

1. Eat enough and sleep enough to keep alive on the way.
2. Don't get eaten up by mosquitoes or bears.
3. Keep from falling into the river.
4. Keep your flatboat from being stove in by hidden rocks, sandbars, planters, sawyers, wooden islands, and snags.
5. Don't let your boat turn upside down, especially when you go over falls.

6. Don't let any Indians or river pirates capture you and your boat.

You can see that was easy as pie. Keelboatmen did that all the time, and went ashore every night and licked everybody they could get to fight between Pittsburgh and New Orleans, just to keep their muscles from getting rusty. If they couldn't find anyone to lick, they'd dance, the way they said in their songs—

> *We'll dance all night,*
> *Till broad daylight,*
> *And go home with the gals in the morning.*

Maybe, to top this off, they'd put in the next day dancing, too. While they drifted downstream, some old codger of a boatman would scrape away at his fiddle, and the keelers would bang their feet on the cover of the boat. And to show their breath was sound, they'd sing, while they danced:

> *The boatman is a lucky man,*
> *No one can dance as the boatmen can;*
> *The boatmen dance and the boatmen sing,*
> *The boatman is up to anything.*
>
> *Hi-O, away we go,*
> *Floating down the river*
> *On the O-hi-o.*

And at times, they'd decide they weren't going fast enough, just drifting the way they were. So they'd row their keelboat, while they sang together:

> *Hard upon the beach oar!*
> *She moves too slow,*
> *All the way to Shawneetown,*
> *Long time ago.*

Those were the ways the keelboatmen kept in shape for what was a man's work on the river—making a keelboat go upstream.

43

Upstream, that's what I said. Flatboats, they were chopped up for lumber when they'd drifted to their stopping place. But a keelboat had a keel and rode high in the water just so it could go up the river as well as down. After they'd drifted down to New Orleans, the keelboatmen unloaded their boats, then took on new cargoes and upstream passengers. Then they went upstream.

There's no secret about the way they got those heavy boats to go up the rivers against the current: they used sheer muscle. That's why a keeler ate four pounds of bacon a day, besides some venison, bear meat, fire-baked potatoes and hoe cake. That's why any boatman worth his bacon licked everybody he could get to fight. He ate and fought that way so he could get enough power to lick the river. (Besides, he liked to eat and fight, of course.) For licking the river was a whopper of a job.

Take just one day Mike and the rest of the crew put in on that first trip upstream. This was above Natchez, where the going was fair-to-middling rough.

The day started off with a spell of rowing. The men sat up there in the waist of the boat and skimmed their oars over the water. Then they sank their oars deep into the river, stood up, and pulled so hard that the handles bent. They did this over and over at a smart lick. After an hour of this, they were all pretty much of a froth.

"Ship oars!" yelled the captain, who was steering.

"Whew!" Mike said. "I'm glad that's over! Now do we get some rest?"

"A few minutes," another boatman, name of Jabe Knuckles, told him. "We rest a few minutes every hour. Looks to me like the next thing we'll do will be some bushwhacking."

"How do you bushwhack?" Mike asked Jabe.

"You just grab hold of those bushes along the shore, and drag the boat along that way," Jabe told him.

Sure enough, after a short rest, they bushwhacked a while. Then they ran out of bushes. Then—

"We're over a sandbar," the captain let them know. "Man your poles!"

44

Mike knew how to pole, for he'd done it before. They got great strong long poles, and took their posts on the running-boards that ran the length of the boat. Half the men had posts on the port side, half had posts on the starboard. What they did was set their poles at the bow of the boat, then put the sockets against their shoulders. Then they started to push for all they were worth, almost bent double. After they'd walked to the stern, pushing this way all the while, they hurried back to the bow and did the whole thing over again.

"Push, mannee, push!" Jabe yelled to Mike.

"Jabe," says Mike, "I'm bent so low my nose is likely to pick up splinters until it looks like a porcupine. I'm pushing so hard that I know, without looking, that two or three of you loafers are loafing and leaving the job to me."

After an hour or two of this, they came to a place where the water was too fast for oars and too deep for poles.

"What'll we do now, for heaven's sake?" Mike asked.

"Cordelle," Jabe told him, wiping his wet face with his bandanna.

"What's that?" Mike wanted to know.

"You'll see," says Jabe.

"Fix the rope to the mast top!" yells the captain. After that was done, he called out, "Now waddle ashore, mannees, and step lively!"

So they went ashore, and shortly Mike found that "cordelling" meant nothing but pulling that big boat along with a rope. With twenty men all tugging like fury, they scrambled over the rocks and through the water, dragging the boat and her cargo. A few hours of that, and the keelers were able to sleep fairly sound that night, even though they were as wet as water snakes and even though the mosquitoes were as thick as the scales on a carp and twice as big.

Of course, it wasn't this hard all the way back from New Orleans to Pittsburgh. Sometimes, when there was wind enough, they sailed the boat, and everybody took things easy. But a good share of the time, the only way to get the keelboat upriver was to row

45

her, pole her, bushwack her, or cordelle her along—and that was work, sure as sunrise. Four months it took to get her from New Orleans to Pittsburgh.

Back in Pittsburgh, though, after his first trip, Mike Fink looked as if the trip had been good for him. The sun had baked him brown as an Indian, and his muscles were as hard as rocks. He wore the butternut britches, the red shirt, the blue jacket and the leather cap that showed he was a keelboatman and that therefore he was spoiling for a fight.

When he walked down the street, he thundered a song that said:

> *When the boatman goes on shore,*
> *All men run when they hear him roar;*
> *But I never saw a girl in all my life*
> *Who didn't want to be a boatman's wife.*
>
> *Hi-O, away we go,*
> *Poling up the river on the O-hi-o.*

"Me for a keelboat," he told the family. "I mean to take a thousand trips like that, fighting men all the way down the river and fighting the river all the way back. For a rough-and-tumble ripsnorter like me, there's nothing like it."

He meant it, too. After a few trips, he went up in the business. Soon he was head poleman, then he was steersman, and finally he was patroon, which was what keelers called a captain. Of course, by this time, he was wearing the red feather in his cap that showed he was the best man, either in a fair fight or rough-and-tumble, on the crew. A patroon had to be.

Even that didn't satisfy him. He wanted to be the head man of the two whole rivers, the Ohio and the Mississippi, as well as all the rivers and creeks that ran into them. So he started out as fast as he could to lick the champion of every crew on the rivers.

A fight those days out West wasn't like a fight other times and other places. People didn't just square off and start trading punches. They had more respect for a fight than that. So first they

46

had a little ceremony, with speeches. The speeches were for the men to tell, in their nice modest way, how good they were.

First, the champion of the other boat would stick out his chest and tell it by shouting:

"I'm a ringtailed roarer, a wild horse and a buffalo. I tell you, I'm a tornado, a cyclone and a snag all rolled into one, and fight's my middle name! I fight against all creatures, human and inhuman, Christian and Injun, white, red, black, and parti-colored. Foot and hand, tooth and nail, knife, gun and tomahawk, or any other way you choose to take me, I'm your man! WHEE!"

Then Mike, who had been standing there and noticing the good points of all that fine talk, would strut around and tell how good *he* was. He'd sing out, as loud as he could:

"I'm a regular screamer from the Ohio, the Mississippi and all the streams that run into them! I can strike a blow like a falling tree, and every lick I make in the woods lets in an acre of sunshine! WHOOP! I can out-run, out-shoot, out-brag, and out-fight—rough-and-tumble or fair play, any man on the rivers from Pittsburgh to New Orleans and back again. WHOOP! Come on and see how tough I am! Haven't had a tussle for two whole live-long days, and my muscles are as rusty as an old hinge! Cock-a-doodle-do!"

When he said "WHOOP," Mike made like a boathorn, and when he said "Cock-a-doodle-do," he made like a rooster, of course. Everybody said it was just perfect—couldn't be improved on.

Well, after this was all over, it was time to start.

And they'd fight, and fight, and roar around, and pant, and grunt, and snort. Then they'd fight some more. You never saw such fighting outside of a battlefield.

Then after a few hours, Mike would be on top, and the other fellow would be on the bottom, rather worse off than he'd been when they'd started.

"Say uncle!" Mike would tell him.

"Uncle!" the fellow would whisper, if he had breath enough.

Then Mike would help him get up, and would carry him, tender as a baby, over to his bunk. "There, there," he'd say, "you put up

47

a good fight, for a poor little old tornado that was up against Mike Fink—a right good fight. Wouldn't have missed it for anything, and I'm much obliged to you."

The list of men Mike outfought would be longer than a whale's nightmare.

There was a fellow named Dick Hanna who, on a bet, had bested a bear, barehanded, near the Big Sandy River.

There was the sheriff down in Westport, Ned Taylor, a little crawfish of a fellow who was hard to get at and lick because he'd lie down on his back and fight with his feet.

There was big Peter Cartwright, the leatherlunged preacher, who could fight just about as well as he could preach.

There was a hard-headed flatboatman, name of Jack Pierce, who used his head in something like a billy goat's way; that is, he just butted the fellow he was up against.

There were a few more—something like one hundred and three or two hundred and seven, at a guess.

After a while, by whopping all the other champions, Mike had won so many champion's red feathers that he didn't dare put them all in his hat at one time, for fear he'd be mistaken for an Indian. He won a name for himself, too—King of the Keelboatmen.

And all this time, since his fights kept him in such good shape, he was doing wonders in the keelboat business. Everywhere you went along the river, you'd hear talk about Mike Fink.

"There's nobody like him," people would say. "He can load a boat single-handed, from stem to stern, in less than half an hour. He can turn a boat around on a dime, float her on a drop of dew, pole, row, cordelle, or bushwhack her upstream without any help. And he can outrun, out-shoot, out-brag, and out-fight—rough-and-tumble or fair play, any man on the rivers from Pittsburgh to New Orleans and back again."

Mike approved of all these remarks, only he felt that they didn't quite bring out all his talents.

"What's more," Mike said, "if ever the time comes when I lose out in a fight, no matter what the odds are, I want to leave the rivers and go to a new country."

48

5

Mike Fink, Mountain Man in the Far West

IT WAS A GOOD MANY YEARS BEFORE MIKE FINK FINALLY GOT licked, in a fight that ranked right up alongside of any fight that ever was fought up to that time or after. Result was, he went to a new country, the way he'd promised. And since this new country was well stocked with snorting hardships, Mike came to be a hero there, just as he'd been on the rivers.

Now, most of these years that Mike was King of the Keelboatmen, the men on the keelboats lived calm, quiet lives, with everything pretty much their own way. Sweet and peaceable, they'd drift downstream, only stopping at night to lick everybody in the district. Then, quiet and peaceable, they'd fight their way upriver. Between trips, they'd take things easy, except for a few ripsnorting fights.

But after a while that fellow, Robert Fulton, back East on the Hudson River rigged up a boat that ran by steam, and first thing you know, some fellows in Pittsburgh and Frankfort were trying the same stunt.

" 'Twon't work," Mike said, after he'd gone and looked one of the contraptions over. "I'd just like to see this new-fangled tub try to get up Horsetail Ripple or the Giant Gulf. It could snort and whistle all it was a mind to, without getting anywhere. Only way to get through *them* is to set poles and push."

Well, sure enough, when the first steamboats put out, they couldn't get across the worst places, no matter how hard they tried. They'd puff and huff like fury, but finally they'd have to give up. Another thing, these machines had a bad habit of blowing up and scattering passengers and cargoes all over the river and both the banks.

People got so they didn't overmuch enjoy riding on them.

But before long, the boatbuilders found that if they built steamboats more like keelboats, the things would run better. Also, they fixed up the engines so they almost got out of the habit of blowing up. It got so a man could climb aboard a steamboat, and take a trip, and be sure, on an average of nine times out of ten, anyhow, that he wouldn't be skyrocketed over the landscape.

Soon, therefore, these steamboats were taking away trade from the keelboatmen.

The keelboatmen did what they could about this, of course. They called the steamboats all the names they could think of. They fought the steamboatmen, fair play or rough-and-tumble, whenever they got a chance—licked a good share of them, too.

But in spite of all the steps the keelers took to stop the steamers from crowding them off of the river, things got worse and worse. Finally, things came to such a pass that some steamboats were towing keelboats upriver. It was strange to see those fine keelboats move along without a crew doing a lick of work to make them move.

It also was as sad a sight, I suppose, as a keeler ever saw.

It was about this time that Mike Fink's keelboat, going down the Mississippi, had come to a point a few miles below St. Louis. It was a dark gray day, with a threat of rain, and Mike was feeling sort of under the weather.

Mike was standing near the steersman, looking at the shore and scowling a scowl that was black as a thundercloud.

The steersman said: "Mike, you look as sour as a merchant that's lost a cargo when the prices are high. What ails you, mannee?"

Mike waved his hand at the shore. "I knew these parts," he said, "when they were wild. I knew them before a squatter's ax had blazed a single tree. Look at them now. Clearings, cabins, even dad-blamed cities! No place along the river—or on the river, either—where a man isn't crowded."

"But most folks think very well of that sort of thing, Mike. They call it progress, you know."

"Progress! Humph! What's the use of it? Whoever caught a bear in a log cabin, let alone twenty log cabins? Whoever found a panther or a fighting Indian in a city? Where's the fun, the frolicking, the fighting? Sleigh bells and panther tails, I'm sick of progress. I want more room!"

It was at a bad minute like that, that a steamboat had to come along.

"Steamboat ahead!" the fellow in the crew sings out.

The keelboat Mike stood on was an old-timer. Back at the start, when she'd been launched, she'd been called the *Lightfoot*, but she wasn't so light-footed any more. The paint was cracked on her, her sail had been in the wind and the rain until it had turned sort of gray, and in general she looked her age.

Mike looked over at this steamboat, prancing up the river with her full cargo. She was brand new and spic-and-span. She was painted white. Her golden fretwork, the glass in the pilot's house, the brass on her decks and cabins, the water flipped from her paddle wheel, all sparkled in the bright light of the sun which began to look through the clouds at the moment she was sighted.

The steamboat, name of the *Western Queen*, had a cargo of polished rice, cane sugar and fluffy white cotton.

The *Lightfoot* had a cargo of dull gray lead.

As the *Western Queen* chugged along, sparks shot out of her chimney. And she went a little faster than a rabbit that's scooting down hill, even if she was going upstream.

"Shall we give her the channel, patroon?" the steersman wanted to know. "Looks as if she means to take it."

Mike looked at that shiny steamboat again, and his face turned black with anger, and he used his whole forehead to frown with.

"Give me that sweep!" he yelled. Then, when he had hold of the heavy sweep they used to steer the boat, he roared out: "Man the oars!"

When the men stumbled to the seats and started to stand with the bite of the oars into the water and sit with the skip of the oars over it, the keelboat speeded up. The steamboat did the same.

The steersman, looking out at the *Western Queen,* said to Mike, "Going to take the channel, isn't she?"

"If she does," Mike said, setting his jaw, "I'll sink her!"

The keelboat went straight ahead, jumping with the bite of the oars.

The steamboat went straight ahead, too, pushed along by the paddles on the sidewheels.

Then Mike stood up there, puffed out his chest, and told the steamboat the following:

"I'm King of the Keelboatmen, King of the Rivers! I'm a ring-tailed screamer from the old Mississippi! I can out-run, out-shoot, out-brag, and out-fight any man on the rivers! WHOOP! I've got the best crew and the fastest boat on all the rivers, and my muscles are as rusty as an old hinge! WHOOP! So come and see what you can do about it! Cock-a-doodle-do!"

Up there in the steamboat, a man pulled a little rope. Some steam went through a pipe and went through the brass whistle. The whistle went "To-o-o-ot!" And it sounded a good deal louder than any noise Mike had been making.

But then, all of a sudden, the steamboat pilot's face turned green. Then Mike could see the pilot's arms whirling as he twirled the wheel, trying to twist the *Western Queen* into the stream.

"She's on the run!" Mike yelled. "WHOOP! Cock-a-doodle-do!"

Soon it was clear, though, that the pilot of the *Western Queen* had twisted the wheel too late. Result was that the two boats came together, almost head on, with a crash that sounded like a bolt of thunder.

The steamboat felt the blow all right. Her chimneys toppled off and splashed into the river, and they sizzed as they sank. Her pretty white starboard guard and her bow were torn to pieces, and she limped away, listing to starboard. But you could still see her name, painted in gold, sparkle in the sunshine—the *Western Queen.*

And the whole side of the keelboat had been stove in, and water gurgled aboard her till she started to settle into the river. The cargo of lead started to pull her down.

"Ashore, mannees!" Mike yelled. "Bail out and swim for the shore!"

So the keelboatmen piled out and splashed ashore. When they looked back, they saw the keelboat sink into the waters. Then all they saw was a big bunch of bubbles.

"Whatever made you do a thing like that?" the steersman asked Mike, when they were sitting on the bank, panting like grampuses.

"I never gave the channel to a man or a boat in my life," Mike answered him back. "And I'm too old to start. But I've been bested in a fight now, and it's time I went to a new country, the way I said I'd do."

By this time, the new country was closer to the sunset, of course, than it had been when Mike had started working on the river. All those settlers that had come West had filled up what once was new country.

The Fur Country had opened up out in the Far West—Missouri, Montana, New Mexico, places like that. You got there mostly by starting up the Missouri River, going as far as you could, and then walking or riding horseback until you got far enough to take fur.

So Mike went to St. Louis, where men started their fur-hunting trips and where traders came back to sell pelts.

In St. Louis, you'd see about as many kinds of people, those days, as you'd see in New Orleans. Leaning up against the post of every doorway, there'd be an Indian in a blanket—and I don't mean a wooden Indian, either: I mean a live one. There'd be keel-boatmen looking for a fight, telling everybody how good they were. There'd be Spaniards from the Santa Fe trail, wearing sombreros, serapes, and tight pants. There'd be French (voyageurs, they called them) laughing and singing. There'd be slaves in rags, rich Frenchmen in top-hats and capes. And there'd be mountain men —trappers—with long beards and with hair falling down over their shoulders, dressed in skin hunting suits.

Well, the two top men in the fur-trading business, General Ashley and Mr. Henry, said in the newspaper that they wanted a hundred men right away. They wanted them to go up the Missouri

River, and then to walk a while or go horseback a while, and then to do some trapping Out West.

Mike went around with a man who'd been steersman on the *Lightfoot*—fellow by the name of Carpenter. Mike had on his red boatman's shirt and looked just the way he did on the river, except that he'd taken the red feathers out of his hat because of what had happened in the fight with the steamboat.

When Mike told General Ashley he wanted to be a mountain man, General Ashley looked hard at him. "See here," he said, "you look like a boatman to me, and the only men I take for this trip out to the mountains are men that can shoot."

Mike was calm about it, because he knew General Ashley hadn't heard about his shooting back there in Pittsburgh.

"Listen here, mannee," he told him, quiet-like, "my name's Mike Fink, and I'm a ring-tailed screamer! WHOOP! They call my gun Bang-all, because that's its nature, and Bang-all takes to my eye, my arm, and my trigger finger like a babe to its mother! WHOOP! I can out-shoot any man west of the Mississippi, and Carpenter here can do the same, because I taught him! Cock-a-doodle-do!"

"Maybe you can," General Ashley said, "and maybe you can't. I'm not saying. But all I ask is you show that you can shoot before I sign you up to be a mountain man on this trip Out West."

He'd hardly finished before Mike was out there in the backyard pacing off sixty-one paces away from Carpenter. By the time Mike had counted fifty-nine, Carpenter had taken a tin cup, filled it nearly to the brim with cider, and put the cup on top of his head. He stood there, still as a stump, with his face turned towards Mike

When Mike started to aim, General Ashley caught onto what he planned to do. "Hey!" yells the general, "you might miss!"

"Stuff!" Carpenter told him. "We do this all the time, just to keep in shooting trim." Then he told Mike: "Blaze away, and take care you don't elevate your piece too low, or you'll spill the cider."

"True as gospel," Mike said, cool as a catfish.

Then Mike Fink threw back his right foot, took a firm stance, and lifted Bang-all to his shoulder, sort of slow-like. General Ashley kept watching that cup on Carpenter's head—couldn't have watched it closer if it'd been a pretty girl, winking at him.

When the rifle cracked, General Ashley jumped.

Carpenter reached up, and took down the cup. Then he looked into it.

"Never spilled a drop," he let Mike know. "You skipped the bullet right over the top of the cider. New it's my turn."

Well, when Carpenter had made the same kind of a shot, General Ashley led them back into the house. "An old-timer," he said, "couldn't do better." Then he hired them both to work under him as mountain men.

They started up the Missouri River, with ninety-eight other mountain men and General Ashley, April 15, 1822. These ninety-eight men were humdingers and screamers, every one of them. Tom Fitzpatrick was there—the fellow they called old "Broken Hand." So was Hugh Glass, the man that fought the grizzly bear, rough-and-tumble. So was Jim Bridger, the fellow that discovered Yellowstone Park. There were some others, too, just about as famous. Only reason Kit Carson didn't go was that he was too young. He wanted to go, but his mother wouldn't let him.

They went in two big keelboats that were loaded down with food and guns, traps and blankets, horses and mules, and all the other stuff there was room for.

It was tough going up that muddy old Missouri River. She cut her way through the loose sand of the valley the way water twines its way through sawdust. Along the way, she picked up so much sand and clay that she was as thick as molasses and almost the same color.

That made the going hard. So did the fact that you couldn't see anything under the water—sandbars, sunken logs and such. But Mike had been on the rivers for so many years that he could smell trouble under the water, no matter how thick the water was. "I'll warn you," Mike promised the men.

Before they finished the trip, they were plenty glad they had Mike along to show them how to work the boats. They didn't have any trouble to speak of at all. They'd pole, or cordelle, or bushwhack, and to keep up their spirits, they'd sing:

She glides along by western plains,
That wild old stream, Missouri.
She changes her bed each time it rains,
Missouri, Oh, Missouri!

She's thick as mud, and twice as brown,
That mean old stream, Missouri.
But she can't get our keelboat down,
Missouri, Oh, Missouri!

Or maybe they'd sing that song they'd learned from the voyageurs:

A frigate went a-sailing,
Mon joli coeur de rose,
Far o'er the seas away,
Joli coeur d'un rosier,
Joli coeur d'un rosier,
Mon joli coeur de rose.

"Haven't any notion under the sun what the thing means," Mike said. "But it's not a bad tune, and it's good for keeping time."

They went past the Tavern Rocks, where the Indians had scratched all those pictures of the birds and the animals. They pulled past Boone's Settlement, where Daniel Boone had spent the last days of his life. When, a good while later, they came in sight of Fort Osage, the Osage Indians, in their buffalo blankets—braves, squaws and papooses—followed the boat and waved good-bye to them. They passed the tepees of the Pawnees, the Otoes, the Sioux and the Assiniboines.

They stopped, finally, at the mouth of the Yellowstone River. There was a little tongue of land between the Missouri and the Yellowstone, where they could build their cabins and their stockade. They christened the post Fort Henry, after General Ashley's partner.

Then they started out on their hunts.

"A man can be a hired trapper or a skin trapper," General Ashley told Mike Fink.

"What's the difference?" Mike asked him.

"Well," the general told him, "a hired trapper gets paid wages, but a skin trapper gets paid only for the furs he brings in."

"I'll be a skin trapper then," Mike decided, "for I aim to bring in so many furs that the company's purse will be lean after I'm paid for them."

"I suppose," says General Ashley, "that we'd better send an old hand along to show you what to do."

"Sleigh bells and panther tails!" says Mike. "I'm no pork-eater. I was born and raised in hunting and trapping country, and I take to the woods like a bear to a honey-tree. WHOOP! Carpenter and

I, we'll go out alone, and we'll get more pelts than any three men in the party. WHOOP! We're ring-tailed screamers, and we can out-hunt, out-shoot, and out-trap any men in the mountains! Cock-a-doodle-do!"

"We-ell," says General Ashley, "maybe you can, and maybe you can't. I'm not saying. But since I'm furnishing the stores on credit, I think maybe I'd better test you. All I ask is that you tell me this. What sort of an outfit would you think you ought to take?"

"I'd take two pack mules and a saddle horse," Mike let him know. "I'd take a rifle, and a pistol, a pound of powder, four pounds of lead, a bullet mold, seven traps, a horn bottle full of beaver bait, an ax, a hatchet, a knife and an awl, an iron kettle, two blankets, and three pounds of tobacco. In my pack-sack, I'd take all my possibles—moccasins, two kerchiefs, three extra trap springs, a skin-sack of buffalo fat, and some trinkets for trading."

"Mm," the general said, "an old-timer couldn't do any better. *Now* all I ask is that you tell me this. How would you set a beaver trap?"

"Well," Mike told him, "I wouldn't set it in rapids, or along bare shores, or in big, deep rivers. What I'd want would be a smooth stream that wasn't very deep, and I'd want to find soft-barked trees along the shore.

"Where I'd found beaver signs on a stream like that, this is the way I'd set my trap at night: I'd take a hard-dried pole, and if it was new, I'd rub it with mud to weather it. I'd set this pole deep in the mud on the bank. I'd wade into the water, and I'd dig a bed for the trap. Then I'd take my trap and put it in the bed, so it would be three inches below the top of the water, and I'd fasten the chain to my pole. I'd strip a twig and shred the end and dip the shredded end into the beaver bait. I'd fix this twig so that the end with the bait on was four inches above the water and so that the other end was in the jaws of the trap. Then I'd wash away any man trail I'd left on the bank, and I'd walk downstream before I climbed up on the bank.

"Next morning, sure as shooting, there'd be a beaver in that trap."

"Mm," the general said. "An old, old-timer couldn't do any better than that. Now all I ask, finally, is that you tell me this. Know anything about Indians?"

"General, I teethed on a tomahawk; I ate mush with an arrow before I was three; and I chased three redskins over a hill before I was ten. I know a redskin's ways like I know the ways of the river. The name they give me is Death and Desolation Fink."

"Mm," said the general. "Well, you can take what you want, and Carpenter can go with you. Now along in July, we have a ron-day-voo. All this means is that all the mountain men and a good share of the friendly Indians come in to the post. Then we buy the furs, have some fun for ourselves, and rest up a bit before people go trapping again. Better be on hand for it."

"We'll be there with a cargo of beaver furs that'll make your eyes pop," Mike promised the general.

So he and Carpenter packed up all the things Mike had said he wanted to take, and went into the woods. They'd thrown away their boatmen clothes now and they were dressed the way trappers ought to be dressed. They had on caps made out of otter skin, hunting shirts made out of antelope skin, britches made out of buffalo skin, with fringes, and moccasins made out of elk skin.

The place where they camped and operated was on the Mussel-shell, in the country of the Blood Indians. It was a good place to be, take it all in all, and they found they liked it there. There was enough sweet cottonwood to give plenty of bark to feed the horses and mules. There were red willows, so the inner bark could be mixed with tobacco, to stretch it out. There was plenty of wild meat—bear and game and grouse.

Since Mike knew so much about beavers' ways, they soon had a good many furs cached away in their caches. So big were the beavers they caught that fifty beaver pelts made a hundred pound bale—instead of the eighty that usually made up a bale. The skins were so prime that, instead of the usual six dollars, they were worth ten dollars and thirty-seven cents a pound.

So they got along fine until, in June, a week or two before the rendezvous, the Blood Indians made some trouble.

Now, of course, Mike and his partner had a note from President Monroe that said it was all right for them to trap in the Indian country. But some Indians couldn't read anything that wasn't written in pictures, and others wouldn't read even though they could. So at any time these redmen might get out of hand. A peaceful Indian wouldn't do anything but steal horses, stores or pelts, all aboveboard and friendly-like. But an Indian at war, along with his whole tribe, could be most bothersome.

Result was that when these Blood Indians began to boil, things got tough. For days and days Mike and his pal had to keep out of sight and stay quiet. They didn't dare build fires, so at night their feet got cold—and then, naturally, the rest of them got cold, too. And pretty soon, the food supply got all-fired low. All they had left to eat was a little parched corn and some jerk.

After they'd lived on this for a while, they were powerfully tired of it. Besides, even if they liked it, they couldn't eat it any more, because there wasn't any left.

Then, one morning as he was creeping along, Mike saw a three-pronged buck, about three hundred yards away. He was as fine a buck as Mike had ever seen anywhere.

"I'm hungry," Mike told Carpenter, "and I mean to have him."

"No!" Carpenter whispered. "They'll hear you!"

But already, Mike was on the way, priming his gun and picking his flint as he went crawling along toward the buck. Finally, he got within shooting range.

Then he saw a fir-branch wiggle, not far away. Lying low, he watched that fir-tree. And then finally he saw a big Blood Indian stalking the buck. This Indian was a mean fellow, name of Laughing Pigeon, that out of sheer orneriness had started his tribe on their war with Mike and his partner.

Laughing Pigeon lifted his gun, slow like, and aimed at the deer.

Then, like a flash, Mike got an idea. He raised Bang-all and pointed it at Laughing Pigeon.

And the very second the Indian's finger bent to squeeze the trigger—Mike could tell of course because it got sort of pink—that very second Mike fired. There weren't two bangs. There was just one. The buck fell down and Laughing Pigeon fell down at one and the same instant. In other words, Mike got himself an Indian and a buck with one shot.

Mike reloaded in a hurry, waiting a while to find whether any other Blood Indians were coming along. Then he hurried over to the buck, sliced off some tenderloin steaks, and he and Carpenter, their pack mules and their saddle horses all were down the mountain trail before you could say "Beaver Bait."

That was how these two mountain men got to the rendezvous on July 1 without starving to death along the way.

It was a good rendezvous that year, with just whole herds of mountain men and whole tribes of friendly Indians on hand for it.

The Indians came from all around to swap thongs, robes, furs, buffalo meat and baskets. They lined up their tepees along the river, long rows of them. Then the squaws screeched, the children frolicked, the dogs barked, and the braves swaggered around in their feathers and their blankets, as was customary.

The mountain men lifted their peltries from their caches, piled them on their pack mules, and lit out for the post. They came in a few at a time, their hair and beards long, their faces about as brown as tree bark, their shirts and britches torn with thorns and blackened with woodsmoke.

There was an old mountain man named Catch'em Ketchum, that happened to be over being friendly with a friendly Indian at the time Mike and his partner first came into view away off in the distance.

"What under the blazing sun are those animals?" Catch'em wanted to find out. "I've hunted all the way from Missouri to Oregon and from Oregon to New Mexico, and I've never seen the like! Can you figure out what they are, Far-sighted Eagle?"

Far-sighted Eagle took a squint. "Five animals," he said. "All got humps—like buffalo—but bigger. Ugh!"

"Maybe they're camels," Catch'em guessed. "But I don't recall ever seeing that many camels together in these parts before. Come to think of it, I've never seen as many as *one* around here—not lately, anyhow."

Catch'em watched them come closer. Then he said, "I see what they are now, but I don't know whether I feel any better or not. They're two mules, a horse and two men. But they're hump-backed, every dratted one of 'em!"

"No," says Far-sighted Eagle, who'd managed to get a good look at them by now. "No humps—furs! Ugh!"

"Sure enough," says Catch'em. "That's a relief, all right. But who ever *saw* such heaps of furs?"

And sure enough, Mike and his partner had loaded the mules as high as they could, and the saddle horse as high as they could, and then they'd still had had piles of furs left over. So they'd put these onto their own shoulders and had staggered into the post with them.

The furs were prime furs, too, the way I've said. So after they'd seen General Ashley, the two men were loaded down with money—just loaded down.

"Mm," General Ashley said, "an old-timer never has done better —never has done so well. Now all I ask is this, that you men have a good time for yourselves."

The way they'd work it at a rendezvous, you see, was like this: the mountain men would turn in their furs; then they'd cut their hair and shave, for the first time in months. After that they'd settle down and have shooting, lying, eating and drinking matches. They'd have horse races, foot races, and fist fights. In short, they'd do everything for sport and amusement that came to their minds. That way, they'd get in a good rest before they had to go back to work.

Some say that it was at this rendezvous that Mike did one of the greatest things he ever did—went and outshot Davy Crockett. Don't ask how Davy happened to be out there. You'll see in the next chapters, though, that Davy got around to almost everywhere. So it seems likely that this match that Mike won over Davy was either at this rendezvous or some place else.

Mike saw this big settler from Tennessee, and Mike swaggered up to him and said:

63

"I'm half-horse, half-alligator, and half-snapping turtle! WHOOP! I've got the handsomest wife—" (By this time, by the way, Mike had married his wife, Sal), "the fastest horse, and the best shooting-iron east or west of the Mississippi, and if any man dares doubt it, I'll be in his hair quicker than fire can scorch a feather! Cock-a-doodle-do!"

When Mike said this to Davy, Davy of course told him: "I won't say you're wrong when you make those claims, but I will say some of your facts are wrong. Let's see whether that shooting-iron of yours really is any good alongside my rifle, Brown Bess."

So they had a shooting match that was a lolapaloosa. They drove nails into a tree, snuffed candles, and knocked flies off of a cow's horn—and each man was as good as the other.

Then Mike looked over the field and saw that his wife, Sal Fink, was going after a gourd full of water from the well. She had a high comb in her hair, and Mike blazed away at it.

He knocked half of the comb off, without stirring a hair.

Then he said to Davy, "I'll give you your choice. Either you can shoot the half of that comb on again, or you can knock the other half off."

"No, no, Mike," says Davy. "Davy Crockett's hand would be sure to shake if his iron was pointed within a hundred yards of a lady like Mrs. Fink. No, I'll give up beat."

It's been pointed out—and rightly, too—that when Davy was beaten this way, it wasn't what you'd call a disgrace: it just proved that he had good manners. If that comb had been on a man, or an Indian, say, he could have cut it off close as a close shave, and no trouble about it. Mike had to admit that he'd been wrong in pointing a gun at somebody that wasn't an Indian, especially this wife he'd promised to love and cherish. And to cheer Davy up, he went on and admitted that, since he'd never seen the woman, that there was a chance that Mrs. Crockett was as handsome as Mrs. Fink.

But, however he did it, it was a great thing for Mike to beat Davy—one of the greatest. That was the only time Davy was ever beaten at a shooting match, or any other kind, for that matter. As the next chapters will prove beyond a doubt, Davy Crockett was

64

one of the greatest heroes ever raised up among our star-spangled hardships.

Aside from this match, that first year Mike spent trapping was pretty much of a piece with all the other years he spent getting hides. Some were worse, but then some were better, so it was more or less average. Year after year, he'd go out to get furs, he'd have trouble with the Indians, and he'd astonish everybody with the huge piles he brought back to the rendezvouses. Last time anyone reported on him, he was still up to those same old stupendous tricks —so he may, for all I know, be up to them to this day.

6
Davy Crockett, Tennessee Settler

FROM THE WAY DAVY CROCKETT'S FATHER AND MOTHER LIVED,
you might guess they were just ordinary people.

They had a log cabin like any other log cabin. The roof was oak
staves held in place by slabs that were laid across them at right
angles. The windows, of course, were made out of oiled paper. In
the fall, Mr. and Mrs. Crockett would put chinks between the logs,
to keep the cabin warm. In the spring, when the dogwood came
out, they'd knock away the chinks so that light and air could come
into the cabin.

Inside, the cabin looked like any other cabin. The floor was
made of wide planks, held in place on the puncheons with wooden
pegs. The table top was a split slab, and the round legs were set in
auger holes in the floor. For chairs, they used blocks or three-legged
stools. Beds were made with poles interlaced with strips of bark.

Hanging on the wall were gourds of all shapes and sizes for keeping salt, soap, lard and such stuff. The punger gourd, the biggest of
the lot, held four or five gallons. Then there were meat and vegetables drying up there in the rafters.

The Crockett family ate about the way everybody else did. To
cut things up, they used hunting knives. For dishes, they used

wooden bowls, trenchers and noggins, and such home-made affairs.

All this, you might say, was as common as an old shoe.

But as a matter of fact the Crocketts weren't ordinary people—far from it. They had great talents, and they lived in a great place.

Davy Crockett's father could grin a hailstorm into sunshine, and could look the sun square in the face without sneezing.

Davy Crockett's mother, even when she was an old woman and had lost a good part of her spryness, could do these things:

1. Jump a seven-rail fence backwards;
2. Dance a hole through a double oak floor;
3. Spin more wool than a steam mill; and
4. Cut down a gum tree ten feet around, and sail it across the Nolachucky River, using her apron for a sail.

At the time Davy was born, his father and mother lived in the Nolachucky River Valley in the state of Tennessee, not far from the Cherokee Indians.

Tennessee was a place where the soil went down to the center of the earth, and government gave you title to every inch of it. You could tell that the soil was rich because if you went and dug a good sized hole, and then threw the dirt back into it, the dirt didn't fill the hole.

The soil was so rich that you had only to kick a dent in the ground with your heel, drop a kernel of corn into the dent, and the corn would grow without work. Some places the ground was so covered with wild strawberries that when a boy walked through them, the squished juice would redden his legs to the knees. Other places, the wild pea vines were matted so thick that a horse couldn't make his way through them. If he took a running jump and tried, he was likely to end up with his legs, his neck and his ears sprawled around every which way, sort of like an octopus.

If Davy's father just sniffed the air of the Nolachucky Valley, it made him snort like a horse.

Well, born to such a ripsnorting family in such a ringtailed roarer of a place, Davy Crockett was the biggest baby that ever was and a little the smartest that ever will be. His Uncle Roarious said right away that he was the yallerest blossom in the family, and he looked so fat and healthy that his Aunt Ketinah said that it was as much fun to look at him as it was to eat a meal with all the trimmings.

Because he was such a ripsnorting big baby, Davy was given an oversize cradle twelve feet long. His pillow was a wildcat's skin filled with the down from thirty-three geese and eleven ganders. Sometimes the cradle was rocked by water power from the Nolachucky River. Other times, Uncle Roarious tied the cradle up on the top of a tree, so the wind could swing the contraption about and Davy could enjoy himself. An alligator skin that Uncle Roarious had spread over some elk horns on top of the cradle kept Baby Davy safe from any rain, hail or snow.

They didn't let Davy stay in the cabin very much, because if he laughed or cried, he did it so loud that it used to set the cider barrels rolling around the cellar.

For a few months, Davy drank buffalo milk instead of regular milk. This made him grow so that soon he was able to eat meat. At mealtime, to get off to a start, he'd eat a whole duck. Then he'd take a big helping of bear's meat, and make it fly.

He liked bear's meat when it was fixed up just right—salted in a hailstorm, peppered with buckshot, and broiled on a flash of forked lightning.

All this food made him grow.

As time passed, he got older, too.

Soon he could float down the Nolachucky River or any other river in Tennessee to the brown Mississippi, paddling with nothing but an old horn spoon, while all the neighbors cheered.

The Nolachucky River Valley was a fine place to grow up in. For one thing, there was plenty of room, even for Davy. For another, it wasn't a noisy place: there was plenty of peace and quiet. There wasn't any sound to speak of at night—just the howls of a wolf now and then, or an owl moaning or a few panthers screaming the way panthers do. In the daytime, it was just about as quiet—with a raven croaking, maybe, or a woodpecker hammering a hollow beech tree, or the whir of a flight of geese.

Finally, it was a good place to grow because Davy's father and mother were busy all the time, and they had to leave this growing business pretty much up to Davy. They couldn't help him because they had to milk cows, cook the mess, spin the flax, plow the field, plant the crops, pick the corn, dig the potatoes, shoot the bears, and chase the Indians away. Left on his own with nobody to help, Davy put his mind to growing, and the way he got along was astonishing.

When he was six years old, Davy had a dog named Butcher who was as woolly as a sheep and as old as a rock. Davy would climb on Butcher's back, and they'd slash through the canebrake faster than lightning splitting a post.

Maybe it would be spring, and the buttercups and shooting stars would be up, and the bears would be coming out of their winter sleeping places—caves or hollow trees. Coming out into the sunshine after all that sleep, they'd have eyes as red as strawberries. They'd be blinking their eyes, and frowning and sort of snarling.

Whenever Davy and Butcher saw any red-eyed bears in a nasty mood like that, they'd scoot after them, Butcher would bark, Davy would screech, and quick as a spark the bears would nip for a hole in a tree or a cave or any hiding place that was handy.

Having got old enough to chase bears, Davy had to get educated now like almost any other boy—had to learn all the useful things that would help him get along. He learned pretty much the sort of thing Mike Fink had learned, up there in Pittsburgh.

Another thing—like all the other boys in the Nolachucky River Valley—he learned how to shoot the bow and arrow, and how to throw the tomahawk. The chief thing to know about throwing a tomahawk was that it would make a certain number of turns at a certain distance. If you heaved it from the wrong distance, it wouldn't strike with the blade. At five steps, though, it would strike with the blade and the handle would point down; at seven and a half, it would strike with the handle up, and so on. Davy learned to judge distances with his eye, and after a while he could walk through the woods and flip the tomahawk any way he wanted it to light.

The exercise made Davy grow even bigger than before, so when he was eight years old, he weighed two hundred pounds and fourteen ounces with his shoes off and his feet washed.

If people wanted to sink tree posts into the bed of the Nola-chucky River or the brown Mississippi for bridge piers, all they had to do was lower them down into the mud and then ask Davy to jump on them. He'd step from post to post all the way across the river, making the tallest posts pop down quick as half a wink. He'd have to swim back, of course, because if he stepped on the posts twice, he sank them clear out of sight, and what's more, got his feet wet.

Swimming back was easy enough for Davy, though, because even at this age he was a ripsnorter of a swimmer. He could swim faster, dive deeper, and come up dryer than half the men in all creation.

Soon Davy was old enough to have a gun and to learn to shoot. The men in the district taught Davy all they knew about shooting, and then he figured out some new ideas of his own. After he'd worked and worked to learn, he finally made up a rule for the best way to shoot. The rule was:

"Be sure you're right, and then go ahead and pull the trigger."

When the leaves were yellow and the sunsets were red and the break of day was gray, that was the best time for hunting. The deer put off his summer suit and put on a winter gray and blue one that matched the scenery better. The buck readied up his antlers—dropped that soft velvet covering and made them hard and white. The bear was fat from eating servings of service berries, and he began to get a mite sleepy.

That was when Davy, by this time too big to ride Butcher any more, would go out riding into the woods on his horse. When he saw an animal, he'd make sure he was right and then pull the trigger. When he'd shot a nice mess of bears, he'd take them home to the family.

Word got around among the settlers that Davy could out-hunt any man in the district, and after while all the other families got so they'd have him do the hunting for them, too. He wouldn't shoot any turkeys for them, because he shot nothing less than forty-pound turkeys (which were rather scarce), and these he saved for the Crocketts. But any time a family wanted a cord or two of bears, say, he'd oblige, and the family would be fixed for the winter.

Before he went after any bear, he could always tell how big it would be by studying its claw marks on trees. It would stand up as high as it could, and make its scratch on the bark—just why, I've no idea. But noticing a little thing like that, Davy always could decide beforehand whether or not a bear was worth the time it would take to kill him.

They tell of the time when Davy had some chores to do, so he had little time for hunting. But the family was low on food. What he decided to do, therefore, was to get as much food as he could as quick as he could. He took along his father's muzzle-loading, double-barreled shotgun, because it scattered more shots.

Well, down by the Nolachucky River, he saw a flock of geese coming along, and he saw a big buck both at the same time. He waited until the geese had flown to just the right place, near the buck, then raised the gun. But just at that minute, he saw a rattlesnake coiled near by, ready to strike.

Thinking fast, Davy made the shot of his life. He let the buck have one barrel, the flock of geese the other, and he shot the ramrod down the snake's throat. (The geese were in a line, of course, so the shot took them one after the other—the whole string of them.)

But that wasn't all. The gun kicked so hard that Davy fell into the river, and when he climbed out, every pocket he had was plumb full of fish. These weighed down his coat and pulled so, that two buttons popped off. One hit a bear and the other hit a squirrel— killed them, too.

Result was, because of his quick thinking and great shooting, Davy got his hunting over with in a hurry.

After a few years, even the animals passed along the word that Davy Crockett was the best shot not only in the Nolachucky Valley but also in all of Tennessee.

He was out in the forest one afternoon, a little before sunset, and had just come to a place called the Great Gap, when he saw a raccoon sitting all alone upon the crotch of a tree. It had the usual look of a raccoon—gray, ring-tailed, white-eyebrowed, and sort of woebegone, downhearted, dismal, discouraged, and sad.

Davy put his gun (which you may remember was named Brown Bess) to his shoulder, and was all ready to shoot, when the raccoon lifted his paw, like a boy at school, and said:

"Is your name by any chance Ripsnorting Davy Crockett?"

Davy told him it was.

"Then," says the raccoon, "you needn't take any more trouble, because I may as well come down without another word."

And he walked right down from the tree, as dignified as a gentleman climbing out of a carriage, because he felt that he was as good as shot, and he said so.

Davy stooped down, patted the little fellow on the head, and said, "I wouldn't hurt a hair on your head, coonie, because you've said as fine a thing about my shooting as ever was said."

"Since you put it like that," says the raccoon, edging off sideways, "I think I'll just walk off right away. It's not that I doubt what you say," the raccoon told him, "but you might kind of happen to change your mind."

By that time, Davy was big enough, old enough and ripsnorting enough to marry and have a family. So he did.

Everybody around came to the wedding. They came, for one thing, because they liked Davy and were grateful for the help he'd given them with the tree posts in the river and with the hunting. For another thing, they liked the girl he married. They also came to the wedding because a wedding was about the only kind of an affair where people didn't have to work. You had to work at a log-rolling or a muster day or a corn husking or a house raising. But at a wedding all you did was race for the bottle and eat and drink and dance.

Davy's wife, Sally Ann Thunder Ann Whirlwind Crockett, was a streak of lightning set up edgeways and buttered with quicksilver. She could laugh the bark off a pine tree, blow out the moonlight, and sing a wolf to sleep.

The children were worthy of such a father as Davy and such a mother as Sally Ann Thunder Ann Whirlwind Crockett. They could out-run, out-jump, and out-scream almost any creature in creation. They could also outfight a middling sized thunderstorm.

The family decided to go to a new country far away from the Nolachucky Valley, where things were less crowded. They piled their bedding and furniture and cooking things into a wagon, and started to travel. All day they'd plod along through the trees, and when the road was bumpy or went uphill, they'd pile out and walk for a while. When the road was boggy, Davy would chop down young saplings and fill holes with them so the wheels could roll across. Some days out, Davy couldn't tell for the life of him whether there was supposed to be a trail or not, except by noticing the blazes chopped on the trees. At night, they'd sleep under the stars.

Finally the Crocketts found a place to settle at the head of the Mulberry Fork of the Elk River, not far from the River Duck.

When a family moved into a new place back in those days, they usually had one party after another. They did this so that they could get people from around about to come and do all the work.

"There doesn't seem to be a cabin in this clearing," they'd say. "In fact, there doesn't seem to be any clearing. So let's have some parties, and make a clearing and raise a cabin, just to pass the time. P.S. Bring some food along, will you?"

The first day, the choppers would fell the trees and cut them to the right lengths; the teamsters would haul them to the place where they were to be used; the carpenters would split the clap-boards and the puncheons; and then everybody would put down the foundation.

The second day would be the day of the house-raising, with everybody invited to pitch in, put down the floors, pile up the logs, make the chimney, and cut the doors and windows.

Next day, everybody would be asked over to help put in the furniture. Then anybody that wasn't too tired would stay for the house-warming, for which there wouldn't be any work left over.

It got so that the minute people saw a covered wagon, with a family and furniture piled up in it, moving into the neighborhood, their bones would begin to ache.

Of course, Davy Crockett, with all his strength, didn't need any help with the clearing of his land or with the building of his cabin or furniture—any help, that is, that his wife and the children couldn't give him. This was lucky, since there wasn't anybody in the neighborhood to help anyhow.

But the family had a riproaring time for itself at the house-warming.

The soil on the Mulberry Fork of the Elk River was even richer than the soil on the Nolachucky. If you planted potatoes there, you soon had a mountain on your hands out there in the vegetable garden. And pumpkin vines grew so fast that they wore out some of the pumpkins just dragging them along the ground. Even when pumpkins didn't wear out but slid along nice and easy over the soft soil, when Davy went out to pick one, he had to run like a shooting star scared by an earthquake to catch up with it.

If Davy so much as sniffed the air of the Mulberry Fork, it made him snort like a team of horses.

The Crocketts ate possum meat, bear meat, corn pone full of cracklings, and wild honey out of bee trees. In the winter, they chunked up their cabin and slept under coonskins, bearskins and fox furs.

There was work a-plenty on that farm of Davy's. Chasing pumpkins and snorting were just the start of it. You had to break that bad habit that squirrels and raccoons had of eating the corn off of all the ears and you had to discourage the liking wolves, panthers and bears had for sheep and hogs. And even when the animals weren't pestering Davy, the trees had a way of falling down here and there and knocking holes in the worm fences so that the cattle would get into the wrong fields. In a case like that, Davy would chase the cattle into the right fields and then would fix the fences.

Davy's wife had to grind meal in the hand-mill, to churn butter, to make linsey cloth out of flax and wool, to tan leather, sew up shoes and hunting shirts, cook the mess and help make crops.

The children had to do the chores that were left over and that they could handle.

So Davy had to think up useful ways to help speed the work. He planted corn, for instance, by shooting it into crevices with his rifle, Brown Bess, and he planted it nice and even that way, too. He figured out a way to harness a hurricane so it would turn a spinning wheel or work the hand-mill. He also tamed animals and taught them to do this and that little thing around the place to help out the family.

He tamed a wolf so that if anyone in the family was cold, this wolf would shiver for them.

A panther that Davy tamed was also very useful. When Davy came home late of an inky night, the panther would light the way to bed with the fire in his eyes. He'd brush the hearth off every morning with his tail, and Saturdays he'd do Sally Ann Thunder

Ann Whirlwind Crockett's heavy work. He raked in all her garden seed with his claws and helped to currycomb the horses with his nails.

Davy thought that the smartest animal the family ever had was a bear that his little girl, Pinette, met in the woods one day when she was out for a walk. The bear used to follow Pinette to church, waddling along behind her and carrying her pocketbook, with the money for the collection, in his mouth. At last this bear got so tame that it would come into the house to warm itself and meet the family.

From the start, this bear thought very well of Davy, and Davy thought very well of the bear.

Davy named the bear Death Hug and taught him how to smoke a pipe. While the bear sat in one corner smoking, Davy sat in the other with his pipe. They couldn't talk to each other, but they would look, and Davy always knew by the shine in Death Hug's eyes what he wanted to say.

Death Hug would sit up nights when his master was out late, and would open the door when Davy came home. Then, with the panther to light the way to the bedroom, it would be a pleasure for Davy to go to bed—even if the night was as dark as a bear's cave.

Death Hug, though, was the greatest at churning butter—did all the churning for the family in less time than it would take a streak of lightning to run around a sweet potato patch, and a little sweet potato patch, at that.

One time when Davy had a race with a steamboat, Death Hug was a big help to him. The two of them walked out to the woods together and cut down a hollow tree. They cut open one side, corked up both ends, whittled a pair of paddles, and launched their boat on the brown Mississippi, just as a sidewheel steamboat came chugging along.

Davy rowed the boat. Death Hug sat in the stern, holding the American flag in his paw, smoking his pipe, and steering the boat with his tail, which he dangled in the water for a rudder.

They left the steamboat so far behind that the thing just quit trying. And that was smart, because if the boat had put on any more steam, it would have blown up its boilers.

7

Davy Crockett, Soldier, Congressman and Comet Licker

FIVE MONTHS AND TWO DAYS AFTER THAT GREAT RACE WITH the steamboat, an Indian chief—a Shawanoe from the Miami Valley named Tecumseh—started some trouble.

This Tecumseh was a fine hunter. Once, when the Indian tribes had a hunting match to see who was the best hunter in the tribe of the Shawanoes, in the day and the night that they had for the match, Tecumseh brought in thirty deerskins, and the most the next man to him could bring in was twelve.

Tecumseh was also a great chief. If he could get enough Indians together and stand up on something and wave his arms and make a speech to them, he could get them onto the warpath, tomahawks, bows and arrows and all, quicker than a buck could jump a thicket.

It seems that this year, he went one place after another and told thousands of Indians what he wanted them to do.

He visited the Seminoles. These Indians lived in Florida and wore clothes with green and yellow and blue stripes. They'd killed off most of the Euchees and had married up with the rest of them, so you can see they were pretty fierce.

Then he went and talked to the Creeks and the Cherokees. These Indians lived along all the creeks in Georgia, Alabama and North

Florida, so there were a good many of them. Most of them spoke the Muskhogean language, which doubtless must have given them bad tempers. They had White Towns to have peace meetings in, and Red Towns to have war meetings in.

Tecumseh said: "Let's have our meeting in a Red Town this time."

Finally, he went to make a speech to the Des Moins, in Missouri. These fellows were great trappers—made quite a fine living for themselves by selling pelts of bear, deer, beaver, otter, raccoon and squirrel at those rendezvous affairs I told you about. But when these Des Moins cut their hair, they gave a hint of how ornery they were. They shaved off all of it except a strip down the middle, called a scalp lock, making it look like a crest.

Nobody liked the way this looked but the Des Moins Indians, and they were glad of it.

Visiting the Creeks, the Cherokees, the Seminoles and the Des Moins, Tecumseh always got up on a high place, waved his arms, and made a speech. In the speech, he'd tell the Indians to climb into their war paint and start a rumpus. So they did the same, and right away quick.

All this time, Davy was doing the same old things, snorting, running down pumpkins, taking care of the farm, and taming varmints. But when news about the Indians came to him, he made sure he was right, and then went ahead.

"The harvest's in," he figured, "all but two or three mountains of potatoes, and Pinette and the panther can finish them up. And I could get back in time for spring planting if I hurried." So he asked his family to excuse him for a while, please, and went off to fight the Indians.

He joined up with Colonel Coffee's army, just as news came that the Indians were marching in that direction.

"That's right thoughtful of 'em," says Davy. "Comes in handy. But we won't be outdid in politeness by any Indians. We'll march in *their* direction."

So the army started marching at a breakneck speed, covering six whole miles an hour, about the fastest an army ever did march.

Davy Crockett, he went on ahead of the army, to be a scout and smell out what the redskins' plans were. He scouted among all the tribes, and then he hurried back to camp, just as Colonel Coffee and his men had decided to call it a day and rest for the rest of the night. The army had been nipping along at six miles an hour all day, and they were all fagged out.

"Take it easy," Davy told them. Then he cooked up a mess of bear for them he'd killed along the way, served it to the men for dinner, and then put up a pup tent for every man in the brave army. Just before the men went to bed, Davy told what he'd learned. Then, when the army went to sleep, Davy stayed up to wash the dishes, keep watch, and get things ready for the fight with the Indians in the morning.

The next day, the fighting was pretty fierce. The Indians were all painted up, of course, and the striped clothes of the Seminoles and the red crests of the Des Moins looked even worse than usual. What's more, all the Indians whooped and yelled, and the Creeks and Cherokees did it in the Muskhogean language. And the Indians, all of them, did anything fierce they could think up.

But Davy yelled so loud that anybody that wanted to couldn't tell about his voice, but had to paint a picture of it. And yelling like that, and banging away with Brown Bess until the smoke blotted out the sunshine, Davy fought the Indians on the Coosa River, the Tennessee River, and the Talapoosa River. Then he fought them on some of the smaller streams.

This went on for several weeks, and became most tiresome.

Then, when Davy had run out of rivers and streams, and the Indians had run out of the country, Davy went back to his home at the head of the Mulberry Fork of the Elk River, near the River Duck.

He got there in time for the spring planting, of course. Davy Crockett always kept all of his promises, whether he'd made them or not.

Davy was as gay as a canary in his cabin in the clearing on the Mulberry Fork. Every morning, before he went to work, he'd haul off and hug everybody in the family—his wife, his children, the dog, the horses, the wolf, the panther, and Death Hug. Then they'd all grin and show their white teeth. And when he came home at night, with three or four cords of bear and a bale of coonskins, he'd give them all a big squeezing hug again, and they'd show their white teeth in a grin.

But before long Davy had to leave this happy home of his again, because the neighbors that had moved into the district by now came to him and asked him to run for Congress. Since they'd heard of the way he'd cut a wide swath through the Indians, they figured that maybe a star-spangled ripsnorter like Davy could go to Washington, D. C., and straighten everything out. Davy thought it over, made sure he was right, and then went ahead and ran for Congress.

To get elected, Candidate Crockett had to make speeches. At first, he found this was harder than it was to pour molasses out of a jug in the Winter of the Big Snow. He'd turn as red in the face as the crest of a Des Moins Indian, and his buckskin collar would get tight around his neck, and the words would pile up on his tongue. Soon, though, after he'd practiced a while, the words flowed as smoothly as the Nolachucky River in the springtime.

In a town where there was a meeting, people could tell where to go and when to get there by looking at the blue smoke that curled out of the long barbecue pits in the grove.

When the people came to the grove, they'd find pigs, shoats, lambs and veal on the spits, smoking and getting golden brown, and smelling heavenly. They'd also find a lot of other people, lined up to watch the parade.

The paraders would be the militia companies that had come in their marching suits—coats with swallow tails and brass buttons, and britches with red stripes down the pant-legs, and funny shaped hats with plumes on them. Ahead of these men would march fellows playing fifes and drums, and that would be the parade.

The men watching this parade would wave their hats, and the women would wave their handkerchiefs. The music made the horses and mules dancy, and now and then an animal would break the sapling it was tied to, and would snort and sniff and run away. Then the owner would have to stop waving his hat long enough to run off and catch the animal, bring it back, and tie it up again.

Things quieted down after a while, though, and people and militia men all sat down to eat. They ate at long tables covered with linen that was as white as snow.

After the things were cleared away, people started hollering for Candidate Crockett to talk. He climbed up on a stand, took off his coonskin cap and his fringed buckskin coat, and hung them on a branch. Then he rolled up his sleeves. All this time, everybody was still, so far as talking went, but the ladies kept waving their turkey-tail fans, and the men looked around for a stick to whittle.

Then Davy started to talk. And he talked so all-fired well that everybody decided to vote for him.

What's more, the insects, birds and animals who lived near the Mulberry Fork, the Elk River and the River Duck all figured it would be more handy to have the candidate (and his rifle Brown Bess) in Washington, D. C., than in the district. So they pitched in and worked for his election.

The crickets chirped "Cr-k-tt."

The guinea hens clucked "Cr-cr-kt."

The bullfrogs chunked "Cro-o-ck-ett."

The wild animals growled "Gr-r-ro-gett."

And the Crockett family's pet animals, who could say things better than the animals that hadn't had any schooling, they showed their white teeth and hollered "Crockett forever," just as plain.

It sounded as if they were all voting for Candidate Davy, along with the people. So their votes were counted, too, and he was elected by a vote that was unanimous and three hundred and seven votes over. This was enough to send the Honorable, Ripsnorting, Star-spangled Congressman Davy Crockett to Congress not once but two times.

Not long before he started to Washington, Congressman Crockett heard that the people there were great dancers. So he taught Death Hug and his brand new pet alligator, Old Mississippi, to do all the latest dances. The Honorable Davy and Death Hug and Old Mississippi and a fiddler would go out into a forest open-ing. Then, while the fiddler played "Grind the Bottle," "The Frog and the Mouse" or "The Crow and the Tailor," Davy taught his pets how to dance.

Then Congressman Crockett and Death Hug and Old Mississippi hugged everybody in the family, including all the animals, and they all showed their white teeth in grins. After that, the three of them said good-by to the clearing on the Mulberry Fork and lit out for Washington, D. C.

On the trip, the Honorable Davy carried along a big bundle of red, white and blue patriotism and a few hurricane speeches tied up in an alligator hide. He rode on the back of Old Mississippi, with

Death Hug waddling along behind. This caused a deal of talk along the way, and people often wondered who this fellow was.

If they tried to sneak up and learn his name in sly ways, Davy fooled them.

For instance, when he and his beasts stopped at an inn one night, the landlord said to him, "Good evening, mister, I don't just remember your name right now."

Davy knew right away that the man was trying to learn his name without asking, so he said: "Makes no difference. Don't worry"—and busied himself with taking the saddle off of Old Mississippi.

The landlord tried again. "I just wondered what might be your name," he just wondered.

"It might be Pine Wing, or Phineas Dowdy, or Jedidiah Crawfish," Davy told him, giving the alligator a bucket of water. "But it's something different."

The landlord said, "I'm sure I've seen you somewhere."

"Very likely," Davy told him, locking the stable door, "I've been there often enough." Davy started to walk to the back door of the inn, followed by Death Hug, and the little landlord trotted along after them.

While they were climbing up the stairs to Davy's room, the landlord panted, "I—was—sure—of it. But—it's—strange—Puff! —I've—forgotten—Puff!—your name—Puff!"

"What you don't know, you can't forget," says Davy, and he slammed the door. And he never let a sly man like this landlord learn who he was or what he could do.

But if people asked him right out who he was, he told them:

"I'm the yallerest blossom in the forest—the Honorable, Ripsnorting, Star-spangled Congressman, Davy Crockett. I can wade the brown Mississippi, jump the Ohio, step across the Nolachucky, ride a streak of lightning, slip without a scratch down a thorn tree, whip my weight in wildcats, and put a rifle ball through the moon."

This rather impressed people.

In Washington, D. C., Davy wanted to stop at Gadsby's Hotel, but the manager, the minute he saw the Crockett party clumping down Pennsylvania Avenue, hurried and hung up a sign. The sign said:

> NO BEARS OR ALLIGATORS ALLOWED

So they stopped at the Indian Queen, instead. Davy wanted to stay in a hotel, of course, until he could find a house with a pool or a creek for Old Mississippi to swim in and with a hollow tree or a cave near by for Death Hug to sleep in that winter.

The manager of the Indian Queen met Davy and Death Hug at the door, and carried the bundle of patriotism and hurricane speeches inside. Then he met the two of them at the register, and showed them where to sign for a room. Next he led them to the dining room and served them their meals. By the time this fellow had turned down the covers on their beds that night, Davy and Death Hug felt they knew him pretty well.

Washington was quite a place. There were hundreds of Congressmen and Senators, going around and clearing their throats and making speeches. Then there were foreign visitors going around and asking questions, so they could write books about America. Wagons piled high with red tape went clumpety-clump down Pennsylvania Avenue.

The most interesting thing to be found in the way of food in the capital was ice cream. Ice cream was new, and everybody was serving it at parties that year. After he'd learned to eat it in little bites so it didn't freeze his tongue any more, Davy often had as much as twenty quarts of an evening. He sent some home to the family in Tennessee.

Washington had built up some since Mr. Long Tom Jefferson had been sworn into office there, but it still hadn't been what you'd call finished up. They hadn't got around to paving most of the streets yet, and everywhere the mud was hub deep or a little deeper. And on these boggy streets stood buildings with wide spaces between them, like Grampa Crockett's teeth.

One thing Davy liked very much about Washington, though, was that there was plenty of pastures right in the city limits, so when a man got tired of hearing politicians make speeches or of answering the questions of foreign writers, he could go and look at the calm faces of the friendly cows. Another thing was that there was a horse race almost every day, and the President was likely to be on hand to cheer for the horses he'd brought all the way from Tennessee.

After the Honorable Davy had got a house and planted a garden, he called on the President, Andrew Jackson. The President lived in a big house called the White House that was on the paved street.

General Jackson was eight feet tall, and his sword was so long that it bumped on the carpets of the White House. Andy Jackson's arms were as strong and tough as hickory wood, so he was called Old Hickory. Old Hickory had red hair, and he smoked a corncob pipe and said, "By the Eternal!" He was a great man—one of the greatest.

When the butler at the White House looked out on the porch and saw who was standing there holding a lantern and waiting to make a call, he hollered out in a big voice, "Make way for Congressman Crockett!"

But the Honorable Davy said, "Congressman Crockett can make way for himself, thank you," and sailed right in.

At the dances in Washington, Death Hug and Old Mississippi were the dancers most talked about, though now and then they had a little trouble finding partners.

In the halls of Congress, Congressman Davy made the best speeches—better than peppery John Quincy Adams, or soft-voiced Henry Clay, or even thunder-voiced Daniel Webster. Davy could spout like a rumbling earthquake, could give any man in all of Congress two hours head start, and still out-speak him.

He gave Congress the best advice it ever got or ever was to get when he said: "Be sure you're right, and then go ahead."

When his two terms were over, Davy went home to the cabin in the clearing at the head of the Mulberry Fork of the Elk River, not far from the River Duck. He hugged everybody in the family—his wife, his children, the dog, the horses, the wolf and the panther. They all grinned and showed their white teeth.

But no sooner had Davy settled down again to the job of shooting a cord or two of bears a day than he had to leave his happy home once more, because he had to go to Texas. He had to go to Texas because his country was at war with the Spaniards there.

In a hurry, he hugged everybody all around, and then took such a lightning start that they didn't have time to grin and show their teeth before he was out of sight. He rode on Death Hug's back, with Old Mississippi wallowing and snorting along behind.

Texas turned out to be a place where there were pears with prickles, cactus plants with thorns, toads with horns, jack rabbits with long ears, lizards with long tails, and fish-storytellers with long arms. It also had tarantulas and rattlesnakes that were so big that they made other tarantulas and rattlesnakes look like garden spiders and fishing worms. In summer, when people went out in the sunshine, they feared they'd get cooked; and in winter, when a norther got playful, they feared they'd get frozen.

But the people that lived there claimed that Texas had the best climate, handsomest women, bravest men, and tastiest barbecues in the world. And, partly, they were right.

In Texas, Colonel Davy Crockett would ride around on Death Hug, or maybe on Old Mississippi, and when they came to an enemy camp, the Spaniards would run like twenty-seven (or at times, twenty-eight) streaks of forked lightning.

Once when Colonel Crockett and Death Hug were scampering across Texas with a message for General Sam Houston, an army of enemies got up enough courage to try to stop them. The army stood under a grove of oaks, waved their arms around, jumped up and down, and hollered, "STOP!"

Death Hug had lived with Davy long enough to know what to do—"Be sure you're right and then go ahead." Death Hug figured out what was right quick as half a wink. Then he did it.

He clawed his way up one of the oaks with Colonel Davy on his back. Near the top, slick as a panther, he scooted out on a limb. Near the end of the limb, spry as a squirrel, he jumped on the limb of another oak, and so on, until the enemy was far behind, camped under that first tree, waiting, and tapping their toes, and pacing back and forth wondering when the bear and his master would come down.

With his trusty rifle, Brown Bess, Colonel Crockett shot enough buffaloes to feed the whole American army and some of their prisoners. "Never found anything I liked so well as this buffalo hunting," he said. "Bear hunting is child's play to it."

He also found a way to cook buffalo steaks that pleased the best eating people in Texas. The wind would have to be big and strong, and then there'd have to be a prairie fire whizzing along in front of the whistling wind. Then Colonel Crockett would run along behind the fire and broil the steaks over the galloping flames. This gave the steaks a good smoky flavor, and cooked them fast enough to save the juice.

Once while he was out hunting buffaloes, the colonel got word of two buffaloes that were ring-tailed roarers even for Texas. When these two fellows got peevish, they'd butt down a few groves of trees and then bore a few holes twenty feet deep before they'd start smiling again.

Colonel Davy, riding Death Hug, came up to these fierce buffaloes one day when they were roaring mad—pulling up trees and tossing them into the air for practice before they really got down to work and tore two or three forests to pieces. They were going to play catch with him, too, which would have been most unhandy and uncomfortable.

But Davy slipped around, as quiet as the breath of a moth, and tied their tails together. Then he drove the ferocious beasts a hundred and seventy miles—and shortly they were as tame as lambs.

One of these buffaloes, once Davy had taught him for a while, turned out to have great talents. When they came to one of the border towns, he and Davy would go to meeting every Sunday. At the meeting, at first, the people would sort of frown and grumble to see this shaggy old buffalo, name of Goliath, taking up two or three of the front pews. But by the time the meeting was over they'd see how useful Goliath made himself, and they'd be all for making him an elder in the church. At the meeting, Goliath would sing the bass part of "Old Hundred" without missing a note. What's more, when the choir leader wanted to get the pitch, this buffalo would let the leader use his horn for a tuning fork.

This was just the start of Colonel Crockett's taming wild things in Texas. He tamed a whole crowd of grumpy animals—snakes, bears, wolves and wildcats—and they all helped him scare the enemy into the running jumps. Taming all these animals, and fighting the Spaniards as hard as he could, kept the colonel busy until the war was over.

It had been a right pleasant little war, and he and Sergeant Death Hug and Corporal Old Mississippi were rather sorry to have it end.

After some more traveling, Davy and his beasts went back to the clearing at the head of the Mulberry Fork of the Elk River, near the River Duck. Davy found that everybody was fine—his wife, his children, the dog, the horses, the wolf and the panther. He hugged the lot of them, and they grinned and showed their white teeth.

Davy found that what his travels had proved to him was that Tennessee was the best place in the world, bar none. Somehow—maybe because he was used to them—he liked the animals and plants and climate better than those he'd found in Texas. He even like the Mulberry Fork better than the Rio Grande, even though the Fork was a mite shorter.

First thing Davy did was get to know two interesting neighbors that had moved into the neighborhood.

One was Skippoweth Branch, who lived by a branch of the Mulberry Fork. Skippoweth slept in his hat, chawed his food with his front teeth, and could scream through his nose. He sunned himself in a thunderstorm and went to church on two horses. He said that he lived in the mountains and ate thunder, that he had a necktie that had been made out of lightning, and that he could never stand up straight until the clouds had hoisted themselves up a few feet. He called himself a West Wind full of prickles.

But then there's a chance that he was only joking.

The second new neighbor was Ben Hardin, a sea-going man who said that he hailed from Captain Alfred Bulltop Stormalong's home town, whatever that was. He had captained boats that had turned over and sailed into port upside down and bottomside up. He claimed that he had leaned his back against a hurricane, that he drank bitters made out of rusty cannon balls, and that he slept coiled up like a rope. He also mentioned that he was a squall and a tornado at a frolic, and that he could dance all the girls out of their stockings.

When Ben called on the Crocketts, he danced a sailor's hornpipe until he wore the stone steps away in front of the cabin.

They were great ones to dance in Tennessee at that time—everybody was. Straight through the night, everybody would dance. Sometimes, they'd sing, too—"Leather Britches Full of Stitches," or "Old Dan Tucker," or "Old Zip Coon Was a Very Learned Scholar"—all the latest and liveliest tunes.

What showed that Ben was unusually good was that he'd not only dance all night but all the next day. When he stopped, not another soul would still be at it—except Sally Ann Thunder Ann Whirlwind Crockett.

But Davy outdid Skippoweth Branch, Ben Hardin and Sally Ann Thunder Ann Whirlwind Crockett, too, the year of the Big Comet.

This Big Comet, which the scientific writers of that day say was all red and blue and yellow and green, took a running jump and started lickety split for the earth. Along the way, it kept giving off sparks, the way a big comet does, you know. It scooted past stars and through clouds, and kept right on coming.

Every night, after the cows were milked, the stock was watered, and the dinner things were washed and put away, people would go out in the yard—front or back, depending on which gave them the best view. They'd sit out there watching that comet getting bigger and bigger.

People began to get rather uneasy.

In Washington, things were in even more of a dither than usual. Senators and Congressmen made speeches and passed laws against it, but the Big Comet kept sailing along, giving off sparks, and getting bigger and bigger. Even after the Committee for the Investigation of Falling Stars, Comets and Misplaced Planets had met five times and had taken testimony, it kept coming closer. And people kept getting more and more fidgety.

So the President of the United States, after a long Cabinet meeting, decided to do the only thing there was to do. He put a story in all the newspapers that said:

WANTED, BY THE PRESIDENT OF THE UNITED STATES: DAVY CROCKETT, THE STAR-SPANGLED RIPSNORTER, TO GO UP TO THE TOP OF A MOUNTAIN AND DO SOMETHING DRASTIC ABOUT THAT COMET.

When Davy read this in the Mulberry Fork *Daily Star*, he ('d what was his life-long habit—made sure he was right and then went ahead. He hugged all the usual people and animals in the family and a few other animals that by now had come to stay with them. While their white teeth were still gleaming, he made his start.

Then Davy went up to the towering top of Cloud Mountain. That was a high mountain from which he could see almost to the Eastern seacoast. Near the foot of the mountain was the Crockett cabin, with Death Hug out in the garden churning butter with one paw and waving the other paw at Davy now and then. Beyond that was Davy's pappy's cabin on the shining Nolachucky River. The next river Davy could see was the brown Mississippi, so far away that it looked like a ribbon. East of that, there was too much mist for him to see anything much.

In time, it got to be time for the dark to come. But the Big Comet was shining so red and blue and yellow and green, and giving off so many sparks, and coming so close, that it lighted up the world like a Christmas tree. This was most handsome, as you can guess.

But Davy remembered what he had to do, and he did it.

He waited until that Big Comet came in reaching distance, and then he grabbed it by the tail. It was a heavy comet, and it had been falling a long time, so it was hard to handle. Davy had to set his feet firmly and fairly wide apart, put his tongue in the corner

91

of his mouth, and grunt a little. Then he swung it around his head seven times, getting up speed, you know.

Then he let go. The sparks hissed and flipped into the snow on the top of Cloud Mountain. But the Big Comet scooted, in a new direction, past the clouds and past the stars. And the people down below, sitting out in their yards, took great pleasure in seeing that, for a change, it was getting smaller instead of bigger all the time.

And so far as is known, it never bothered people any more.

This was the second best thing Davy Crockett ever did. The best thing Davy ever did, he did one cold morning in January. That day was a cold day, for fair.

It was so cold that the day-break froze as it was trying to dawn.

In a way, it was good that there weren't any shadows, for if there had been, they'd have frozen, turning some of the snow black, of course. And offhand, I can't think of anything much more ridiculous than black snow.

Well, anyhow, it was powerful cold. The wood in Davy's fireplace would no more catch fire than a raft at the bottom of the South Seas.

"So," thought Davy, "I must strike a little fire from my fingers, light my pipe, travel a few miles, and see about it."

Then he cracked his knuckles together, getting some real nice bright sparks that way, but the sparks froze up before he could so much as begin to collect them.

So out Davy walked, sort of stiff-legged, trying to be careful not to wake up the family. The trees, all full of ice pearls, stood still because even the breezes had frozen and had fallen with a plop into the snow drifts. There wasn't a sound, because the noises had frozen, too, you understand.

With his sort of stiff legs, Davy tried to keep unfrozen by going at a hop, step and jump gait, and whistling a tune called "Fire in the Mountains."

At last he reached Daybreak Mountain. Then, after a good deal of stumbling and slipping on the ice along the way, he reached the top of Daybreak Mountain.

This was even above Cloud Mountain—you could see the top of

Cloud Mountain from there. You could see all the things you could see from the top of Cloud Mountain, and then beyond that to the Washington Monument, in Washington, D. C. which wasn't built yet. In another direction, you could see Texas, maybe, and beyond that, Brazil and Haiti. I mean, you could see all these places on a medium cold, clear day. But this day, account of the sun not being up, this day wasn't a clear one—just a mess of blackness.

Soon, though, after some scouting around, Davy figured out what was the matter:

The earth had frozen fast on her axis, and couldn't turn around in any direction.

The sun had got jammed between two cakes of ice under the wheels, and there he had been shining and working to get loose until he'd frozen fast in his own cold sweat.

"My stars and comets!" thought Davy. "This is getting serious. Something must be done!"

So he thought things over, made sure he was right, and then went ahead.

He poured some oil on the sun and the earth's axis—about a ton of bear oil, it was, that he happened to have along with him. The oil was stiff with the cold, but Davy warmed it with his hands so it would flow better, and when it finally got near enough to the sun, it thawed out and moved along nicely. Then when the oil had got to running, Davy gave the earth's cog-wheel a kick backward, until he got the sun loose.

Then he whistled "Push Along, Keep Moving."

And in about fifteen seconds, the earth gave a shiver. Then it gave kind of a grunt, like a red-eyed bear climbing out of a hollow tree in the springtime. Then the earth began to turn.

The next thing that happened was this: The sun walked up beautifully, fanning Davy with such a wind of thanks that it made him sneeze.

He lit his pipe by the blaze of the sun's top-knot, and walked along toward home, introducing people along the way to fresh daylight with a piece of sunlight in his pocket.

The breezes had unfrozen, and were tugging and pushing at the branches of the trees. The branches were limbering up and flipping off some of their ice pearls. Fires in cabins along the way were getting thawed out, and blue smoke was beginning to come out of the chimneys.

Breakfast was just about ready when Davy got back to the cabin in the clearing at the head of the Mulberry Fork of the Elk River near the River Duck. Everybody was sitting around the table—Sally Ann Thunder Ann Whirlwind Crockett, Pinette and the other children, the dog, the wolf, the panther, Death Hug, Old Mississippi, and the other animals that had come to stay in the cabin. They all looked up when Davy came in, waved their hunting knives and cane forks, grinned, and showed their white teeth.

Breakfast was put on the table just as the sun was sailing over the clearing, with his flame top-knot trailing behind. The ice pearls and the white snow sparkled in the sunshine. So did the hunting knives.

And for breakfast that morning the Crockett family had corn pone full of cracklings and wild honey out of bee trees.

8

Johnny Appleseed, Planter of Orchards on the Frontier

THE NEXT FELLOW I'M GOING TO TELL ABOUT IN THIS HISTORY of America may or may not be a hero. There are good points to be made on both sides of the question. This fellow, name of Jonathan Chapman (or Johnny Appleseed) never fought anybody rough-and-tumble, never killed any whales or varmints or Indians, the way Stormy and Mike and Davy did. Fact is, he made it a point never to hurt a fly. Another thing, he wasn't smart like old Stormy and the others. Some claim that he was crazy as a coot—maybe a little crazier, and there may be something in what they say.

Still there are some people that set their jaws and say: "There wasn't anything gaudy about him, I'll agree. But he was a hero anyhow." And when you think of what this little rascal did, in spite of all his handicaps, you see that there are reasons for agreeing with these people.

Johnny Chapman was born about the time old Stormy made his first trip to sea. About the time Mike Fink took his first keelboat trip, Johnny found his calling, and he stuck to that line of work a good many years after Davy unfroze the frozen sun down in Tennessee.

Back there in Massachusetts on the day Johnny was born, there was one of those Massachusetts May storms that rain cats and a fair number of dogs. But along about when Baby Johnny had polished off his first big cry, the sun came out and made a handsome rainbow.

One end of this rainbow was hitched to Monadnock Hill, where the great carbuncle sparkled in the sunshine. From here the rainbow arched up in the gray-blue sky until the other end swooped down right smack into the Chapman dooryard near Ipswich. There, this end of the rainbow got all tangled up in a big Spitzenberger apple tree which was so loaded with blossoms that it looked more or less like a big snowball. Result was the rainbow colored up the blossoms with all the colors you can think of, off hand, at any rate.

The nurse that was taking care of Johnny and his mother claimed that she picked him up and carried him over to the window for a look at the tree.

"You'll never believe the way he carried on," she said. "Why, he humped and gurgled and stuck out his little white paws as if he wanted to pick all those blossoms! And he was only forty minutes old, too!"

Well, frankly, some of us historians *don't* believe this story—sounds fishy to us. But it's a known fact that as long as Johnny was a baby, each spring he'd whoop and squall and holler around, not giving the family a lick of peace, until they handed him a branch of apple blossoms to hang onto. Then he wouldn't bang the petals off, or eat them, like other babies would. Instead, he'd just lie there in his crib, looking at those apple blossoms, sniffing at them now and then, and smiling as happy as an angel plumb full of ice cream.

When Johnny ended his babyhood and started in being a boy, his mother got to feeling that he was concentrating a little too much on apple trees. "Sonny," she said, "you've got to branch out a little. Apple blossoms are fine things, I agree. But you can't depend on them for all the joy you get out of life. Wild flowers and animals, in some ways, are more or less like apple blossoms, and you might come to like them, too. Come on and see."

So she'd take the little fellow and meander around in the woods with him, introducing him to plants and squirrels and such. Since she was part Indian (Pequod, I believe), Mrs. Chapman knew many of these things almost as well as she knew her kinfolk. And after a while, when Johnny had caught on, there wasn't anything that gave him as much pleasure as taking a stance in front of a wild flower or forest animal and just standing there to admire it until dinner time.

If a flower or weed had a name for making a body well, he'd just about go wild the minute he set eyes on it. Hoarhound, catnip, pennyroyal, ginseng, dog fennel—these were the growing things he favored above all others. Some of these things were ugly as sin and smelled to high heaven, too, but he didn't seem to care a hang. And if the family didn't keep a close watch over him, dear little Johnny would haul whole messes of these herbs home and come close to stuffing the house with them.

He was keen about birds and animals, too. He'd rather listen to a wild bird tuning up his pipes—even if the bird was a hoarse old crow—than eat a piece of pumpkin pie with blackberry jam on it. He was never happier than when he was lugging around some little animal or other, even if, say, it was a skunk, an animal many people sort of tried to avoid. And whenever an animal in the neighborhood was sick or had a broken leg, the neighbors would say:

"Take the brute over to Johnny Chapman; he'll fix him up for you."

Any time he got hold of an animal in a fix like that, he'd wrap bandages around scratched places or put splints around broken legs. Or if a dog or cat was sick, he'd feed the beast some of the bad-tasting medicine he'd made out of herbs.

Before long, the animal would perk up and go kiting it for home, as fast as four legs and a tail would carry it. So it appears that this cure worked pretty well.

When he wasn't doctoring helpless little animals, Johnny would be reading. The book he liked best, for some years, was the one by Aesop, the old Greek slave, that told about animals who kept doing human things—such as lying, cheating, or stealing from one another. Naturally, an animal lover like Johnny was tickled no end by a book that flattered dumb brutes that way.

But in time Johnny's father, a preacher, began to call his attention to the Bible. "There are animals in the Bible, sonny," his father pointed out, "all those animals in the Garden of Eden that were friendly, for instance, and didn't eat one another up, and those animals that took the excursion on Noah's ark, and Balaam's ass, and the four horses of the Apocalypse. Matter of fact, the Bible swarms with animals."

Result was Johnny started to read the Bible for the animals in it. When he found that this book also had a good many parts about apples, that made him think the book was just about perfect. And after a while, when he could catch on to the ideas, they were as much to his taste as the animals and the apples.

They say that Johnny got to be so fond of these two books, *Aesop's Fables* and the Bible, that even after he'd gone to Harvard College and got highly educated, he still couldn't find any books that came within twenty yards of giving him so much pleasure.

It was shortly after Johnny got thoroughly educated that the Chapman family picked up and went to Pittsburgh. And it was in Pittsburgh that something happened to Johnny that made him behave the way he did the rest of his days.

He didn't change, mind you—just got to be more so.

Just what happened isn't clear. Some say that a woman somehow found she couldn't keep her promise to marry Johnny, and that affected him. Some say Johnny got malaria, and it did things to him he didn't get over. Some claim that he got kicked in the head by a horse he was trying to doctor. Still others incline to the idea that it wasn't any one of these things, but all three working together. And if all three of these things did happen to him within the space of a short time, you can understand that there'd be likely to be some noticeable results.

Whatever the cause was, Johnny hit on the idea of getting into this business—or "mission," as he called it—of spreading apple trees all over the Middle West.

His idea was that there ought to be more apple trees in the pioneer parts of Pennsylvania and Ohio and Indiana, and he was the fellow to see to it that there were. So each fall, in cider making time, he'd get around to the sweet-smelling cider presses in Pennsylvania. There he'd collect the pomace, the mashed up stuff that was left after the juice had been squoze out of the apples. Then he'd wash the seeds out, and let them dry in the sun. There were only a few things he liked better than rubbing his finger tips over the slick seeds.

The next spring, he'd bag these seeds, some in old coffee sacks or flour sacks, some in little deerskin pouches. Then he'd start tromping westward, carrying seed packets of one kind and another along with him. He'd hand out the little pouches to the movers West, one to each family. The big bundles he'd tote along to use himself, stopping here and there to plant the seeds all along rivers, in meadows, wherever people would let him or there weren't any people. Even after the seedlings got a good start in some of the orchards, Johnny Appleseed (as he was called by now) would drop around every so often to tend them.

What Johnny would do, in short, was to go traipsing all over the country, sleeping out in the open, eating whatever was handy, stumbling through the trackless forest or tramping through mud and snow, to get these apple orchards started. As the years passed, he covered plenty of ground, too—made it as far south as Tennessee and as far west as the Rocky Mountains.

Some people claimed it was pretty silly.

Maybe you'll ask what people thought was foolish about it. The answer they'd give would be that he wouldn't take any money for going to all this trouble—not a red cent. And it's well known, these people point out, that the only reason that makes sense for doing things is to make money.

"Money?" Johnny Appleseed would say, "*that* for money!" And he'd snap his horny fingers. "I've got a mission, that's what I've got. What do you do with money? Just spend it for clothes or houses or food, I understand, and a saint doesn't care a snippet for any of these. Fact is, he sneers at them, every time he gets a chance. Only thing I want is to get these apples, and herbs that're good for folks, scattered all over the Middle West."

So he'd give those pioneer families appleseeds—free. And if

they'd let him have a little ground for his tree nurseries, he'd plant whole orchards for them, and tend the seedlings, too—free. In the course of a few years, he had nurseries all along the shores of Lake Erie, along Elk Creek, Walnut Creek, French Creek, along the Grand River, the Muskingum, the Tuscarawas, the Mohican, and hundreds of other lakes, rivers and creeks. And instead of selling the seedlings from these nurseries (as he easily could have done), he'd heel them in and wrap them in wet straw and give them to the movers—free.

People that held Johnny was on the queer side said that if these facts didn't prove their point, they had other facts about the way he'd go wandering around in the Indian country, even when the redskins were on a rampage, without a gun or even a knife on him.

"Indians?" the little cuss would say. "*That* for Indians!" And he'd snap his bony fingers. "What'll Indians do to you if you go along peaceful-like and don't hurt them? Nothing—that's what they'll do. A saint gets onto some facts that other people don't, and one of them is that Indians are our brothers."

Well, there is some reason for saying that this was a cracked idea—one that, on the face of it, was plumb crazy. But there's one little detail that keeps it from being a clincher—the fact that, somehow, the Indians *didn't* hurt him—just the way he'd said they wouldn't. Whether the redmen were scared off by his strange looks, or whether they thought he was a heap big medicine man, or what it was, is hard to say. Anyhow, he got along with Indians better than a good many white people got along with white people.

When anybody brought up the matter of animals, Appleseed was likely to go through that finger-snapping business again. "Leave animals alone," he'd say, "and they'll do the same by you. They're brothers and sisters to you, sort of, only they don't borrow clothes and other truck and they don't misunderstand you the way human brothers and sisters do."

And he'd do the strangest things about varmints you ever heard tell of. One night some of those Ohio mosquitoes came along—some of those pests that are so big that, to set them apart from the common little ones, some people call them gallinippers. Well, Johnny had a fire out there in the woods, and considerable smoke was coming out with the flames. He noticed that these gallinippers kept getting into the smoke and choking to death, or maybe flying into the flames and getting cremated.

At a time like that, most people would just say, "Yaah, serves the brutes right," and chuck more wood on the fire.

But Johnny said, "Poor things! Guess I'll have to put out that fire." Then he sloshed water over the blaze, and lay there shivering in the dark—and being et by gallinippers, the rest of the night.

Then there was the time that Johnny was going from Mansfield to Mt. Vernon one cold winter's day, slushing through the snow in those bark sandals of his. Night came, no cabin was near, and he looked around for some big hollow log to sleep in. He found a dandy, built a fire near by, cooked his mush, slupped the stuff up, and started to crawl into the hollow log.

When he'd got in about to his hips, though, he heard a groaning grunt. Peeking in, helped by the light of the fire, he saw a big bear lying in there with his paws crossed on his chest, enjoying his winter snooze.

Johnny backed out, inch by inch, slow as a snail, being quiet so as not to interrupt the bear's sleep. "Beg your pardon, Brother Bear," he whispered. "I didn't mean to bother your sleep. Saints love bears too much to disturb them any."

Then he yawned, stretched, and curled up in the snow.

People that claimed Johnny was touched said that if all these facts didn't show it, they could mention at least three more. One was that he never ate meat, because of this liking he had for varmints. A second was that he kept planting dog fennel, as well as appleseeds, all over the country. "Dog fennel," he said, "keeps away malaria and typhoid, and heaven knows what all." (He was wrong, of course: all it does is smell bad and choke up vegetable gardens.) A third was that, though he never exactly came out and said it, he kept hinting all the time that he was a saint.

But some people kept arguing against anybody that tried to run down Johnny Appleseed in any way. "He was a hero and a saint," they'd say. "He had something he believed in, enough to suffer for

—and he went to a lot of trouble to bring it about. Talk about overcoming hardships! Why he'd go traipsing around without any shoes, in his bare feet, dressed up in a gunny sack, in the coldest weather. He didn't even have a decent hat: either he'd wear that pan he cooked mush in or he'd wear that cardboard affair he'd made that looked like a conductor's cap. And why? Simply because he was sweet and good and he wanted to get orchards scattered all over the countryside to look pretty and grow apples for folks."

Well, you can see there are arguments for both sides.

If you want to figure which side you want to take, it might help for you to have a look at Johnny when he was paying one of those hundreds of calls he paid on the farmers scattered through the Middle West.

This particular call was one he made back in 1839 when Mr. Martin Van Buren was president. Mr. Van Buren was a little plump bald-headed man, chiefly famous, at the time, because he perfumed his sidewhiskers and ate his White House vittles out of silver dishes.

The Merritt family, out there in a clearing near Perrysville, Ohio, was a powerful long way from anything as elegant as perfume or silver dishes. Whatever perfume there was around the Merritt place came from the flower garden and the farmyard, and the dishes they ate out of had been whittled out of wood. They had this farm, this big house and this big barn, and they worked from dawn to sundown—Mr. and Mrs. Merritt and the three children—Paul, Rose and little Phyllis.

When bedtime came, because they'd worked so hard, the Merritts usually just fell into bed and slept like logs. But this May night, Mrs. Merritt woke up, listened a while, then poked her husband.

He stopped snoring and said, "Huh?"—the way husbands do at a time like that.

"Henry," she said, "those night birds out there are making so much noise they went and woke me up with all their singing."

"Well," says Mr. Merritt, "I'll go to the window and politely ask the nasty old things to shut up. That what you want me to do?"

"Listen," Mrs. Merritt told him.

When he stopped grumbling long enough to listen, it was clear that the nightbirds really were having a jamboree out there. They were near the barn, just whooping it up, singing their best and loudest—even letting go with a cadenza or two every now and then.

"They are noisy, for a fact," Mr. Merritt said.

Mrs. Merritt by now had got out of bed and had gone over to the window. Mr. Merritt could see her there in the moonlight, in her long white nightgown.

"Come back to bed," Mr. Merritt told her. "You'll catch your death."

"Henry," Mrs. Merritt said, "they're out in that apple tree near the barn. You can see dozens of them, black against the apple blossoms."

"Thank you," Mr. Merritt said. "I'm glad to know where they are—didn't have a ghost of an idea where they were before. But you're catching your death. And you and those dratted birds, between you, are keeping me awake. Come back to bed."

After Mrs. Merritt had listened a while longer, she said: "Henry, there's somebody snoring out there in the barn! I can hear him snore!"

"He's probably asleep," Mr. Merritt figured. "Don't worry. I expect it's just some old tramp, asleep in the haymow."

"But why didn't the dogs bark?" Mrs. Merritt wanted to know.

"That *is* a puzzle," Mr. Merritt said. He got a hand out from under the covers and scratched his head. Then he said, "I've got it. It's probably that no account Johnny Appleseed out there. Dogs never bark at him. And wild animals and snakes and such, as a rule, don't think he's worth the trouble of hurting. And that would explain those blasted nightbirds in the apple tree, too. Now come on back to bed."

"We should have figured it out before," says Mrs. Merritt. "I'm a-coming."

Well, the next day, just before breakfast, Johnny came marching from the barn to the house. The three Merritt children stood there in the kitchen window and goggled at the man with all their might and main as he crossed the barnyard. He was a sight, for fair.

First thing the children noticed was his gray hair and gray whiskers. He had more of both of them than a mountain man coming in for rendezvous, because he'd let them go longer—for a matter of a good many years. The hair was down over his shoulders and down over his chest, and it waved every which way in the breeze. Next thing they noticed was the way he was dressed. He had a pasteboard cap with the wide bill on it. Instead of a shirt, he had **an** old sugar sack with holes chopped out of it for his head and

arms to go through. His pants were old and short and shredded at the bottom of each leg. One suspender had the job of holding them up, and it was worn until it looked a mite insecure. One foot had a boot on it, and the other was bare. Next the children noticed his bright gray eyes, shining from under bushy eyebrows and through tangles of hair.

Last thing they noticed was that Johnny was marching at the head of sort of a parade. Behind him, in line, more or less in step too, and looking proud as peacocks, marched the Merritt dogs Spotty and Snip, then a ewe, and finally a white hen. They were all talking to Johnny, passing the time of day so to speak, as they marched along.

When the parade got close enough, Mrs. Merritt called out: "Good morning, Johnny. We thought you'd be along one of these days, to tend the orchard. Come right in, and find a chair."

"Good morning, everybody," Johnny said, taking off that pasteboard cap. "Shall I bring in my brothers and sisters to breakfast with us?"

"We won't have any of those animals in the house, except Spot and Snip, if that's what you mean," Mr. Merritt told him.

Johnny, looking sad, turned to the animals. "It's just the way I feared," he said. "They're narrow-minded—won't let you in. Well, I'll join you later." The animals looked sad too, complained a bit, then marched back toward the barnyard, looking dignified as a squad of judges.

After Johnny came into the house, he sat down in the kitchen. The children made kind of a circle around him, and stared and stared, their mouths wide open—didn't stop even when he stroked their hair.

"Sleep well?" Mrs. Merritt asked Johnny, while she busied herself around the stove.

"Yes and no," he answered her. "Of course I wanted to lie down on the nice hard floor out there—sleep better on the floor, you know. But that dear old horse asked me to leave—said it was his stable. So I had to sleep on that soft hay in the hayloft, which rathered bothered me. But I was all fagged out, I could smell the sweet apple blossoms, and there were nightbirds singing—so I got some sleep in anyhow."

"Those confounded birds woke us up with their cluttering and clattering," says Mr. Merritt. "We'd rather you'd slept on the floor in the parlor."

"Oh, no, Mr. Merritt. I didn't want to wake you up so late at night," says Johnny, smiling sweetly. "Saints with missions are thoughtful of people, you know."

With the same sweet smile spread all over the lower end of his leathery face (so far as you could see through the whiskers), Johnny turned to Mrs. Merritt. "And how," he asked her, "have the big Merritts and the three little angels been since I last broke bread with them?"

"Well," Mrs. Merritt told him, "all three of those little angels went and caught themselves the whooping cough in January, and I had lumbago in February, and Mr. Merritt had the miseries in March. Aside from that, we've been fine and well."

"I still have the miseries now and then," Mr. Merritt said.

"I never have the miseries," Johnny said. "I live in the great out-of-doors, think high thoughts and such, and eat up all my mush. That way, I never have miseries."

Mr. Merritt got middling red and started to say something, but by now little Phyllis had taken her thumb out of her mouth to ask a question: "Why do you wear only just one boot, Mr. Appleseed?"

"Well, I'll tell you, little Phyllis. This bare foot here, he went and stumbled his big toe the other day, so I'm punishing him for a while."

"Oh, I see," nods Phyllis.

The last few minutes, Mrs. Merritt had been taking hot things from the stove and sailing into the dining room with them. Now, hanging up her apron, she said: "Well, I guess everything's ready. Henry, will you bring in an extra chair?"

Mr. Merritt grunted while he carried the kitchen chair into the dining room. "The trouble isn't that there aren't enough chairs," he said. "It's that there are too many people."

When they all were sitting around the table, Johnny asked a

question: "Is there enough for all the animals and for the three little angels?"

"Of course there is!" Mr. Merritt said, getting reddish again, this time with a touch or two of purple.

"Good," Johnny said. "Make it a point never to eat a bite till I've made sure. Saints are thoughtful of others that way."

"We're lucky to be fixed so you can eat with us," says Mr. Merritt. "Now, can I have the pleasure of giving you a big helping of sausage?"

"Dear me, no," says Johnny, holding up his hands as if something scary was coming at him. "Never eat a four-footed friend, as I've told you before; it'd make me feel like a cannibal. Just give me a little mush and a few pancakes. Saints are never very heavy feeders."

So Johnny ate his little meal of two bowls of mush and eight pancakes, and then leaned back in his chair. "That was perfect, Mrs. Merritt, just perfect," he said. "Only thing that might just possibly make it a smidgeon better would be some apple sauce or maybe a piece of apple pie."

"Apples?" says Mr. Merritt. "I think they disagree with me— give me the miseries."

If Mr. Merritt had whacked the Appleseed Man over the head with a plow, Johnny wouldn't have looked more astonished. He blinked his gray eyes, back of all that hair, and stood up in a daze, like a fellow setting out to do a little sleep-walking. He put his napkin down on the red-checkered tablecloth, cleared his throat, took a stance, and made one of those speeches of his about apples.

"Apples," he started out, "never, from the beginning of time, disagreed with anybody. They were in all the great countries of the earth; they were in the Hanging Gardens of Babylon that were one of the Seven Wonders; they were in the Garden of Eden; they—"

"Seems to me," Mr. Merritt interrupted him, "they caused some trouble in the Garden of Eden."

"That's wrong!" Johnny said, excited-like. "I don't know who started that story, but he was a bad man. Look in the Good Book, and you'll see that all it says is, they ate of 'the fruit of the tree.'

Now that could be anything—a peach, a plum, a persimmon, a lemon—anything, in short, except an apple. Be sure the Lord wouldn't keep anyone from eating an apple. How many times is the apple spoken of in the Good Book in a favorable way? Eleven times, that's how many.

"Now you take an apple tree, and put it alongeside of any other, and what do you find? Well, you find there isn't any fruit tree that lives so long and still gives fruit. An apple tree will bring good fruit a hundred and fifty years without even getting stooped over. Apple trees have got the handsomest blossoms, too, that smell the best of any fruit blossoms. Apple trees grow anywhere—north, south, east or west. Then take the fruit itself—how long does it last? Well, it'll last a sight longer than any other fruit you can name. Keep an apple, and a tomato, and a peach, and an orange in the same cellar, and after all the rest are squashed and nasty looking, the apple will be firm and crunchy and good to gnaw on. Then think of the things you can't make without apples. There's cider—"

"How about cherry cider, Mr. Appleseed?" asked Paul, who took after his father and liked to argue.

"That's not cider," Johnny answered, speaking very quickly. "That's just cherry juice. They pay it a high compliment when they call it cider. Only way to make real cider is out of apples. There are other things you can't make without apples, too—prime things—vinegar, apple butter, apple dumplings, apple sauce, even apple pies. Where'd the world be today if it wasn't for apples? In a horrible fix, that's where!"

Then Johnny got ready to wind up his speech. He stood up very straight, brushed a hank of hair out of his eye, and stared at something in the distance. "I see America," he said, using his quivery deep voice, "a nation of apple orchards. The apple trees bloom in the spring, and the men and women and children love the blossoms. The birds sing, the sun ripens the fruit, and the pickers carry the fruit to the cool cellars. Then men and women and children everywhere become strong and good and healthy, like me, because they eat apple pies."

Johnny sat down, wiping his forehead with the table napkin.

"I'm sure," says Mrs. Merritt, starting to rid up the table, "that Mr. Merritt will try some of those apples some time. Sounds to me as if they might cure those miseries of his. Won't you, Henry dear?"

Mr. Merritt sort of grunted.

"What are you going to do today, Mr. Appleseed?" Paul wanted to know.

"I'm going to get some nice herbs planted, so you won't be ailing around here so much. I'll plant some hoarhound, to take for a cold, and some dog fennel, that'll keep away malaria, and pennyroyal and catnip and rattlesnake weed. Then I'm going to put some new Russet appleseeds into the moist brown earth, and tromp them down just right. And I'm going to tend the seedlings in the nursery and the orchard. Guess I'd better get started."

"Can Paul give you a hand?" Mr. Merritt wanted to know. Mrs. Merritt gave him a quick look, and then traded a smile with Johnny.

"Of course he can—and the other angels, too," says the Appleseed Man. "Come on, angels!" And he started out of the door.

"Psst!" whispers Mr. Merritt to Paul, pulling him aside. "You watch where he puts those dratted dog fennel seeds. They don't do any more for malaria than hay does, they choke the vegetables, and they smell to high heaven. Run along, and keep your eyes peeled."

So Paul went out to the barn, along with the girls, and got there just as Johnny was picking up his seeds. He couldn't find one bag, however, even after he'd hunted all over for it. Finally Rose, who was helping, said:

"Here it is, in Nanny's stall! Nanny ate all the seeds! Oh, you naughty, naughty goat!"

But Johnny just said, "I don't mind, Nanny. I don't care, Rose, if animals eat all my seeds. And rattlesnake weeds won't hurt a goat. Nothing hurts a goat, you know. So come on, brothers and sisters, to work."

With the dogs, the ewe, the hen and the Merritt children trailing behind, Johnny set to work. For all he was such a skinny little runt, he could work like a horse. So, though he took time out to set a squirrel's broken leg and to make a willow whistle for Paul, by supper time he'd finished all the work he'd laid out for himself.

After supper, he was at his best. He'd reach a knotty fist into his knapsack and pull out presents for all the children. Rose got cloth for a doll dress, little Phyllis a sparkling string of beads, Paul a brace and bit. Then he told them stories—about the people he'd visited, about the heavenly angels who came calling while he sat alone by his campfire, about the way he saved the settlers from the Indian attack.

"When I was visiting in this tepee and learned what they were up to, I lit out. I'd stop at all the settlements, and holler: 'The tribes of the heathen are upon your doors and devouring flames followeth after them!' That way people were warned—"

"Well," Paul said, "I don't see why you didn't just say, 'The Indians are coming.'"

"Prophets don't talk that way," Johnny answered him back, and he went on and finished his story.

After the children had gone to bed, Johnny played his fiddle a while. Then he said, "Let me read you some news fresh from heaven." He read out of the Bible then, until Mr. Merritt started to snore. After the Merritts had gone upstairs, Johnny stretched out on the floor—slept fine there, too.

The next morning, after the Appleseed Man had waved good-by, Mrs. Merritt said, "Henry, don't you think he's wonderful? Isn't he just a saint on earth?"

Mr. Merritt sort of grunted, and asked Paul to show him where that dratted dog fennel had been planted, before he forgot.

So for years and weary years, Johnny Appleseed went on his saintly way, planting appleseeds and bad-smelling herbs. Through good weather and bad he traipsed, and his bags of seeds were a weight on his scrawny little shoulders.

When many years had passed and he was old and stiff in his joints as seven new hinges, one stormy day he caught his death of cold tending an orchard he'd planted.

As soon as Senator Sam Houston of Texas, back in Washington, D. C., heard Johnny had died, he stood up and made a speech. Along toward the end, "This old man," he said, "was a great citizen. His was a work of love, and in time to come people will call him blessed." This was a good guess: though some people run him down, the way I've mentioned, others still speak highly of Johnny Appleseed.

And it's claimed by some that, even today, if you
1. Go to a certain part of Ohio in apple blossom time;
2. Get up before sunrise;
3. Go to a certain old apple tree—
you'll see the smoke from Johnny's fire as it dies out. Maybe you'll even catch a glimpse of Johnny's spirit as it moves along westward with the spring, on his mission of waking up the blossoms and tending the orchards.

I haven't looked into this, never having been in the right place at the right time. But quite a few people say that Johnny Appleseed was a queer one, of course, and they wouldn't be at all surprised if it turned out he really was carrying on that way.

9

Mose, New York Fireman and California Miner

ALL THIS WHILE, BACK EAST AND DOWN SOUTH, CITIES HAD
been growing as fast as pumpkin vines in the Crockett clearing—
New York, Philadelphia, Charleston—places like that.

These cities haven't got into this history so far because, somehow,
they hardly ever managed to raise up any heroes. But along in those
years when old Johnny Appleseed was taking some of his last trips
West, New York had a humdinger of a hero. So it's time I told
about New York and this hero, Mose the Fireman.

The history of New York goes away back to 1609 when a Dutch
explorer, Henry Hudson, tried out a new dodge for doing what
Columbus hadn't managed to do—sailing to India. Henry had it
figured out that maybe if he sailed far enough up the Hudson
River, he might get to that country and sail home with a shipful of
silks and spices and suchlike.

Well, he sailed as far as Albany without seeing hide nor hair of
India, got discouraged, and sailed back down the river. At 209th
Street, West, he went ashore on Manhattan Island and discovered
New York.

Soon as they heard about this, a good many Dutchmen left home
and came over here. They built a fort at 39 Broadway, by sheer

good luck, of course, since the street hadn't been built in front of the fort yet. Then they settled on Bowling Green, which wasn't there at the time either. Finally, after they'd made up their minds that they liked the climate or something, they scraped together twenty-four dollars, and bought a mess of fancy trinkets, and swapped the whole island away from the Indians.

After everything had been made legal that way, more and more people settled there, just the way I've said. Even after the English took the town over and even after the city came to be more or less a part of the United States following the Revolution, people kept moving in.

Along in those years when Mose was a hero and when James Polk and then General Taylor were presidents, New York was three times as big as Boston, even without counting the dogs, cats and pigs. Since Boston was even bigger than Baltimore, you can see that New York was a whopper of a city.

In those days if you looked at New York from the bay, first you'd see a regular forest of masts with sails flapping and flags waving on all the ships docked alongside the city. Then, farther along, you'd see regular heaps and herds of buildings, some as high as five stories, with here and there a spire or steeple standing up above them.

When you went ashore, first thing you'd think was that New York must be an easy place to live in. There were great quantities of white or red brick houses, all with glass windows, some even with plaster on the walls. Wherever you had a mind to go, you could go without much work, in a cab, a coach, a tilbury, a carriage or a horse car. And you didn't have to grow or kill your food, the way people did Out West in those days: you could buy it in stores. You could buy your clothes, too—velvets, rainbow silks, and pink and blue bonnets for the ladies; and green, blue or purple pants and coats—and vests that would knock your eyes out—for the men.

But just the same, New York had plenty of hardships for a hero to overcome.

Don't think that all those tilburies, horse cars and such didn't make it tough to get around. These things would be thick as three in a bed out there in the street. They'd be flashing by at a speed as high as five miles an hour, regardless of consequences. So if you wanted to cross a busy street like Broadway, say, you'd have to set your teeth, watch your chance, and then just dart through the bunch of them. And if you weren't a first class darter, it might be smartest not even to try, even though staying on one side of the street all the time did get monotonous.

Another thing, a good many people in New York that had pigs but didn't have any pig-pens would simply turn the critters loose in the morning and let them stroll around the streets all day. And it was most unhandy to bump, rub up against, or step on one of those pigs.

What's more, the place was worse than a boiler factory for noise. The pigs grunted, squealed and went "Whuff! Whuff!" And you'd find more people howling in a way of business than you'll find nowadays hollering for fun at a football game. Newsboys, bakers, fruit peddlers and locksmiths all threw back their heads and bellowed. Woodsaws buzzed. Oystermen blared on their horns. Ragmen banged bells. Mixed up with all this blimming and blamming there was the clatter and clutter of traffic joggling and jolting over the bumpy cobblestones.

Mose, it happens, never put his mind to fixing up traffic, penning up pigs, or cutting down on those awful noises. There were some men that hung out on the Bowery and that were lively and playful, and that therefore were called the Bowery Boys. These Bowery Boys had even bigger jobs to handle, two of them—keeping the Plug Uglies under control and putting out fires. And Mose helped the Bowery Boys.

One of the finest streets in New York, those days, was the Bowery. Daytimes on the Bowery, people bought stuff at the fruit stalls, clothing stores, or hardware shops, and the place was all business.

At night, though, the street was all lit up like a three dollar Christmas tree, and pretty nearly as gay. There were black mammies peddling mint, strawberries, hominy and hot yams. There were fellows selling hot chestnuts. There were pretty hot corn girls, carrying hot roasting ears in big cedar buckets, paddling around in their bare feet and chanting:

> *Hot Corn! Hot Corn!*
> *Here's your lily white corn.*
> *All that's got money—*
> *Poor me that's got none—*
> *Come buy my Hot Corn,*
> *And let me go home.*

Along with this, there'd be music from all the concert halls and some of those show houses and such along the street. The Bowery Theatre was not only the biggest on the Bowery but also the biggest in the whole town. There'd always be a gaudy show at the Bowery—*Hamlet, Macbeth, The Drunkard or the Fallen Saved,* or some regular thriller of a play.

There were people of all kinds and sorts wandering and strolling around on the Bowery at night, or hissing and cheering in the theaters. But from top to toe and up again from toe to top, the Bowery Boys were the handsomest men and the Girls were the handsomest women.

A Bowery Boy wore a shiny plug hat that slanted forward on the left front corner of his head. His hair was cut short in back, long in front, and rubbed with bear grease until it shone like a bottle. He wore a black frock coat that even went below his knees. He had a fancy velvet vest that was big enough to see, of course, but that was cut low enough so you could likewise see plenty of his swank shirt and some of his bright suspenders. His trousers were tight to the knees and then belled out from there on, until they almost covered his boots from heel to toe.

The Bowery Girls, in the clothes they wore, outdid those elegant belles who were always mincing along Broadway with their noses in the air. The feathers on the Bowery Girls' hats were bigger, the Girls' dresses were shorter, and their clothes had at least twice as much color to them.

Seeing these Boys and Girls strolling around on the Bowery or dancing and prancing in a concert hall, you might think they were just gay butterflies, without a lick of work to do. But both the Girls and the Boys worked like fury all day and were free to play only at night.

As I've said, for one thing, the Boys had to keep the Plug Uglies in order. The Plug Uglies were a Five Points Gang that hung out over on Paradise Square. They got their name because they were ugly as sin and because they wore those huge plug hats. They'd stuff these hats with wool and leather and pull them down over their ears to use for helmets. Then they'd wander around, with a brickbat in one hand and a club in the other, looking and hoping for trouble. They were bad, they were ornery, and the watchmen couldn't handle them. So of course, the Bowery Boys had to whop them, to preserve Law and Order.

They'd fight the Plug Uglies along the Bowery or at the Five Points or over on the place north of Grand Street that was called Bunker Hill.

At first, this was a great trial for the Bowery Boys. But in time they came to rather like a fight or, as they got into the habit of calling it, a "muss." After a while, when things were dull, now and then they'd go wandering around, looking and hoping for a chance to preserve Law and Order.

The other thing that kept the Boys busy was putting out fires.

That was quite a thing to do, those days, because the buildings weren't fireproof, of course, and scientists and people like that hadn't hit on a good share of the stunts we use nowadays to put out a fire. So a building was likely to blaze up and then turn to ashes— fast—unless the firemen rushed and stopped it.

The Bowery Boys were the firemen. They'd scoot to fires, and save any people that were in need of it, and put out the flames. They weren't paid to do this, either: they did it for the same reason they whopped the Plug Uglies—because they wanted to be helpful. That was at first, anyhow. After a while, they came to enjoy it.

A whole mess of things happened, those days, whenever a fire started. The watchman in the part of town where the blaze was would run around and tell at least five people—the Common

Councilman, the engineer, the firewarden, the foreman and the bellringer. Then he'd sort of larrup around the place in general, hollering "Fire! Fire! Thirty-third Street!" (Or whatever street it was.)

As soon as people in that part of town woke up, they'd crawl out of bed, stumble over some chairs, make some remarks, quiet the baby, light candles, and put the candles in the windows. The candles were supposed to help people find their way around the dark street when they went to the fire.

By this time, bells would be ringing in all the churches. But the bell that told where the fire was to be found was the one in the City Hall tower. The number of strokes this bell made would show what district, and there'd be a light hanging on a stick up there, pointing out the direction.

Well, the boys might be dancing, or taking a stroll, or snoozing. Whatever they were doing, they stopped and legged it to the fire-house, making whatever changes in their clothes they had to as they ran. When they got to the engine house, they'd have their pants legs rolled up. They'd be in their red shirts and those rainbow suspenders with double-headed eagles on them. All they needed was to get fire hats, and they were ready.

The first man there threw open the doors, kicked away the chocks, and rolled out the machine. This was a beautiful thing, all shiny and painted up, with a hose on it. Only trouble was, the firemen had to catch hold of a long rope and lug her to the fire, because horses weren't being used on hose wagons those days.

Before long, though, enough Bowery Boys would be on hand to do this, and the foreman would yell through his trumpet, "Start her lively, boys!" Then he'd yell, "Let out more rope!"

When she was well started, he'd holler, "Now jump her lively! Every man lay to his work! Pull heavy!" So they'd hurry to the fire fast as ever they could, unless, of course, they got tangled up with another company along the way.

Then, naturally, they'd have to stop and have a muss.

After they galloped like mad, that way, to the fire, the first thing they had to do was find a hydrant. Probably one of the company had seen to it that one had been reserved, for there wasn't hardly any disgrace as disgraceful as failing to get a hydrant. So some fellow probably had taken an empty barrel and put it over a hydrant, so only his company could find one there. Sometimes, though, there'd be a company onto every hydrant, and of course there'd have to be a few fights to see which company had to go without.

Once they got a hydrant, one way or another, the Boys would run out their hose until the nozzle was close enough to the fire to do good. Then the foreman would yell, "Man your brakes!" "Brakes" were what they called pumps; I've often wondered why. A fire engine, chiefly, in those days, was just some big pumps on wheels that took twenty men to run them.

Then the men pumped like all fury, and a stream started. The man that had got to the firehouse first was the one that got to hold the nozzle, which he did. The steward of the company, who was in charge of the vittles, went around passing out drinks and food, to keep up the Boys' strength.

Firemen would do other things, too, in addition to pumping and holding nozzles—chop holes, save people, and whatever was needed.

That was the way things went at a fire, as a rule. But when Mose got into Company No. 40, the Lady Washington Company at 174 Mulberry Street, things were different.

If you asked a Bowery Boy that was in Company No. 40 about Mose, you might have trouble figuring out what he said, unless you knew two things—1) that a Boy, as a rule, said "d" wherever most other people would say "th"; and 2) that his grammer was of a sort to make your hair stand on end, it was that awful. What he'd say would be:

"Mose Humphreys is de pet of de Bowery. He's one of de Boys, he is. Everybody knows Mose and dose dat don't know Mose don't know nobody dat is anybody. A spree wouldn't be one widout Mose was dere. He's at home in a muss, at home at a concert hall, at home any place in New York. He walks into a row or a fire like a ton of brick. He always has a friend to help and a foe to lam, and neider has any trouble findin' him."

Mose had red hair and tended to be sort of large. He had feet like East River barges, his beaver hat was two feet from crown to brim, and his fireman's helmet was about the size of a pup tent. He could swim the Hudson River in two strokes, go all the way around Manhattan Island in six strokes (five, if the weather was a little chilly.) But if he wanted to cross the East River to Brooklyn, he simply swung his arms a while then jumped it, with room to spare.

When he had nothing else of interest to do, Mose was as likely as not to take a horse car off the tracks and carry it on his shoulder,

the way a waiter does a tray. This annoyed people in the car, because Mose would be chuckling all the time, and they'd be more or less shaken up. Even people that weren't in the car would be riled when he pulled a stunt like that, because when Mose laughed, the trees along the street would bend as if a storm was blowing them, and there'd be a roar like Niagara Falls.

Mose didn't carry a car very far as a rule, though—the longest trip on record was only from Chatham Place to Broome Street, along the Bowery.

Mose, like all the rest of the Boys, loved a muss. "Haven't had a muss for ever so long," he'd say, "except for a little blowout last night, when I gave dat Plug Ugly thunder over de coconut. It goes against me grain."

So he and the other Boys would look around for some Plug Uglies that needed to be taught what was lawful and orderly. "Bring on a cord or two of 'em," Mose would say. "We can lick de crowd, *we* can!" Those Plug Uglies would carry brickbats and staves, the way I've said. But Mose would carry a hickory wagon tongue.

When the chance came, "Huzza!" he'd yell. "Now I'm goin' in!" And the way he'd lay about him was something to see. Only trouble was, sometimes he'd break that wagon tongue. But Mose knew what to do in a case like that. He'd uproot a tree, right out of the ground. Then he'd hold this tree by the branches and swing it around. (You'll find that some histories say that the mulberry trees of Mulberry Bend were chopped down to build up the city. Fact is, though, that Mose pulled them up to fight Plug Uglies.) Or if there weren't any trees handy, but some paving stones were there, he'd rip the stones up and fling them in all the right directions.

Even Plug Uglies couldn't stand up long against Mose. First thing they knew, they'd be making tracks for their hideouts in Paradise Square, and the muss would be ended.

After Mose had helped out that way, the Bowery Boys in No. 40 would try to tell him how good they thought he was. "You're one of de Boys," they'd say, "you ain't nothing else. We ain't stuffin' you."

Then Mose would look kind of shy and puzzled, and he'd answer them back, "Ain't I doin' me duty?"

Mose was just as keen on fire fighting. "De engine No. 40's got is one of de seven wonders of de world," he said. "She's painted up wid white and gold paint, and she has dese pitchers of Marda Washington on her. I loves her better dan my dinner. Last time she was at de corporation-yard, we plated de brakes and put in new condensil pipes; and de way she works is about right, I tell you. She throws a four inch stream de purtiest in town, and I go to de hub for her. It'll make me mussy if dere's not a fire soon. I likes to go in when I'm at a fire, just to keep cool!"

Soon after that, there was a fire. Some of the No. 40 Boys that were bunked at the station got down to the engine room mighty quick. They threw their boots from an upper window and were down before their boots hit the sidewalk. But Mose, who was a few blocks away, just jumped and got there first.

Then he pulled out the engine and ran for the fire with it, while the Boys of No. 40 raced to catch up with him.

At the fire, Mose found that the Boys of No. 28 had taken the best hydrant. "Lookee here, hoss flies," he told them, "it makes me mussy if No. 40 don't git de best plug. I'll lam you if you don't let No. 40 in here. I won't do nothin' else."

So of course the generous Boys of No. 28 were pleased as Punch to let the best engine in New York plug in where it could do the most good.

Since he'd been the first to get to the station, Mose had a right to hold the nozzle. But this time, like other times, he let his pals take turns holding it—because Mose had a heart as big as a house. Meanwhile, he manned the brakes alone and made the Martha Washington fire engine throw up a stream that was the thickest and longest at the fire.

While he was pumping, Mose sang the company's song, as was customary. It was a fine noble song that went this way:

Huzza for brave Old Forty,
Ever prompt at de fire-bell's call;
Tree cheers for brave Old Forty,
Huzza for de firemen all!
When de red flames wildest flash
On de startled midnight air,
Where de crackling embers crash,
Old Forty's men are dere.

Secure may de mudder sleep,
Wid her babe upon her breast,
Brave hearts deir watches keep,
To guard dem when dey rest.
When sudden fires alarm dem,
In de dwellin' where dey lie,
De fires shall never harm dem—
Old Forty's men are nigh.

This was the fire where there were a mother and her three children caught in a room away up on the fourth story. Standing in the window, they were, with the mother waving her hands and the children all wailing and crying. Right off, the Boys tried to get a ladder up to that terrible height, but naturally none would reach anything that high.

When Mose heard about this, he told the No. 40 Boys, "Here, hold de butt and man de brakes, hosses. I'm goin' in."

So he went over, sized things up, and figured out what to do. "Lookee, hosses," he said. "Go git dose barrels dat you put over de plugs. I want eight of dose barrels, and be hasty about it!"

When they brought the barrels, Mose piled them one on top of the other. Then he hoisted the ladder onto the top of the top barrel and stood back to size things up. The ladder reached plenty high, if you added Mose to it, but it looked a mite shaky.

"I'm goin' in," says Mose, rolling up his red shirtsleeves.

"Don't, Mose!" some of the boys yelled. "She's not steady, and she's apt to spill ya!"

"Gas," says Mose, and he took a step to the top of the first barrel, then the second, then the third, and so on, until he was on the

top one. By that time the ladder was waving around like a whip. But Mose kept going until he stood up there at the top of the ladder, sort of balancing himself by waving around his left leg.

"All right," he told the woman and the three children. "Jest climb down and hold on to me suspenders, de bunch of ya."

The mother and two of the youngsters made it nicely, and then they just hung on to Mose's suspenders like so many tassels. But the littlest baby stood there and whimpered, twisting his nightie in his little dimpled fists.

"Don't be scared," Mose told him. "I go fer babies to de hub, I don't do nuttin' else." Then he took the baby tenderly in his left hand and lifted him down, as careful as you'd take one of those thin glass balls off of a Christmas tree.

"Look at that ladder," the mother told Mose. "It's weaving around like a *couple* of whips. Oh, my poor babies!"

"Just hang on tight," Mose asked her. "We'll git down okay."

"I know we'll get down," says the mother. "But the question is, how?"

"Like dis," says Mose. And with that he jumped down light as a feather and lit feet first, like a cat, before the mother and the babies had time to break loose or even to worry any.

"Huzza for Mose!" everybody yelled a few times. Then they dashed back to work to put the fire out some more.

The mayor of New York was on hand, of course, yelling with the rest for Mose. He had to go to every fire, the law back in those days said, all togged out in the proper outfit for a mayor to wear at an affair like that.

After the blaze was out, the usual commands were given—

"Vast playing!"

"Back your lines out!"

"Take up!"

Then the mayor herded a crowd together and made a speech at Mose and the rest of the Boys.

"In behalf of the government of the city of New York," says the mayor, "and in behalf of the boroughs and such, I'd like to thank and felicitate Mose Humphreys for his great work at this fierce fire. He's one of the Boys, and I am not stuffing him."

"He ain't nothin else," roars the crowd. "Huzza for Mose!"

Then Mose looked bashful and sort of puzzled, and he answered the mayor and the crowd back, "Ain't I doin' me duty?"

When the firemen had their parades, Mose gave No. 40 an edge on every other company. Every company, of course, would have its band playing its songs. Every company would polish all the metal on its engine and fix her up with flags and streamers and

flowers. But every company would have four horses to snort and neigh and pull the float the engine was on—every company but No. 40. You see, Mose would pull Old 40 himself, alone, and easily.

And everybody watching the parade would wait until Mose came along to give his loudest huzza. "What you yellin' about?" Mose would ask them. "Ain't I doin' me duty?"

You can easily see why, when Mose went away for a while, the Bowery Boys in No. 40 found his being away made a whale of a difference. Mose went away because, in 1849, there was the Gold Rush to California.

Those years that Mose was putting out all the fires in New York, you see, were the years when Texas came into the Union and the United States took in places like Oregon and California.

In January, 1848, a man by the name of Sutter down in California had a fellow named Marshall at work building a sawmill for him. On January 28, it was raining cats and cataracts—or, as Californians would put it, the weather was being unusual.

Marshall, all spattered with red mud and drenched with rain, came sloshing up to Sutter, said "Shush!" and led Sutter into a room. Then Marshall locked the door, stuffed the keyhole and peeked under all the tables and chairs to see that no one was hiding.

"Look here," he finally whispered, and he pulled a little bundle wrapped up in a red bandanna out of his pocket. "This here was washed out by our new tail-race, and I think it's gold!"

Sutter looked at what was in the bundle, then—"Vell! Vell!" he said. (Sutter was Swiss, and that was the way he said "Well! Well!") "Dot," he went on, "is somedings I hadn't egspegted!" Then he scowled and said, "Dunder und blitzen! If de men find out dere iss gold here, dere vill be no more work at our mill!"

You know how it is when gold is struck somewhere: the news gets around in short order. And even though Marshall had whispered in a locked room, and even though he and Sutter both kept the thing hushed up the best they could, before long the news was pouring all over California and then all over the whole country.

And by 1849, people from everywhere were pouring into California to get the gold.

126

Back in New York, there was a newspaper called the *Sun*. Mose went up to the hub for it, because it had said once that No. 40 was the best-drilled fire company in all New York. Result was, when the *Sun* said there was gold out there in California, Mose knew it must be a fact.

After ciphering a bit, Mose figured out that if he had a good deal of money he could do some fine things with it. He could give some to his best friend, Syksey. He could use some to marry his girl, Lize. And he could spend the rest on a new engine for No. 40, a house, and some duds.

Having seen how useful great quantities of gold would be to him, Mose scraped together what money he needed for a trip to California—about a hundred and ninety-eight dollars, and told the Boys of No. 40, "I'm goin' in."

Then he booked passage on the clipper ship *Apollo*, and went around to the stores on the Bowery to stock up with cigars, spades, hoes, shovels, pickaxes, rifles, pistols and bowie-knives, red shirts and big hats, beans and Blake's Bitters. (Blake's Bitters was a wonderful medicine that cured about everything, all the way from a headache to pneumonia.)

All this time, as was to be expected, the Boys of No. 40 were getting up a farewell banquet and ball. This put them to heaps of trouble, because getting together enough grub for Mose to make out with was a staggering chore. Days before, all the butchers at Center Market were as busy as Bowery Boys at a fire, chopping up hogs and cattle. And days before, the Boys of No. 40 were rushing about buying vegetables and fruit.

When the big night came, the hall where they were having the feast and the shindig was all decorated up with streamers and flags and the fire engine. (The metal parts of the engine had been shined up until they sparkled like diamonds, and the Boys had given Martha Washington a new coat of paint.) On Mose's right sat Lize, on his left sat Syksey. On the table in front of Mose was his first course, four quarts of oysters with catsup on them.

When everyone was seated, Mose, being polite and thoughtful the way he was, wanted to find out whether everybody was served. He stood up, rapped for order, and said: "Are you all on hand at the station, Boys?" When they told him they were, "Then," says Mose, "start her lively," and they all began to eat.

After the oysters, Mose had a barrel of soup. After that, he had a few fresh hams and a few legs of roast beef, served up with fiery sauce. To finish up, he had three or four watermelons and a keg of coffee. (The coffee, in line with a happy idea Syksey had had, was served in a keg that No. 40 was going to use after that to hide hydrants under.) The rest of the Boys couldn't eat quite as much as Mose did, but they did their best, which was very good.

On seeing that all the plates were empty, Mose stood up and said: "Back your lines out, Boys, pull up, and we'll do some dancing."

They danced until it was time for Mose to board his ship, about three o'clock in the morning. At Pier No. 10, North River, Mose shook hands with all the Boys, patted Syksey on the shoulder, kissed Lize and the No. 40 engine (which he'd pulled to the pier). Then he stepped aboard the *Apollo*, making her list a bit.

There wasn't enough of a wind to make the ship start. That meant that Mose had to step down into the bay, take a drag on his two-foot cigar, and puff at the sails. The *Apollo* got under way with a swoop; it's said she got clear beyond Staten Island before the pilot could do anything with the helm. By the time he got her under control, Mose had waved good-by to his friends and had jumped aboard.

Somehow, the historians don't seem to have found out much about what happened to Mose on this trip to California. All we have a record of is the song he sang while he was on the trip around the Horn and a few facts about his life at the diggings.

The song, to the tune, "Oh Susannah," went this way:

> *I've put from New York City*
> *Wid me washbowl on me knee;*
> *I'm goin' to California,*
> *De gold dust for to see.*
> *I soon shall be in Frisco,*

128

And dere de gold I'll spy.
I'll pick de gold lumps from de ground,
So, Syksey, don't you cry.

    Oh California!
    Dat's de land for me.
    I'm goin' to San Francisco
    Wid me washbowl on me knee.

I jumped aboard de Apollo ship,
    And left widout much fuss,
But I'm homesick for de Bowery,
    For a fire and for a muss.
But when I get to Frisco,
    I'll drain de rivers dry,
And I'll lug back a pile of gold,
    So Lize, dear, don't you cry.

    Oh California!
    Dat's de land for me.
    I'm goin' to San Francisco
    Wid me washbowl on me knee.

All we know about Mose at the diggings is this: he used that washbowl, which was about the size of a bathtub, to wash out the gold with. The first day at the diggings, he found a solid lump of gold that weighed one hundred pounds, ten ounces, fifteen pennyweights and three grains—a rather large one, you see.

And after such a start, his luck held out good and strong until finally he filled his tent chock up with gold, and he had to sleep out in the open air, with nothing but his boots to shelter him.

So there was this day a while later when Syksey and Lize were standing and looking out to sea, heaving sighs every now and then and wishing that Mose was back. All of a sudden, they saw a huge shadow moving across the water, more or less like a cloud, but with more arms and legs. Then they knew that someone had jumped across a good stretch of water, and then they knew he was standing beside them. It was Mose with seven kegs of gold in his arms.

After hellos, handshakes and kisses, Lize said to him, "Oh, Mose dear, are you going to marry me and settle down now?"

And Syksey said, "Oh, Mose, are you goin' to buy a new engine for de company and run wid No. 40 to de musses and de fires?"

And Mose said, "I ain't goin' to do nothin' else."

10

Windwagon Smith and the Santa Fe Trail

Two years after Mose came back from California, a newspaper story came out. It was in an issue of the *Nickport* (Mass.) *News,* and it was as follows:

SEAMAN SAYS PRAIRIES ACTUALLY ARE OCEANS

"Prairies or plains, I tell you, have got the wrong name. They're oceans, that's what they are."

This was the main idea developed in a speech that Tom Smith made yesterday in Sharp's General Store. Tom, who is the eldest son of the late Capt. Ezra Smith of this village, came to port as a crew member of the clipper ship *Zipper,* which docked here Monday.

"I've been reading books about the western prairies," Tom said in part of his speech. "They call these land, and in a way they are land—sort of. But they're so different from any other land that in some ways they're not land at all. Keep in mind that they stretch on and on, and you can't see the end of them. It's the same with the ocean. Some parts are long green swells, and some are wide level stretches. It's the same, again, with the ocean. Then look at the weather in that part of the continent—gales, storms, tornadoes and the like. You don't find weather like that anywhere else on land; but you have it all over the ocean. So I'd say, as a matter of fact, that what you've got there is a sort of a dry ocean."

Jed Sharp wanted to know why no one had ever noticed this before Tom did.

"I'll tell you," Tom answered. "The trouble, mainly, is that all the books were written by landlubbers that didn't know a wave from a typhoon. But even landlubbers out there," he went on, "seem to have some idea that they're not really talking about land. Look here, when they talk about getting some place or another, they call it 'making port,' just like a sailor. The wagons in those parts are called 'schooners'— 'prairie schooners.' Looks to me as if they had a glimpse of the truth."

The fellows around the stove in the store were so interested in this speech that they forgot to reach into the cracker barrel and swipe any of Jed's crackers, even forgot to whittle. They asked Tom what he meant to do about it.

"Think I'll sail out there and see whether a sea-going man can get them to begin on a new tack," he said.

Tom Smith plans to leave Nickport next week to go to Baltimore. From Baltimore, he aims to go Out West on the National Road. Good luck, Tom.

A good many hundred miles west of Nickport, Massachusetts, where this newspaper story was published, was the town of Westport, Missouri. Today, you won't find Westport on the map, because she went and got swallowed up by Kansas City. But back then Westport was a young town that was growing as fast as Jack's beanstalk, and there appeared to be a good chance that *she'd* swallow up Kansas City.

The reason Westport was growing so fast was that the town was at the eastern end of a good many trails people were following West those days—the Oregon Trail out to the Northwest, the Santa Fe Trail out to New Mexico and another trail or two. It was a town that thrived on the prairie schooner business, both the freight business to Santa Fe and the emigrant business to other points westward.

Out on the prairie on the edge of Westport, one day several months after Tom Smith had made his speech in Sharp's General Store, several parties were camped. As was customary, they'd stopped there for a few days so they could finish stocking up before they shoved off for the long trip to California.

These parties were different looking, of course. They all had sun-burned faces, sure, but their eyes and noses and figures and clothes had a good deal of variety to them. This wasn't what you'd call odd, since they were people of several races, people both of the city and the farm, people from all parts of the United States. Only thing alike about them was that they were all Americans going West for a new start.

But the covered wagons that were dotted around through the camp, they were as much alike as peas in a pod. Look at one of these "Pennsylvania wagons" and you'd see the way the whole batch of them looked. Such a wagon had a sky-blue underbody, a bright red upper body, topped off with a white canvas roof. It was made chiefly out of white oak and hickory, seasoned and strong, so it could take a good deal of jolting. The long deep bottom was curved up at the ends, so that the load couldn't jolt out when a body drove up or downhill. This wagon was about nineteen feet long along the canvas top, fourteen feet along the bottom. (The five feet extra made a shelter front and back to keep out rain and sunshine.) The front wheels were close onto four feet high, and the back wheels were five feet and a half. And there was a lot of metal on those wheels, too, since each of them had an iron tire that was six inches wide—a good six inches.

You can easily figure that when you got a wagon with all that lumber and metal in it, and loaded it up with tools and furniture, not to speak of a good-sized family, you had something that took plenty of strength to pull it. It certainly did—maybe as many as ten strong mules or oxen, all tugging till their eyes bugged out.

That's what made some members of the Russell family get so scared when they first sighted this wagon.

This wagon was different.

133

Little Charity Russell was over giving her dolls a bath in Cave Spring when she saw it. White as a particularly pale ghost, she came running lickety-split to her mamma, howling like a pint-sized banshee. Mrs. Russell, sitting on a camp chair over near the campfire, had a lap full of sox and shirts she was mending.

Little Charity gave one jump, burrowed into these clothes like a gopher, and hid her head, all but the yellow curls. Her mother dropped her sewing bag.

"What's got into you, child?" she asked. "What under the sun's the matter, dear?"

Charity's talk was blurred, but Mrs. Russell thought she heard her say, "That wagon! No oxen!"

Mrs. Russell could hardly believe her ears. Then in a minute, she could believe that was what she'd heard; but by then she was having a hard time believing her eyes. Other things took up her attention—such as all the camp animals making more noise than ever, and trying to tug loose from their tethers. But she was looking here and there, sort of wild-eyed, and just chanced to be looking in the right direction when this wagon went flashing by, throwing clouds of dust behind it.

Just about as fidgety as Charity she was, too.

"John!" she hollered, in a quivery voice. "JOHN RUSSELL!"

Mr. Russell was under the far side of the prairie schooner, greasing an axle with a mixture of tar, rosin and tallow that he'd bought in Boone's Grocery in Westport. He crawled out, looking tolerably smudged up around the left side of his nose.

"Martha!" he said, when he saw his wife. (*She* was looking white as a ghost by now, herself.) "Martha, what's got into you?"

"That wagon!" she said.

"Huh?" says Mr. Russell.

"John, I saw it with my own two eyes, scooting along like a jackass rabbit. It was going along like fury, and it like to scared me out of my wits. It's against nature, John, it's—"

"Martha! What're you talking about?"

"It was a—a—a wagon, John, and it was going like mad."

134

"Nothing wrong with that, Martha. Our wagon goes right fast, when the oxen put their minds to pulling it."

"That's just it, John—just it. There wasn't hide nor hair of an animal of any sort hitched to that wagon—not a single, solitary ox or anything else."

Mr. Russell got more worried. "Your head hot?" he asked, putting his palm on Mrs. Russell's forehead. "You've been in the sun too much, dear. You'd better lie down a while. You're seeing things."

Just then Charity lifted her head out of her mamma's lap. "Is that wagon gone yet?" she wanted to know.

"What wagon?" says her father.

"That wagon that didn't have oxen hitched to it and that was kiting along so fast."

"My poor little Charity," says Mr. Thomas, and he was feeling her forehead when Junior strolled up.

"Paw," Junior said, "I just saw a wagon. It was moving across the prairie faster than a ship on a windy day."

"Did it have any oxen hitched to it, son? Did it?" Mr. Russell asked him in a sort of grated voice.

"Course it didn't, Paw. Going that fast, it'd run over any slow old ox team."

Mr. Russell lifted a shaking hand and felt his own forehead. Then—"That settles it," Mr. Russell said. "We're packing. We're going back East as fast as we can. The whole family's going crazy." And he started to throw stuff into the Russell wagon.

By this time, naturally, the wagon that had caused all this trouble had got into Westport and had flashed down Main Street. It had about the same effect there, too, only the effect was multiplied, because there were more people and animals to get scared out of their wits.

Westport was booming and busy, the way it usually was those days each spring as soon as the grass got high enough to feed the stock. The streets were middling noisy, what with mules braying, oxen bellowing, horses neighing, movers and Indians jabbering, and drivers cracking their long black whips.

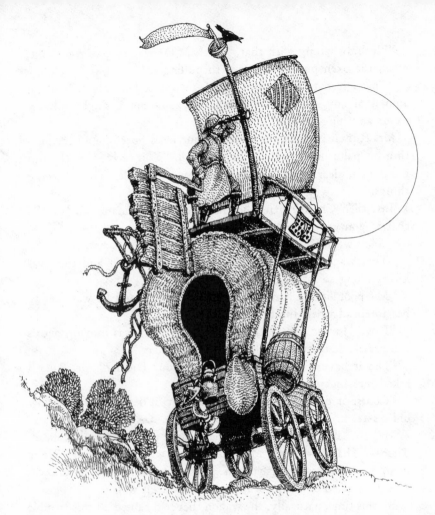

But when that wagon got into town, there was a noise that made the earlier ordinary noises sound like a Sunday School at prayer-time. The horses and oxen made more and louder noises than ever. The mules, naturally, headed for something to kick—fences mostly, though one of them got a window or two in Boone's Grocery. The splintering of boards, the crash of glass, mixed in with the scared howls of humans and Indians, reached up and stabbed the clouds.

The minute Yocum's hound dog, two Pawnee Indians and two hens came into Yocum's Tavern, howling, chattering and cackling, the people in the tavern sort of suspected that perhaps something out of the ordinary was happening. Quick as they could, they pushed back their chairs and spilled out of the front door onto the piazza.

First thing they saw, after they'd blinked at the bright sunlight, was this oxless wagon coming to a stop in front of the tavern. She looked pretty much like any other prairie wagon, except that above the canvas top there was a wooden deck, and out of that a mast was sticking. A man up there had just finished furling a white sail that was rigged on the mast. Now he walked over to the stern and flipped down an anchor. Then he swarmed down a rope ladder over the side and stood squinting up at the people on the piazza.

He was different from prairie men. He was ocean brown, so was a little more on the mahogany side than prairie brown, for one thing. For another, he was wearing a tarpaulin hat instead of a sombrero. He had on a dark-blue sailor suit and big gold ear-rings. Where his sleeves were rolled up, you could see tattoo marks—a mermaid on his right arm and an anchor on his left. And when he walked towards the piazza, he did it with a roll, careful-like, as if he was prepared to keep his balance if, at any minute, Main Street was to tip up to the east or to the west.

"Ahoy, my hearties!" he yelled. "I thought I'd drop anchor here and see what kind of mess comes out of your galley. I'd sure like to stow away some lobscouse. Want some water to store in the scuttled butt, too—it's dry as a bone."

"Light and squat," says Cy Yocum, "and we'll see if we can figure out what in tarnation you're trying to say."

So he rolled into the tavern and went over the whole business again, slowly, as if he was talking to foreigners. He talked for ten or fifteen minutes more, while everybody got more and more confused. He was getting nowhere fast until Cy Yocum's son Dick stepped out of the crowd and spoke up.

"I know what he wants, Pop," says Dick. "He wants some food —stew if you've got it. And he wants some water to put in his water cask."

Cy stared at the boy open-mouthed. "How'd you ever learn

to savvy such an outlandish lingo, son?" he wanted to know.

"They talk that way in the books I read," says Dick, "everybody but the noble hero, leastwise. In *The Witch of the Wave or the Rover's Captive* and in *The Black Avenger of the Spanish Main*—books like that. It's sailor lingo."

"Do tell!" Cy said. "Well, after this, I swear I'll never burn another yellow-backed dime novel again, no matter what your maw says against them. Sure," he says, turning to the sailor, "we can give you some stew—buffalo stew. Bring some in, Molly. And the man's welcome to all the water he wants. Now, Dick, see if you can get out of him what he's up to with that contraption of his."

The seaman had been listening and smiling a kind of a puckery smile. Now he said, "I can tell you. Trouble was I'd been cruising around on the dry ocean out there, and when I docked at a town that had 'port' in its name, I figured I wouldn't be sounding off to a crew of landlubbers that couldn't understand sea talk. My name's Tom Smith, Able-Bodied Seaman, and I'm from Nickport, Massachusetts—over to the northeast there on the Atlantic Wet Ocean. Last wet ocean cruise I took was on the clipper ship *Zipper*. She was becalmed in the South Seas, and for want of something of interest to do, I got in some reading. Read about this plains country."

"Never learn anything from books," Cy said, "unless maybe from dime novels. Horse sense beats books any time, I say."

"All right, Cy," says Doc Parker, who was standing by. "Next time you get sick call in a horse doctor that never read a book."

"Might be worth a try at that," Cy snapped back. "But what did you think you learned from these here books, Mr. Smith?"

"Learned enough," the sailor said, "learned enough so that when I used a little *sea* horse sense, I figured out something about this country that you landlubbers don't seem to know. I learned—Ah, lobscouse! Excuse me."

Molly, the waitress, had come over to the sailor's table with a bowl of buffalo stew, cooked up Pawnee Indian style. Soon as she set it down, Tom fell to with a will and with his spoon.

"What did you figure out?" Ben Newson, the Indian agent,

wanted to find out, soon as several spoonfuls had disappeared.

"Gentlemen, I'll tell you," Smith said, waving his spoon. Then, between bites, he told the crowd pretty much what he'd told the men back in Sharp's General Store in Nickport—about this dry ocean idea of his.

"We-e-ell!" Cy says, finally, looking even more like an owl than usual, "that seems good horse sense to me—land *or* sea."

"Bah!" Doc Parker said. "Just shows what nonsense a man can

think up if he isn't a scientist. Now when I went to Harvard College with Oliver Wendell Holmes and the rest of the Class of 1829, I took a course in Geology. One thing I remember from that course is that land's land and water's water, and they're as different as a salt is from an acid."

Tom stopped scooping up stew and pounded on the table with his spoon, looking wrathy. "Sheer off! Sheer off!" he yelled. "Nobody made any fool claim that land and water *were* the same—nobody in this tavern, at any rate. I spoke of a dry ocean, didn't I? Well, that's land. And a wet ocean's water. Of course they're different. You can't drown in a dry ocean, I know. But they're more alike than they are different. Drowning is smothering, isn't it? Well, you can smother in sand or dirt. You can't drink out of the ocean, any more than you can drink the dust out there, without bad effects. Or take the matter of schools."

"I beg your pardon," says Doc Parker. "Did you say schools?"

"Aye, aye, sir. In the wet ocean, you have schools of fish—codfish, sharks, whales, grampuses and the like. Well, in the dry ocean you have schools of animals—buffalo, wild horses, coyotes. Or there's fleets—ships on the wet ocean, prairie schooners on the dry one."

"You can't overcome an argument like that, Doc," Ben Newson said.

"Only thing I want to know," says Cy, "is how you can put a fact like that to any practical use. You've discovered something, I'll grant you, and it's interesting, too. But how can you turn it into money?"

"Gentlemen of Westport, I'll tell you," says the sailor, standing up and taking a pose like a preacher or a congressman—straight, you know, with his chest swelled up and his hands put away. "I'll talk about this thing in dollars and cents ways that even you landlubbers can understand. Now this Santa Fe Trail, my hearties, if you count the curves, is seven hundred and seventy miles long. It takes about two months to travel her in an ox-drawn prairie schooner. Put a sail on your wagon and you know how fast you can travel her? Two weeks! Just fourteen days! Or maybe less, since you won't have to follow the rivers to water your stock. That's what a windwagon can do!"

"I thought you were going to talk dollars and cents," Cy said.

"I've been leading up to it, mister, leading up to it. Listen. You have capital invested in your wagons and goods, don't you? All right. If you sail that course in a fourth of the time, you can make four times as many voyages—four times the profit you're now making carrying freight. You make thirty per cent now. Gentlemen, you'll make a hundred and twenty per cent with a fleet of windwagons."

"By golly!" Cy said, his eyes beginning to shine like stars.

"That's not all. You won't have to waste all the time you waste now, waiting for the grass to come up to feed the stock in the spring. You can travel that trail mighty near the whole year around. Or another thing: think of the cargo space you waste taking those slow trips. Each man going West needs ten pounds of clothes, fifty pounds of flour, fifty pounds of bacon, ten pounds of coffee, twenty pounds of sugar, three pounds of salt—a total of a hundred and forty-three pounds in all. On a windwagon trip, each man'll need only a fourth of that amount, and you can save all that space for cargo space. What's more, there won't be any trouble with Indians, for a windwagon can run circles around any Indian pony you ever saw. No loss that way, you see—and that'll increase your profit."

"Whee!" Cy said. "Let me in on it!"

"Gentlemen of Westport," Tom said, "that leads me up to why I'm telling you all this. At first I thought you were as dumb as they come, but now I see that, for landlubbers, you're fair-to-middling smart. I want to form the Westport and Santa Fe Dry Ocean Navigation Company, Inc., and I'll let you in on the lower deck. You subscribe for stock; we'll build a fleet of windwagons, and we'll be sloshing around in floods of money before you know it."

"I'll buy some stock—all I can afford," Cy said, making for the safe.

Hank Sager, who hadn't said a word all this time, broke in. "Just a minute," he said, quiet-like. "I'm a wagon-builder myself,

141

and I think there may be something in this. But we ought to be sure, Cy, don't you think? Suppose you show us, Mr. Smith—test it out."

"Exactly," says Doc Parker. "Let's be scientific."

"Fair enough," the sailor said. "What test you want me to make?"

"Hum," Hank said, thinking a while. "I'll tell you. Suppose you run over to Council Groves and back. Let's see how fast you can make her. Take somebody along, of course, so you can prove you went all the way. Then we'll see whether you can make it or not, and if so, how fast."

"Aye, aye, sir!" the sailor said, heading for the door. "Who wants to go along?"

When there was a good deal of silence, the sailor stopped, turned around, and said the same thing louder. Still there was silence.

"Cy," the doctor said, "I thought you were sold on this wind-wagon idea."

"Oh, I am," Cy said, "I certainly am. But the tavern, you know. Got to run the tavern."

After a little more silence, Dick spoke up. "Could I go, Pop?" he wanted to know. "Could I?"

"Well, if your maw doesn't object," Cy told him.

"Maw's over at Boone's Grocery," says Dick, "and she can't object if we hurry. Oh, Mr. Smith, I'll fit the yards, rig the fly-blocks for the topsail halliards, bend the deck and swab the spanker and such."

The sailor looked at him something in the way a chicken looks at a snake, scared and interested at the same time, but mostly scared. "Not on my ship, you won't do *those* things," he said. "But come along. You'll do for ballast, anyhow."

So they took on supplies, weighed anchor, and sailed away before Mrs. Yocum could get back from the store.

The next few days things were only normally noisy in West-port, except for talk about Tom Smith and the windwagon. It was while the sailor and Dick were on that trip that someone thought up the nickname that Tom had ever after. "We can't always take

142

the trouble to say 'Tom-Smith-that-fellow-that's-got-the-wind-wagon,' " says this man. "Let's call him Windwagon Smith." After a good deal of talk this idea was adopted. Then there was a good deal more talk—and a certain amount of betting—about the time the windwagon would get back. Result of all this talk was that the days until she came back passed quickly.

She arrived in Westport on the seventh day after she'd started.

A few things happened just before this. There was a pack of wolves that went scooting through town, howling as if they'd all sat down, unbeknownst, on a cactus. Then there was a party of trappers that came through, whipping their mounts to a lather, yelling, "Run for your lives! Here comes a ghost-wagon!" The pack ponies looked twice as scared as the trappers.

Naturally, this readied the people of Westport for what was coming. Therefore, when the windwagon sailed into town, Main Street was lined with people standing along the side the way they did for a minstrel show parade. They didn't have to wait long before somebody yelled out, "There she comes now!"

Coming down the stret, Windwagon Smith was up on the deck, bowing and waving his hat to the left and to the right, similar to a politician. Dick, it appeared, had talked him into letting him handle the sail, and he was fiddling around, tacking so that the ship would zigzag slowly down the street, in order that everybody might get a good long look at him. Everybody was cheering, and a mule got a brand new window in Boone's Grocery.

There wasn't a boy in Westport that wouldn't have given an arm or two to be up there where Dick was.

As soon as the windwagon was moored, and everybody there was room for had gathered in the tavern, Doc got out his pencil and made what he called "some scientific calculations." Turned out that the windwagon had averaged about seventy miles a day, even better than Windwagon Smith had guessed it would do.

But Windwagon had had some time to do a little thinking on the trip. Result was, he had to make another speech in which he scolded himself for being blind as a bat and not seeing that what was needed was a big windwagon.

"Ladies and Gentlemen of Westport," he said, "I'll tell you what I've decided. I've decided that you can double the keel-length of a prairie schooner if you use wind to make her go. Take advantage of power that way, you see, that you couldn't get from an ox team, because the sail could be twice as big. That means just twice the cargo space and twice the speed I figured on before. When we get us a fleet of these super-windwagons going, we'll make something like sixteen times as much profit as folks make on ordinary Pennsylvania wagons."

He made a few other remarks about the glories of Missouri and the great future of the West—the sort of stuff everybody threw into a speech in those days just to warn the audience that he was winding the thing up. But nobody was listening: everybody was doing arithmetic in his head to work out how much money he could spare to buy stock.

When the papers for the Westport and Santa Fe Dry Ocean Navigation Company, Inc., had been fixed up by Lawyer Martin, quite a few people bought stock. There was Cy Yocum, of course, and then there were Tom Adams, Ben Newson, Hank Sager, Windwagon Smith and a few others. The last minute, after doing two or three pages of figuring, Doc Parker decided he'd buy some stock too, "now," he said, "that the validity of the hypothesis has been semi-demi-demonstrated by scientific methods."

At the meeting over at Henry Sager's Wagon Yard, where Windwagon showed the stockholders his final blueprints, there was an argument that stopped just short of whisker-pulling. Windwagon and Cy, you see, were all for getting into quantity production right away. But Doc Parker held they should make just one big wagon first, so they could make what he called "scientific tests" of the contraption. Cy made a speech in which he set forth that a fleet of forty windwagons, he figured, could make ninety-six hundred per cent profits. Even after somebody had showed this was a miscalculation, Windwagon Smith told in a speech how people had mistreated Columbus and Old Captain Stormalong when they had great ideas, and won over three stockholders. In the end, though, when the company voted, Doc's idea of starting with one super-windwagon, instead of a fleet, won by two votes.

Windwagon Smith, wanting to make sure that this one super-windwagon would work, naturally took great pains with her. He had the sailcloth shipped all the way from Nickport, because he claimed his home town made the best sailcloth in the world. The steel for some of the fittings was shipped in from Pittsburgh, and some of the lumber came from St. Louis. After all the stuff was assembled, though, Sager made good progress by putting a good many men to work on the super-windwagon.

When he could spend enough time away from the yards, Windwagon Smith went out now and then in the first—or little—windwagon, and gave Dick Yocum lessons in navigation. "Dick'll do to help out on the trial trip," he said. "Course when we get our fleet really started, we'll want to recruit a good many wet ocean sailors. Most landlubbers can't learn to tell a tiller from a trussel-tree."

Just the same, Dick did very well, and before long the way he could skid the little windwagon all over the map was a wonder to see. Got so he'd charge four bits to run some of the braver people over to St. Joe, and make pocket money that way.

When work on the super-windwagon was far enough along, the company made plans for a big launching ceremony. They were unanimous about inviting President Franklin Pierce, who'd just come into office and was still popular; but they couldn't get together on the other invitations. Doc Parker said that since the super-windwagon would be running between nations, scientific logic showed they should ask Secretary of State Marcy. Cy and Windwagon said it was a matter of common sense to see that they should ask Secretary of the Navy Dobbin. Ben Newson, who was in government service, naturally solved it all by working out a compromise—inviting both Marcy and Dobbin. As it turned out, it really didn't matter, since neither the President nor his Secretaries could come.

Regardless, there was a fine crowd on hand for the launching—some Congressmen in top hats, some Governors, likewise, and hosts of people, some from as far away as Council Groves. They gathered on that level stretch on the edge of Westport, and cheered when a team of twenty oxen pulled up the brand new super-windwagon.

This super-windwagon, with a cigar store Indian for a figure-head, red, white and blue stripes, and a great white sail, looked most fetching. She was a whopper, too—twenty-five feet long, seven feet a-beam, with wheels twelve feet across which had hubs as big as barrels.

The Congressmen and the Governers naturally tried to make speeches, but naturally Windwagon Smith beat them to it.

"Ladies and Gentlemen, Congressmen and Governors," he started out. "I'll tell you something about this super-windwagon. To my mind, it's on the small side, but we intend to build us a fleet of good-sized ones later. This tiny affair, though, will give you land-lubbers a hint of what our super-super-windwagons will be able to do—a fleet of them, of course, a navy of them. Soon the whole world will be dotted with these good-sized ships that can cruise on either wet oceans or dry oceans, irrespective, so to speak. And of course, Westport will be a center of navigation, like Liverpool or New York. I thank you."

With this, Windwagon Smith put on his admiral's hat, gave the ship a quick once-over, and yelled, "All ashore that's going ashore!"

Since nobody was on board but Windwagon and Dick, this confused people a little. But the only people that were to be allowed to take the trip—the stockholders—climbed up the gangplank. Everybody did, that is, except one stockholder, Doc Parker. Doc sat there on his cayuse and said, "I'll trail along behind with some liniment and some splints. Got to be scientific about this, you know."

When the gangplank had been pulled in, Dick stepped up to the prow and busted a bottle of Missouri River water over the wooden Indian's head, similar to a wet ocean launching. The crowd and the stockholders yelled, Windwagon Smith hoisted the sail, and with a creak or two the super-windwagon started to move.

"Git up!" Doc Parker told his cayuse, and started to move after her, fast as he could.

At first the stockholders smiled and waved good-by to the

crowd. Then, when the people were out of sight and all they could see was Doc Parker, galloping along behind them, they all started to shake hands and slap one another on the back, laughing like mad. For there was no doubt but what the super-windwagon was sailing along like a bird.

Then Windwagon Smith called out to them, "I guess she's ship-shape, mates! Now it'll be safe to let her really take the wind."

It was at this time, they say, that some of the stockholders began to get slightly worried. If not, it was soon after—just as soon as the super-windwagon doubled her speed. Doc and his cayuse, left far behind, dwindled to a speck in the distance. Then two stock-holders lost their best hats, and seeing how fast these hats turned to specks, a third stockholder—Ben Newson, I understand—turned green.

Soon everybody aboard except Dick and Windwagon had turned a strange color somewhere between the color of prairie grass and that of hay. They were groaning, too.

And soon every last one of the landlubber stockholders began to say nasty things about Windwagon Smith.

"We think you're a skunk," they said. "We hate your dratted super-w-w-windwagons. We don't ever want to see one of the dratted things again. We resign."

They all said about the same thing—even Cy Yocum. "Let us off or we'll sue you," they said. Then they said, "We'll sue you anyhow."

You know how a baby looks when he has had his little stick of candy taken away from him when he's just got started on it, how a little girl looks when she first hears there's no Santa Claus? Well, that's how Windwagon Smith and Dick Yocum looked, only on top of it, they looked scornful.

"Landlubbers!" Windwagon said, in the tone of voice he'd use to start making a speech to a convention of snakes.

"Landlubbers!" Dick said.

Windwagon Smith pushed his lips tight together until they were about as thin as a toothpick. "All right, Ensign," says he. "Let's bring her about. Step lively!"

147

So they did things to the sails, and circled back toward Westport.

First they passed Doc Parker, going slow on his cayuse toward town. The minute he looked up and got a view of the stockholders' faces, he spurred his horse to follow as fast as ever he could.

Soon they were nearing the crowd again. A Congressman, evidently, had got started on a speech as soon as the super-windwagon had disappeared. He was up in front of the crowd, waving his arms and flapping his jaw. The crowd, of course, stopped listening and started to cheer the super-windwagon.

The crowd was still yelling when she slowed down to a stop. But they chopped off the noise as soon as the stockholders started to wobble down the gangplank. They came down jerkily, one after the other, and just flopped down on the prairie grass, green and panting, until there was quite a row of them.

Windwagon Smith watched the last one do his flop, just as Doc Parker rode up, leaped from his cayuse, and knelt down by Ben Newson, the first in the row.

"Landlubbers!" yelled Windwagon Smith, as he pulled up the gangplank. "Anchors aweigh, mister!"

"Aye, aye, sir!" says Dick, pulling the anchor aboard.

"Man the sails!" Windwagon Smith yelled. "Hoist sails!"

The super-windwagon began to move away again. It gathered speed, began to get smaller. Dick's voice, yelling "Landlubbers!" sounded very small shortly before the super-windwagon was a pin-prick size. Then there wasn't a sign of her on the horizon.

And that was the last that Westport saw or heard of Ensign Dick Yocum, Admiral Windwagon Smith, or the super-windwagon.

11

Feboldson and Bridger, Western Scientists

WINDWAGON SMITH AND ENSIGN DICK WENT SAILING AWAY from Westport right on the eve, you might say, of the Civil War. From that time on, for several years, the war came closer and closer. After a while it began, and then after a while it ended. As usual, people were mighty glad to have peace come along after the end of the war.

There were heroes a-plenty along in those times, as is well known—Honest Abe Lincoln, for one, on the Northern side, and General Robert E. Lee on the Southern side, to mention only two of them. Since you can find plenty of facts about these heroes and others, and about the war, in other histories, this history won't say any more about them.

But this chapter will bring up (more or less exclusively) a point that isn't generally noticed—that along in the years just after Windwagon Smith made his great discovery about dry oceans, Americans had more trouble with weather, geography and animals than they'd ever had before.

What had happened, maybe, was this—that Americans had got started operating in a part of this great land where all three of these things were simon-pure American.

The weather in a good many other parts of the country was imported. Along the eastern coast, it came mostly from one part or the other of the Atlantic Ocean. People in Florida and California boasted that their weather was *un*-American, because it was so much better than the average run of American weather. All along a good share of the northern edge of our country, the weather seeped in from Canada. But out on the plains, deserts and mountains of the West, the weather was of an ornery sort that it'd be just too mean to blame on any other country.

And the same was true of the lay of the land and the varmints. Probably the most American things about all three of these were two in number: 1) They were on a big scale—a whopping scale, and 2) they provided new kinds of hardships for Americans to cope with. And an interesting thing about Americans at this time was that—in ways that fitted in with Doc Parker's ideas—they dealt with them scientifically. Partly this was because science was getting to be very popular about this time. Partly it was because there wasn't any other way of getting anything accomplished.

Two great natural scientists of the day were Febold Feboldson, out in Nebraska, and Jim Bridger (nickname, Old Gabe) around the Yellowstone Park and points east, west, north and south. These weren't all the great natural scientists there were in those days— not by a long shot. But they were good samples of hundreds that now got into the habit of using science to solve all kinds of problems.

Nebraska, at the start, was big enough so great hunks could be chopped off and handed over to Colorado, Dakota and Idaho without anybody in Nebraska getting worried. After these gifts had been passed out, it was seen that every dratted mountain in the whole vicinity had been handed over to some other state. Result was that the whole of Nebraska was nothing but valleys, tableland and rolling prairies, all with a southwestern exposure. This meant that all the weather and all the wild life that came along had plenty of room to work and play in without natural let or hindrance.

Febold Feboldson settled down out there about the time the weather began to feel its strength. He got his farm and his family started, took on the job of Indian Agent for the Dirtyleg Indians, and then started his great work as a natural scientist.

One of the first things he had to cope with was the Great Fog that came along the year of the Great Heat. The Great Heat was bad enough, Heaven knows. Looking back, many people said that one of the most fiendish things about it was the way the mercury in thermometers everywhere shot up the tubes and spewed out the top like a fountain, so people couldn't *tell* how hot it was. Over in Saline County, though, one fellow with a big thermometer that'd take two hundred and thirty-two degrees, stood by it day and night with a cake of ice, bound and determined to save his thermometer. And he said the heat never went below a hundred and fifty degrees all those weeks, leastwise when he could see the thermometer with the help either of the sun, the moon or a lantern.

That was bad enough, as you can imagine. But one day Febold looked at the sky, fiddled around with some of his instruments, and made a horrible discovery. "That's bad," he said. "Got to do something drastic."

What he did was send a cable to London that read this way: "Send along a gross of your fanciest fog-cutters soon as possible, C.O.D. Febold Feboldson."

Being a scientist, you see, Febold had figured out right away what a horrible time Nebraska was in for. He told Mrs. Feboldson about the steps he'd taken that very evening while they were sitting in the sitting room trying to cool off a bit.

"Cabled over to London today for a gross of fog-cutters," he said.

Mrs. Feboldson's eyes stuck out so far they appeared to be on stems. "Fog-cutters?" she said, dazed-like.

"Yes, fog-cutters, Mother," he said. "You see, they have the thickest fogs in London that they have anywhere except on the ocean. And they're inventive there, you know—a right smart race. So they've doubtless got the best fog-cutters you can find anywhere."

"Of course, Febold, but I can't see as we need any fog-cutters. What would we do with them?"

"Cut the fog."

"It's been hot enough to make me wish we could cut the heat," says Mrs. Feboldson. "But if you look out the window there, you'll notice there's no fog—nothing but level land and sky, as far as you can look, with a hundred thousand heat-waves, just what you usually see out that living room window."

"Some unusual things out there, too," says Febold. "What's that dark gray thing up in the sky yonder—a dark gray thing no bigger than a man's hand?"

"Why!" Mrs. Feboldson said. "It's a cloud—first one I've seen since the Great Heat started pestering us. Looks as if it might be a rain cloud."

Febold nodded. "How about that little toe of yours that warns you when we're to have rain? How's it feel?"

Mrs. Feboldson noticed her toe for a minute, then, "I'll swan, it's a-twitching," she told him.

"I've fiddled around with my barometers, looked at the moon, and listened to the bullfrogs, and they all say the same thing," Febold said. "What's more, they say it's going to be a regular Bible storm—forty days and forty nights. Oh, we'll need those fog-cutters all right, Mother."

"Do they cut rain as well as fogs?"

"No, they just cut fogs, I reckon. But we'll need them. You'll see. Let's turn in."

Along toward morning, there was the beginning of that horrible sound that people in Nebraska (and parts of the neighboring territories) kept nearly being driven crazy by for the next forty days and forty nights. People that tried to describe it later said it was like the sound of steam shooting out of three million tea-kettles at once—big kettles, too, boiling like fury—just one long burbling hiss.

As soon as Febold came in from milking, Mrs. Feboldson asked him what that horrible noise was.

"It's working the way I figured it would," he said. "The rain's coming down like a dribbled ocean. But up there ten miles or so, it's spattering down on the hot air that was piled up around here

152

by the Great Heat. As soon as the rain hits the hot air, it turns to steam and makes that hissing noise. The steam will be the fog."

"But the steam's staying up there," Mrs. Feboldson said. "Out the window, all you can see is level land and sky as far as you can look, same as usual, only gray because there's no sun today."

"Pretty soon, Mother, the rain will hammer the fog down to the ground, and what'll pile up will be the fog. Hope those Englishmen hurry up with those fog-cutters. Things are going to be bad."

Febold was right, as usual. There was a little fog at first, then more and more of it, until taking a walk alone was impossible. At least two people would be needed so one could part the fog and hold it apart while the other one walked through. Cattle didn't have to be watered, because they could drink the fog. But the dirt farmers were scared speechless, because their crops were in a bad way. You see, some of the seeds had figured that the closest sunshine was in China, and had started growing downward.

Around Thanksgiving, when the fog was so thick that portions had turned to three hundred thousand gallons of slush, both farmers and stockmen by the hundreds had about decided to pull out of Nebraska. "Too crowded by this danged fog," they said. "We need elbow room."

It was when things had come to this kind of a pass that the fog-cutters arrived, C.O.D. Febold used one of them to cut red tape so he could pay for them out of his Dirtyleg Indian fund. Then he started to use them on the fog—to slice it into big neat strips. Soon, when he had great piles of these strips, it was needful that he figure out where to put them.

"Can't leave them lying out there on the fields," he told Mrs. Feboldson, "or all the seeds will keep growing downward. I know! I'll lay them out along the roads."

Upshot was that he put those fog strips end to end all along the dirt roads of Nebraska. And before long some of the slush-fog seeped down, and some got so covered with dust that nobody could see where Febold had buried the Great Fog.

Only one serious bad result came of the whole thing. Every spring, when the sun begins to shine and the thaw comes, some of

this old fog seeps up on the dirt roads, turning them into the gooiest mess you ever got stuck in.

And if you don't believe this, just go out to Nebraska some spring and try driving on one of those roads.

This is only one of the stories they tell about Febold that show how scientific he was and, in addition, how much good sense he had. He handled a good many weather problems in ways just as smart—the Year of the Two Winters, for instance, and the Year the Rain Came Up from China.

On top of being a weather handler, he was quite a mechanic. He solved the fence post problem out there in the treeless district—to cite one instance—by applying the principles of meteorology and varnish. What he did was dig the post holes in the fall, then let them freeze all winter. Along towards spring, he'd put a chain around the top of each of those holes and then have an ox team jerk each of them out. After he'd varnished them, there was nothing better for stringing barbed wire onto.

The Year of the Big Drought, when Pecos Bill was fixing things down in Texas in ways a later chapter will tell about, Febold was fixing things in Nebraska. What Febold did, when you had to go so deep for water, was hit on the trick of driving post holes into the ground, one right on top of the other, until he got down as far as was needed—about a hundred and thirty-one feet.

Then, to boot, he was a great man with animals. No one but another scientific genius—with the best of luck—would have thought up some of the ways of doing zoological stuff Febold thought up. Take, for instance, the way he used this animal called the happy auger to bore post holes. Or take the gag he figured out for catching fish with raisins, when the bait supply was low in Civil War times.

This last showed he knew a heap about physics as well as another heap about fish. He knew fish liked raisins, of course, the way they always had: that was the start. But on top of that he had to know that raisins had iron in them, and he had to know about magnets attracting iron. Then it was easy for him to work it out that you could feed the fish raisins, then use a magnet to pull them out of the water.

The thing that best showed Febold's all-around-genius, though, started with the grasshopper trouble. Maybe you know how horrible hoppers are when they go on a rampage in Nebraska, but if you don't, you're lucky. They cloud up the sky like the Milky Way, only more sloshed around, and then they swoop down and eat everything in sight, regardless of its taste. That's the way it is as a

155

rule. But this Year of the Grasshoppers was worse than ordinary—about four times worse, maybe five.

Febold and Mrs. Feboldson were sitting in the sitting room one evening, trying to get a little relief from the hoppers. Looking out the window was most monotonous, for all you could see was hundreds of thousands of grasshoppers, roaming and flitting around in search of supper.

Febold, who'd been thinking and thinking (as was his habit), finally spoke up. "Only result of it all," he told his wife, "will be those prairie dogs. And I don't think anybody will mind them, do you?"

"Prairie dogs?" says Mrs. Feboldson. "Never heard of them. Will they bite?"

"They won't bite people," Febold told her. "And they'll be kind of cute. Little they'll be, you see."

"What's the good of having the critters?" Mrs. Feboldson wanted to know.

"Get rid of this plaguey plague of grasshoppers, Mother."

"Well, anything will be better than them, Febold. Go right ahead."

"I knew you'd say that," Febold said. "So today I went and sent for the flying fish."

"Flying fish! Whatever do you want with them?"

"Well," says Febold, "I've been experimenting. I seemed to remember something about fish liking hoppers. So I took a handful of those grasshoppers today, and dipped them in the creek. Sure enough, the fish like to took my arm off, trying to get them. 'Hm,' says I, 'if the fish could get out and get at the grasshoppers—' Then I recalled flying fish. '*They* could,' says I. So I sent off for a hundred thousand of them. Hope people in Nebraska don't mind the prairie dogs, though."

"How do they connect up with this?" Mrs. Feboldson asked him.

"You'll see," says Febold. "Let's turn in."

The flying fish, when they hit Nebraska, were a whopping success. They winged and wheeled and swooped around all over the state, snapping up the grasshoppers and licking their chops for more—seemed as if they couldn't get enough to suit them.

Pretty soon, the hoppers weren't bothersome any longer, but there was a new trouble: the fish were a tarnation pest. They'd try to scoot down some of the post hole wells, and would stop the things up. They'd flip against somebody's face at night, and not only startle him but make the chills run down his spine. They'd flutter down and light in milk pails without farmers noticing, and give city folks wrong ideas when they were delivered with the milk.

Febold, of course, had foreseen all this. So when the committee came to protest, he was ready for them. "Gentlemen," he said, after they'd been seated in the sitting room, "within a few days, everything will be under control. The timber wolves and the baby cottonwoods came today."

"What good are the timber wolves?" the chairman of the committee asked him.

"They'll eat the flying fish," Febold told him.

"Good," the chairman said, and the rest of the committee nodded. "But how about the cottonwoods?"

"Gentlemen," says Febold, stern-like, "you wouldn't want those poor timber wolves to be unhappy because they don't have any timber, would you?"

"Well, no," says the committee, looking sort of ashamed.

"All right," Febold told them. "Nothing grows faster than cottonwood, nothing I know of anyhow, so they'll have timber in no time. But before you go, let me ask you a question. You know how the South, these days before the Civil War, is looking for slave states to join up with it. Do you want Nebraska to be a slave state?"

After thinking a little while, "No-o-o-o, we'd rather not," the committee said. "Most people in these parts are from the North, you know."

"That's what I thought," Febold said. "I'll work it out that way. Good night, gentlemen."

It wasn't until time had passed and the cottonwood trees had grown quite big that the committee remembered this little talk.

This was when they read in the papers that some Southern planters had arranged with Febold to let them send some slaves up to Nebraska, to pick the cotton from the cottonwood. Febold had said that he was glad to promote good feeling between the North and the South, and the newspapers had editorials headed, "WILL NEBRASKA BE A SLAVE STATE?" and mostly agreeing that things ought to be viewed with alarm.

Knowing Febold, though, the committee didn't worry overmuch.

First off, everything went fine as a fiddle. The slaves liked the shade of the trees they worked in better than the hot sun down home, and they picked sack after sack of Grade A cotton. While they picked, they sang a song they'd make up—went this way:

> *Pickin' cotton offa dese trees,*
> *Pickin' cotton offa dese trees,*
> *Please, Ole Massa, please O please,*
> *Lemme pick among dese trees.*
>
> *Hates de hot sun, lubs de shade,*
> *Hates de hot sun, lubs de shade,*
> *So, Ole Massa, like Ah sayed,*
> *Lemme pick in dis here shade.*

But after a while, they'd picked all the cotton that was down low enough for them to reach it. The overseer came calling on Febold, and sat down with him in the sitting room.

"Suh," the overseer said, "those black men cain't seem to get at the cotton that's higher up than they-all can reach. They haven't had any trainin' for climbin' trees, you know."

"Yes," Febold said, "I foresaw that. I'll tell you what I've thought up—if you'll take the blame for doing it. We can bend those trees over, you know, and stake their tops down close to the ground."

"Fine, fine, suh," says the overseer. "Of course, I'll take the blame, such as it is—be right proud, suh."

"All right," Febold said, "I've got the stakes and the ropes ready. We'll get going on it in the morning."

Well, everything appeared to go fine, and the overseer got a good many compliments for thinking up that tree bending stunt. The slaves got all the cotton easily, and made up and sang some new songs about what they called "de hump-backed trees." Then they went home to spend the winter. It wasn't until the next year that the overseer saw why Febold had asked him to take the blame.

He figured it out right off when he came up to Nebraska, with the slaves, and saw that all the trees had grown completely into the ground.

When the overseer called at the Feboldson house, Mrs. Feboldson told him, "Febold's out there some place cheering up the timber wolves. They're sad, you know, without those cottonwood woods to run in. Want to wait?"

"No ma'am," the overseer told her. "You can tell him, though, for me, that Nebraska no longer may hope to have the privilege of bein' a slave state. Good day, ma'am."

When Febold heard the news, naturally he wasn't upset in the least. "That's the way I figured it'd be when I asked the committee that question," he said. "Only thing I've worried about right along has been those timberless timber wolves."

"How are they, by the way? How'd you cheer them up?"

"It wasn't hard, Mother. I simply gathered a pack of them together, turned them into a school (which wasn't hard, after they'd eaten all those schools of flying fish), and then taught them where the trees are—underground. When I left them, they were busy as a bunch of Presidential Bees, digging down to the trees."

"They'll be happy then, will they, Febold?"

"They'll be gay enough. Of course, without overground trees and dug down into the ground where there's no sunshine, they'll fall off a good deal in size in the next few years. Wouldn't be surprised if they got to be around about the size of a squirrel, but maybe fatter. But they'll be happy."

It worked out the way Febold foresaw, naturally. Those timber wolves, in spite of the fact that they were plenty carefree, did get smaller and smaller, the way he'd predicted. And if you don't believe this, run out to Nebraska and have a look at them some time. Don't ask for timber wolves, though, for the natives have changed the name.

The way Febold foresaw they would, Nebraskans call them prairie dogs.

Well, if all these things don't show you that Febold was a great scientist, maybe the story of what became of him will. Along about the time San Francisco had that little thunderstorm that non-Californians called an earthquake, California sent for Febold to hurry out there and see that they got the most unusual, sunkist, vitaminized weather a genius could line up for the place.

Of course, Californians don't like the news to spread that they *need* anybody like that, so there's nothing about it in the papers. But by and large, he does give California pretty good weather, and there are stories in the paper, every now and then, about that good weather. And the way Californians talk, you can gather that they think highly of Febold's work.

I mentioned this other natural scientist, Jim Bridger, before, back where I said he was on that fur-trading trip with Mike Fink, after Mike had left the river. Jim was only about eighteen when he made that trip, though: he did his scientific stuff—and told about it—a good deal later, along in the years just after the Civil War ended. It's important to notice that he told about it, because science, as you may have noticed, gets to be useful to other people only after it has been passed along. Well, along in there when Andrew Johnson was president, Jim passed along a powerful lot of science. He did it in what might be called Campfireside Talks.

By that time, Jim was pretty generally known as Old Gabe. He'd been a hunter, trapper, fur-trader and guide so many years that he was the best known old-timer in any of those lines in the West. He'd also discovered a mess of places scattered all over the West— Salt Lake, South Pass, parts of Yellowstone Park, and so forth. Even more—he'd figured out what to *do* about some of the strangest of these places, and he'd been most generous and open-handed in telling people.

Letting people know was his favorite pastime. Let Old Gabe corner somebody in a tavern or a trading post or by a campfire, and he'd just pour out wisdom by the gallon.

One night in a camp in the Teton Mountains, for instance, he got started in a talk about using nature in a scientific way. There was a bunch of men there, sitting around in the shadows, with the firelight showing their faces in the darkness now and then. There were only three men, it happened, though, that did much talking that night—Old Gabe, another old-timer named Jack Something-or-other, and the tenderfoot.

"Trouble is," Old Gabe said, "that though we've got more wonders of Nature out in this country here than there are in any other part of the world, very few folks make much use of them. Take the way people fail to reckon time. They do it with trees, sure, counting the tree rings. But why don't they do it other ways that don't put a body to the work of chopping down a tree?"

This uppity young tenderfoot that had got himself educated at Yale said, "What, precisely, do you have in mind, Mr. Bridger?"

"I'll tell you," says Gabe. "You see that hill over there, that one that's shaped something like a Ute Indian's nose? Well, that used to be a hole in the ground. But in this salubrious and healthy climate, the thing went and grew into a hill."

"Indeed?" the tenderfoot said. "And how, pray, did you know that?"

"Saw it with my own eyes, back in 1820, when it was a hole. Jack here did the same. Didn't you, Jack?"

The other old-timer shook his head. "No," he said, "I didn't come along and get my first squint at it until in 1825, when it was more in the nature of a mound. But it's sure growed since then, the way you say."

"Course it has," Old Gabe said. "Point I want to make is, if you knew about the rate of growth in a thing like that, you could measure time. Or take that stone I heaved across the Sweetwater a good while back. Go and look at it now, and you'll see it's grown up and got to be Independence Rock. We've got a lot to learn about how holes and rocks grow, but when we learn it, it'll be right helpful. And another thing we haven't learned to use properly out here is the handy arrangements of the scenery."

"Perhaps," the uppity tenderfoot said, slapping at a mosquito, "you will provide me with a specific example or two."

"Of course," Old Gabe said, "and I'll show you how I worked it once or twice too. Don't suppose anybody here—"(he looked at the men around the fire) "—anybody outside of Jack, at least, remembers the Year of the Big Snow. The way you could tell it from other winters is this, that for seventy days a foot of snow fell every single day. Let's see, that added up to a good deal of snow, as you'd find out for yourself if you multiplied and so forth. Let's say, roughly, that it came to about seventy feet of snow—that's the depth I found by measuring some places, anyhow. Well, I was scouting around Salt Lake the next spring, and I saw all these white statues that looked like animals—buffalo mostly, but here and there a bear or a deer. What they really were, you see, was real animals that had friz. So I toted them over to Salt Lake, and heaved the varmints in. The lake then pickled and cured them—and I had vittles on hand for me and the Ute Indians to last for years."

"Mr. Bridger," the tenderfoot said, "that sounds dubious. Can you establish the veracity of your allegations?"

Bridger had been throwing some wood on the fire. Now he dusted his hands off, sat down, and answered the tenderfoot back. "Of course I can, and I can prove what I said was true, too—or you can do it, if you're a mind to. Just hunt all over the Wasatch and Humboldt Mountains, young man, and if you find a single buffalo, or a married one, I'll eat the critter, horns and all. There's not a buffalo in the whole district. Ain't that true, Jack?"

"True as gospel," Jack said. "I can tell, too, of another time Old Gabe took advantage of the way things had got laid out—over in Yellowstone. I only had a chance to eat that salted buffalo, and had to take his word for how he'd saved it. But this time I was along, to see with my own two eyes. In this camp we had, just before we turned in for the night, he'd holler out, 'Time to git up!' Six hours later—"

"Six hours and seven minutes," Jim Bridger cut in.

"Six hours and seven minutes later, the echo would come back and wake us for breakfast," Jack said. "Gabe knew, by testing it out, about acoustics and such—knew how long it took a medium-sized echo to travel. After we'd been woke that way, we'd catch our breakfast in Fire Hole River—just pulled our trouts out, took them off the hooks, and ate them, then and there."

"Ate them?" says the tenderfoot, looking sickish. "Raw?"

"Course not," Jack told him. "Fire Hole River's a body of water Jim went and discovered. It's cold on the bottom, so trouts live there, but it biles on top. These trouts would be cooked beautiful by the time they'd been landed—all except the seasoning, which we'd take along with us when we fished."

The tenderfoot didn't look so sick any more, but by now he looked more or less like a little boy that had gone to bed at home in the usual way, and then had wakened up in China—a mite astonished and puzzled.

Old Gabe thought a minute, then said, "It wasn't far from Fire Hole River, as I remember it, that my pony got some ideas—logical ideas, too—that in the end went and killed him. He was a right fine pony, too, and I hated to lose him."

Gabe got his pipe going good before he went on. "It was along toward sundown, and I wanted to get to a camping place I was fond of before dark. Well, I tried a short cut. And that's the way I happened to get into this here peetrified forest."

"Peetrified?" the tenderfoot said.

"Sure. Everything was turned plumb to stone—the green grass, the trees—"

"Pardon me," says the tenderfoot. "I presume that you mean petrified."

"I presume I don't," says Old Gabe, sort of sharp. "Maybe forests get petrified back at Yale, but out here in this man's country, where everything's on a big scale, they get peetrified. Everything there, like I said, was peetrified—the sage, the spruce, the varmints. In the air was the peetrified perfume of the stone flowers and the songs of the stone birds. The fruit was turned to stone, too, and I picked me a pocketful of rubies, emeralds and such stuff without

163

bothering to get off my pony. But I had to hurry, so I spurred the critter along.

"What we did, finally, was come to a great wide canyon that appeared to cut me off from where I was going. At first, I was worried, but then I got an idea, drove my pony to the edge of the canyon, and says 'Git up!' He turned around for a look at my face, naturally, to see if I was joking, the way I sometimes did with him, for we were old friends, you see. When he saw I wasn't, of course he stepped right ahead. He pranced right across the air in the canyon, the way I knowed he would. And well before sundown—"

"Wait a minute!" the tenderfoot said. "That's going too far! That's impossible!"

"Not there," Old Gabe told him. "You're educated and can see why, too, soon as I tell you. You see, *there, even the law of gravity was peetrified.* That's what I'd figured would be the case—and well before sundown, we got to that camp."

"Sounds logical," the tenderfoot had to admit. "Have you any additional proof, however?"

"Well, lemme see—Oh yes, Jack saw what happened to that pony later, didn't you, Jack?"

Jack took his pipe out of his mouth to answer. "Sure did. Some time later, that pony got together three or four other ponies on the edge of Wildcat Bluff—lined them up to watch him, you know. Then, with a smug smile on his face, he pranced out over the edge of that bluff. I never saw a horse look as surprised as that pony did when, all of a sudden, he started to fall. We figured he was loco till Gabe here told us why he went and done it."

"He was a good pony," Jim said, looking sad. "Logical, too. Only thing he didn't know, you see, was that in most places—like Wildcat Bluff, say—the law of gravity *isn't* peetrified. A while back I myself had good reason to wish he'd been right instead of wrong. If the law of gravity had been peetrified everywhere, I'd have been saved from what was just about the most horrible thing ever happened to me."

"Please tell us about it, Mr. Bridger," the tenderfoot said.

"It was when six big Indians ambushed me, and started to chase

me. I was on my pony, not this one but another, and naturally, I kept a-twisting around in my saddle, and picking off the lead Indian. Got five that way, so there was only one left—and I had only one cartridge in my gun.

"He was coming fast at me, this last one, just as we came up to the edge of the Grand Canyon. No horse on earth could jump across a ditch that size, and a fall to the bottom meant sure death. I turned my horse sudden, and the redskin was upon me, whooping like mad. We both fired at once, and both our horses were hit and killed. We now got into a hand-to-hand ruckus with hunting knives. He was a powerful Indian, big, too—about nine feet tall. It was a long fight, with one on top, then the other. Finally, though, I began to tire. He edged me over to the edge, and howling like a panther, he gave me a horrible hard push. I couldn't grab hold of anything—started to fall—"

"Good heavens!" says the tenderfoot, standing up in his excitement. "I do not see how you survived!"

Old Gabe looked at him, even sadder than before. "I didn't," he said. "That dratted Indian killed me. Time to turn in."

12
Paul Bunyan, Northwoods Lumberman

PAUL BUNYAN WORKED AT LUMBERING A LONG TIME. HE started lumbering back there in Maine, where he was born, in the early days of lumbering. Along in the days of Feboldson and Bridger, he moved to Wisconsin, Minnesota, North Dakota—along in there, and logged that part of the country. That was a great time in his life, as this chapter will show. A later time in his life that was also a great one, when he was a Scientific Industrialist, in a nice way, will be told about in a later chapter.

Whenever there's any doubt about where a great man was born, any number of places are likely, through their Chambers of Commerce, to fight for the honor. It was that way, for instance, with Homer, the Greek poet, and Captain Stormalong.

It was so with Paul, too, as was to be expected. But there is some reason for saying that he *may* have been born several places all at once, since he was large enough, even at the start, to need some scope for being born in. Mostly, though, he was born in the state of Maine.

At three weeks, baby Paul got his family into a bit of trouble by kicking around his little tootsies and knocking down something like four miles of standing timber. This was in Maine, and remembering the old saying, "As goes Maine, so goes the nation," the government took action right away. They told Paul's family they'd have to move the little fellow somewhere or other where he'd do less damage.

With the timber Paul had kicked over, the family made Paul a cradle, which they anchored off Eastport. Everything went well until, getting playful, Paul began waving his arms and legs around, the way babies do. That started the cradle rocking, and that started a bunch of waves that larruped around and came close to drowning every town along the New England coast.

So they had to move him again—keep him some place ashore until he was a year or two old and could shift for himself and watch out about hurting people. By that time, Paul had invented fishing and hunting, modern style, and had started, so to speak, to invent logging. People had done some logging, if you could call it that, on a small scale B.P.B. (Before Paul Bunyan). But since Paul figured out all the best dodges in the business, you might say he invented it. Then he went out and perfected it in his own way, and trimmed it up with Efficiency and Mass Production, until nobody could come within ten miles of doing what Paul could.

When Paul came along, all lumbermen did in the way of logging was chop trees down any old way and then, in a haphazard fashion, get the logs to the sawmill. Sometimes it would be so much bother and take so long to do this, that it was scarcely worth the trouble.

But Paul changed all that in short order.

At the start, for instance, the way ax-men kept their axes sharpened was most awkward. The ax-man would go up to the top of a hill, find a big stone, and start it rolling. Then he'd gallop downhill alongside the stone, holding his ax against the stone.

"That won't do," says Paul, just like that. "If the stone's bumpy, or if the hill is, you get the ax sharp, maybe, but the blade's likely to have too many scallops in it, pretty much like a washboard. Guess I'll invent a grindstone."

Which he did. And that ended that kind of trouble, and saved the men the work of running so much.

Two other inventions of Paul's were the Two-Man Saw and the

Down-Cutter. He didn't need either of these, to be sure, as long as the Seven Ax-men from the Bay Chaleur Country were working for him, because they could fell trees as fast as anyone could ask. They used axes hung on long rope handles, the kind Paul showed them he'd invented, instead of using the sort with old-fashioned wooden handles. Big and strong the way they were, they kept swinging these axes at a steady pace from sunup to sundown. Each of them kept three axes going. They'd each use one at a time, that is, but each fellow's two helpers would be kept busy running to the river to cool the blades after they'd got sizzling hot from chopping. By the time the axes had been tempered that way for four or five days, they were hard enough to scratch diamonds, if anybody had been fool enough to want to do that sort of thing.

But when these ax-men drew their pay and went down the tote road for good, Paul had to think a while before he could work out ways to keep up production. Finally he hit on the scheme of getting a strip of steel long enough to reach over a quarter section, notching it and sharpening it along one side, and putting handles on each end. "Here's a Two-Man Saw I invented," Paul said, soon as he finished it up.

To work this, Paul would pull one end, several men would pull the other end, and the trees would tumble like tenpins all over the quarter section. Paul always told the men at the other end, "I don't care if you ride the saw, but for heaven's sake, don't drag your feet."

This saw, however, wasn't worth a hoot in hilly country. There, though it'd cut the trees on the hilltops right and properly, it'd take off only the tops of the trees in the valleys. This led Paul to invent the Down-Cutter—a rig like a mowing machine (which gave him the idea)—only enough bigger so it would fell a swath of trees five hundred feet wide. So using either the Two-Man Saw or the Down-Cutter, Paul felled the trees at the proper rate in any kind of country there was.

But there still was the problem of turning logging sledges around.

In logging, the men would find their trees, fell them, shave the

169

branches off close and clear, cut the logs into the right lengths, and then roll them down to the road. Then the teamsters would come along with their little flat wooden sledges, to pull the logs down to the skidways.

It was when the teamsters came along with their sledges that the trouble came in. The road, you see, was narrow, and the trees on both sides of it made turning around impossible. So the teamsters had to twiddle their thumbs (which was awkward, with those mittens on) and wait until Paul came along, picked up the four horses and the load, and headed them in the other direction.

"We're wasting too much time this way," says Paul. "Guess I'll invent a round-turn." After he did this, turning around without Paul's help was easy as falling off a log—easier, so far as loggers were concerned—old-timers, at any rate.

Well, everything men did in logging had to be worked out like that by Paul. He had to figure out how to mark his logs so they wouldn't be swiped by other companies, how to get the logs down river, how to break up log jams—how to do most everything that had been done either very badly or not at all before Paul came along.

After he'd perfected processes and methods all along the line, things went smoothly everywhere they'd gone roughly before, pretty nearly half of the time. And when he'd lined up his help, both animal and human, Paul Bunyan had a set-up that couldn't help but be world famous.

Babe, the Blue Ox, was the most useful of the animals. They say he was sky-blue because of his being born in the Winter of the Blue Snow, though most of us historians think this explanation is a little silly. If this was so, we'd like to know, why'd he have a black nose and white horns? Anyhow, Babe was a big beast—forty-two ax-handles and a plug of Star tobacco between the horns—and strong in proportion.

Some ways, Babe was a bother. Supplies for a monster animal like that were naturally a problem. Every time Babe needed to be shod, they'd have to open a new iron mine on Lake Superior. Then there was the problem of feeding him. In one day, he could eat all the feed one crew could lug to camp in a whole dad-blamed leap year. Another thing about the brute that was bothersome was his sense of humor. Nothing he could think up seemed cuter to Babe than sneaking up behind a drive and drinking up the river, until the logs were as dry as a skeleton and even less likely to move. And his other playful pranks were likely to be similarly gruesome.

But all in all, Babe doubtless was more useful than he was bothersome. He could pull a down-cutter with the greatest of ease, something no single animal, or quadruple one, for that matter, could do. He could haul logs to the landing quicker than a scandal could travel—a whole section of them at a time, regardless of how big the stand of timber had been.

Or you take the way he had with crooked roads. That stretch on the St. Croix in Wisconsin showed what he could do—a road nineteen miles long as the sober crow flies, but much longer if you had to follow it, because it jogged and jiggled around and doubled back on itself so often. When the teamsters kept twisting around until they were dizzy, and then, on top of that, kept meeting themselves on the way back, they began to get the jumping jimjams. Result was, Paul decided to hitch Babe to the end of this road and straighten her out.

Hitched onto the end of this wiggly road, which by good luck was on a level stretch, Babe scowled, put his tongue in one corner of his mouth, hunched his shoulders, and just about touched the ground with his belly. His legs were quivering like daddy longleg legs before he could get started moving. Finally, though, after he'd started going, he kept going until he'd pulled her straight. And there was enough road left over—fifty-three miles and a fraction— to do a number of useful things with, I don't recall exactly what.

Things like that, helpful little things, seemed to more than make up for all the trouble Babe brought to Paul's men. Besides, Paul was most fond of the animal, and Babe had a great liking for Paul. Babe would do anything in his power for Paul, unless it was impossible.

Another useful animal—by and large, that is—was Paul's cow

Lucy. Since, like Babe, she tended to be largish, she was likewise a problem when it came to feeding her. At first, they never could keep her and Babe at the same camp at the same time, for fear both of them would eat one another out of house and home.

Still, Lucy had to be kept somewhere near camp so that use could be made of her milk. She gave so much milk, they say, that it took six men to skim it—and the cream made enough butter to feed the camp and grease the skid roads, to boot. It was a big problem, worth Paul's best thinking.

Paul worked the thing out though, in time, as was his habit. What he did was train her to eat evergreen boughs, which, of course, were plentiful up there in the woods. Turned out that this was a pawky idea in more ways than one, since it solved the feed problem for Lucy and the health problem for the camp at one and the same time. Lucy gave enough milk for everybody to have plenty, you see, and this milk had so much balsam in it that it could be used both for cough medicine and for liniment.

It's hard to stop talking about the animals Paul gathered around him and made useful. There was the reversible dog that came in so handy for hunting. There was the goat that could be depended upon to do any of the butting that was called for around camp. There were the pigs that could be used for the pork in the pork and beans that the loggers ate. And there were any number—any big number, that is—of other animals.

All of them brought up problems, and Paul or one of his men had to solve them. It was Brimstone Bill, they say, that worked out the big pig problem. Bill, who was in charge of all the camp animals, including Babe, was troubled by the roving habits of these perambulating porkers. He shortly thought of keeping them in log pens. But then the pigs (who were as smart as they were fat) thought, almost as quickly, of the idea of burrowing out and escaping into the woods. This wasn't because the woods were better or more comfortable than the pens; it was simply because the pigs were ornery.

Brimstone Bill figured and figured, and finally started work on a new fence. When it was finished, he went swaggering around for

a while, then he called Paul over to have a look at the thing.

"My stars," says Paul, "that's the craziest and crookedest fence I ever saw. Whatever did you build a thing like that for?"

"Just watch that pig that's almost dug his way under the thing," says Bill, "and you'll see."

Well, this fat fellow came hunching out under the fence. Then he stood on the outside of it, brushing the dirt off, wearing a proud look on his snoot that seemed to say: "No little old log fence can hold *me!*" Then he curled up his tail and made ready to prance off into the woods. But he'd hardly taken a step before he bumped up against a scallop in the fence. He looked at it with a puzzled look, as much as if to say, "Again?" Then, giving a disgusted grunt, he started to burrow under the fence again.

"See?" says Brimstone.

"I see," says Paul. "Looks like you've got her solved, Bill."

Brimstone was a sure enough wonderful hand with animals. He took care of Babe so long that, as he said, he knew the critter as well "as if he'd been through him with a lantern." When the Winter of the Deep Snow came along, and Lucy couldn't get at the balsam trees, account of their all being covered, Bill worked out a way to keep her from starving. What he did was outfit her with snowshoes, put green glass goggles over her eyes, and turn her out to graze among the snowdrifts.

Bill was always working out smart dodges like that. Paul couldn't have done what he did without Brimstone Bill's help—never under the sun or the stars.

Another great man that helped Paul a lot was Paul's cousin, Big Joe the cook. Joe, who came from three weeks below Quebec, started working for Paul the year he was logging on the Big Onion. That was when Andrew Johnson, from Tennessee, was president, or along there close to that time.

Joe was the only man ever found that could make hotcakes fast enough for Paul's crew, even though Paul always gave any cook as many cookees to help as he needed. (Joe had four hundred and sixty-two that first winter.)

"Nothing a lumberjack likes so much as hotcakes," Paul told

this cook when he hired him. "So you've got to see they get all they want."

What Big Joe finally did was get Big Swede Ole, the camp blacksmith, to make a griddle so big that on a day that was a bit foggy you couldn't see all the way across it. Then he got together several dozen cement mixers, to stir the batter, and some cranes and spouts to pour it onto the griddle. To keep the griddle greased, he hired a bunch of pickaninnies, who'd go skating around with slabs of bacon tied to their feet. After Big Joe got this set-up, he could keep the hotcakes cooking fast enough so that all four hundred and sixty-two cookees could cart them to the tables in bushel baskets in a steady stream.

Then there were other men on Paul's crew just as interesting— fellows like Johnny Inkslinger, who invented bookkeeping along about the time Paul invented logging, and who kept books for Paul's camps. There was careless Shot Gunderson, who got his logs boomed in the round lake that didn't have any outlet, the Year the Rain Came Up from China. There was Sourdough Sam, the cook, who filled the round lake with sourdough, so that when the stuff riz, the logs riz, too, and finally were carried over the hill to the river. Oh, there were plenty of men in Paul's camps worth writing about even in a history as choosy as this one is.

Now, though, I'd rather tell you instead about Paul's family and about one of his most famous jobs of logging.

Paul met up with his wife in a way that was most romantic.

Paul was working with one of his men grading a new road when he heard a most musical screech, followed by two or three of a similar sort.

"That," says Paul, "must be a woman. It's too musical and too loud to be a wildcat, and it's not musical enough to be a bird. Maybe she's in trouble."

So Paul and this man ran over to the Big Rapids. It was Carrie that had been screeching that way, and her reason for doing so was that her sister out there on the water was drifting along toward the falls. Having seen in a flash that the sister, Mary, would be likely to be banged up most terribly if she went over those Big

Rapids, what with the rocks and all, Carrie was calling for help.

Paul sized things up right away. "This can't be stood for," he said. "Think I'll throw enough rocks and other truck above her so we can dam up the water and she can walk ashore on dry land."

Then he started to splash in logs and boulders and hills and anything he could lay hands on. What made Paul notice Carrie (on

top of her musical screech) was the way she lit in and did the same. Quick as a quarter of a flash, she saw what Paul was up to and pitched in to help. And the way she'd uproot trees and cliffs and fling them into the water—not the way a woman usually does, awkward and sprawly, but overhand—the way she'd do that warmed Paul's big heart.

As soon as the dam had stopped the water and Mary had walked ashore, Paul looked at Carrie. Most considerately, she was kicking a hole in the dam, so the boom of logs below would have water to float on.

"Say," Paul said, "you're a ripsnorter. You've got a musical screech; you're smart; you're strong, and now I see you're thoughtful. What's more, you're fair-to-middling handsome, and when you get your growth, I think you'll be tolerably big. Will ums be my ickle wifie?"

"Sure," she said. And that's how Paul won his wife. Later on, she admitted that the way Paul had saved Mary and the way he'd talked so sweet had made her think kindly of him, but it was mostly the baby talk that swept her off her feet. No one else, she said, had ever been of a *size* to talk to her like that before.

She was young at the time, but, the way Paul had expected, she grew until she was of a size proportionate to Paul. Then it took a round dozen Hudson Bay blankets to make a skirt big enough to go around her; and she usually used a mainsail from a clipper ship to build herself a waist. They say that's the way the idea of using sailcloth for girls' and women's blouses got started. Very few women, however, need anything like a whole sail for this purpose.

Mrs. Bunyan was helpful around any camp Paul ever ran. She could split logs to beat any ordinary man, she could fix almost anything with a hairpin, and she was a great hand at cooking, too—specially when there was chicken or soft-nosed pancakes.

In time the Bunyans had a daughter named Teeny and then, a few years later, a son named Jean.

Like her mother, Teeny was smart and helpful. She was the one that figured out that hens alone couldn't furnish enough eggs for a camp the size Paul was running. Result was, she planted and tended a great huge eggplant on a fertile mountain forty-nine miles away from camp. With the plant up high like that, she could roll to camp on the eggs and have them all beaten up by the time she got there, ready for her mother's soft-nosed pancakes.

She was careful about saving the shells, unbroken, after they'd been emptied. She made pin money by selling these shells for Eastertime ornaments. You may have seen some, with white rock candy spread around them, and a peep-hole at one end to squint through and see beautiful scenes. The eggs tended to be big, like everything around Paul's camps, and people often wondered why they were called Teeny Eggs.

Some say that Teeny finally married Ole the Blacksmith. It's a known fact that Ole did court her beginning when she was seventeen, that he made her a handsome brooch out of one of Babe's ox-shoes, and that they had tastes in common, both of them being very fond of coffee. But I haven't been able to find any records that definitely show that they were married. Of course, the records may have been lost, I suppose.

Little Jean, Paul's son, was a chip off the old log. He wasn't more than three weeks old when he jumped out of his cradle one night, grabbed an ax, and chopped the four posts from under Paul's bed.

"Didn't wake me up, or Carrie either," Paul said, proud as a pouter pigeon. "He just let that bed down as gently as a mother panther lays down a panther kitten. That boy's going to be a great logger."

Last that was heard of Jean, he was Down South somewhere, helping Tony Beaver do his logging on Eel River.

All these facts about Paul, his helpers and his family may have got the gentle reader of this history educated up to a point where he—or she, if that's what he is—is ready for the story of one of Paul's famous jobs, the logging of North Dakota.

Maybe, in other words, without telling first about logging the Big Onion, which was tough, and then about logging on the Round River, which was even more so, it may now be possible just to skip to this high spot in Paul's biography.

What started Paul on this North Dakota job was the letter that came to him shortly after he'd finished up logging Minnesota the Year of the Two Winters. This letter was all decorated up with coats of arms and wax and royal seals and big ribbons, so Paul suspected right off that it was from some king or another. But when he'd untangled all that wrapping stuff, made sure there wasn't any "Do Not Open Before Christmas" seal, and pried the envelop open, he couldn't read the foreign language.

Now, in a camp the size Paul had, there were men from almost every country in the world that had a king. So Paul called these men in, one at a time, and had them take a try at reading that there royal epistle. When Swede Ole the Blacksmith tried it, he got results right away.

As excited as a Swede his age and size could be, Ole told Paul it was from the King of Sweden. "He says," Ole told Paul, "that there are too many Swedes over there—country's getting crowded. And he'd pay you well to get ready some land for them to live on over here. He says maybe you can decide on a good place."

"Of course I can," says Paul. "Everybody knows that the right place for a Swede is North Dakota. I'll just see whether President Grant knows any reason why I shouldn't open up the country to those Swedes."

When President Grant said that he thought very highly of Swedes, himself, and it was all right to go ahead, Paul had Ole write back to the King, using a picture of Babe for a coat-of-arms, a hunk of spruce gum for a seal, and a few strands of hay wire—in place of ribbons—to hold her all together. "Sure I'll do it," says Paul, translated into Swedish. "And you might send me a few hundred thousand Swedes, right away, to help me do the logging." (Paul knew the logs had to go, because what the King had in mind was wheat land, so the Swedes could help supply flour. He knew that Swedes couldn't make coffee cake without flour—and where'd a Swede be without coffee cake?)

After Paul had settled on the price with the Swedish Ambassador, he took a two-day trip across North Dakota—a rather slow trip, you see—to size up the way the job of logging ought to be handled.

First thing he saw was that there were several animals that had to be dealt with. And one reason he took two whole days on that trip was that he dealt with the critters then and there. He got rid of all the Hodags, for instance, and all the Tote-road Shagimaws, by stopping up their caves.

Then he tackled the Teakettler. A Teakettler was a small animal, but the steam that boiled out of its nose with a whistling sound was likely to scald people. Studying this animal, Paul found it had a strange habit: it always walked backwards, because it didn't give a hang where it was going, but it was always interested in looking back where it had been. (It was sort of like some historians.) So he arranged for it to bump into sticky things until, full of panic, it moved to Alaska—Kiska, I understand.

When he'd got rid of the Luferlangs, the Snow Snakes and the Rumptifusels, he figured that North Dakota was a safe place to work in—as far as animal life was concerned, at least.

But he needed a camp, of course, and to set that up he took another four-day trip. The camp he built for this operation was ten times bigger than any he'd built before. So, instead of digging the hole under the old pancake griddle, he had a whopper of a new griddle built at Moline. He had Babe tow this great hunk of iron to the top of a hill about five miles from camp, then let it roll down hill to where he wanted it. When it arrived at the right place, it spun around until it stopped, digging a deep pit and then lying down on top of the pit, just as even as you'd want. He fixed the pit so a fire could be built in it. Then he arranged to have the hot-cakes delivered on horseback by twice the usual number of cookees.

That pretty well took care of breakfast, but the tables were big enough to be problems at other meals, too—so long that some might feel that it was hopeless to serve men seated from one end to the other. Not Paul, though—he invented roller skates, and taught all his cookees to use them. Hired other fellows, too, he did, to drive salt and pepper wagons up and down the tables. By driving at a good clip, a pepper man or a salt man could make a round trip in forty-seven hours and seventy minutes—fairly close, I think, to two days, if you want to work the thing out by mathematics.

He worked up a rig for cooking pea soup, too, that was mighty clever. There was a medium-sized lake about three miles from camp. Well, Paul would fill her up with split peas every so often, and throw in six or seven medium-sized pigs for soup stock. He'd have a salt man dump a wagonload of salt in, for seasoning. Then he'd pile up slashings all around the shore, and set fire to them. When the soup began to boil, he'd have seven cookees climb into row boats and paddle like fury here and there on the lake—keep her stirred up that way. And, oh yes, he piped all that soup down to camp, so that, when mealtime came, it could be turned on and off like a faucet.

There had to be buildings made, too—a cookhouse, a dining room, bunkhouses. All of these were built to the right scale. You can get an idea of the size of the cookhouse from this fact—that a cook got lost between the flour bin and the root-cellar once, and he nearly starved to death before he was found. (His name was Smitherson—Archibald Smitherson.)

But the big bunkhouse, maybe, was the most interesting. This soared high in the air, with the top seven stories on hinges to let the moon go by. Since having the rooms fold down that way on a moonlit night was uncomfortable, only the best sleepers, or fellows that couldn't sleep anywhere but enjoyed swooping, would take rooms up there.

All these things were fixed up before logging work began. Then, because of all that forethought, a day in camp would go along wonderfully well. In later years, lumbermen that were there would think back to those happy days time after time, and always they'd get sentimental and homesick for them.

There'd be thousands and thousands of loggers sound asleep in their bunks, used to sleeping through the thousands and thousands of snorting snores of one another, and not likely to wake up because of any little noise like, say, the firing of a cannon or two. But the Bull Cook would take the baton that Big Swede Ole had made and would pound the big triangle with it until the echoes got going every which way, bumped into one another, and started to wrestle. This made such a huge and interesting din that everybody piled out immediately or even sooner.

After a hotcake breakfast, eaten while the thud-thud of the serving horses' hoofs made music, the men would hike out to the woods in the dark—before sunup. They'd fall to, and before you knew it, all over North Dakota you'd hear the cry go up, "Ti-i-im-berrr! Down the line! Watch out!" People in the neighboring states heard it, too. A good many of them used it for an alarm clock.

When the sun came up, everything was fresh and clean, and it was more of a pleasure than ever to swing axes, pull saws, drive sledges, or nudge around logs. Babe and Paul would come around every so often, to help any way they could. And there'd be split-pea soup for dinner, and baked beans or something just as good for supper. Then there'd be a fine night's sleep, with everybody snoring like a sawmill.

With conditions so good, the timber kept coming out at a great rate, until it was piled mountain high and then somewhat higher. Finally, it was piled so high that the lumberjacks would no sooner get over it or around it into camp than it would be the start of another day.

"This won't do," says Paul, when he sized up what was happening. "I want my men to get some sleep before they go out to work. Got to do something about all those logs!"

One thing he did was build his Big Sawmill, right away, using what he had on hand and ready to use so he could finish it quickly. He made a circular saw out of the hotcake griddle. (The men had to go without hotcakes for a few days while a new griddle was made and delivered from Moline, but Carrie cooked popovers for them.) For smokestacks, Paul used the barrels of his shotguns, fixed up with cloud-parters at the top, so the clouds could go around them. And he taught Babe to pile the lumber with his tail. That way, the log piles got cut down some in size.

Another thing Paul did was have careless Shot Gunderson take out one of the biggest booms of logs in the history of the world

and drive it down the Mississippi River. Shot was as haphazard as a North Dakota winter night was long, but Paul kept hiring him, year after year, because he brought up so many interesting problems. Paul could always depend on Shot to double the hardships he had to overcome.

This time was like others. Shot was supposed to take those logs down to St. Louis, but he didn't recall this, somehow, until he'd taken them all the way down to New Orleans.

"Have to fix *that*," says Paul, laughing and laughing fit to kill at Shot's forgetfulness.

What Paul did was feed Babe a big salt ration, then drive him over to the upper Mississippi to drink. When Babe started to slake his huge thirst, the Mississippi started to run upstream, much to the puzzlement of Mark Twain, who was taking a trip on the river at the time. (He wrote about it on page 528 of *Life on the Mississippi*, they tell me, and then had to leave it out because there wasn't room.)

Johnny Inkslinger was on the shore, making hundreds of figures on a cliff with a slate pencil, keeping track of how fast those logs were coming upstream. At the right minute, Johnny said, "OK!" Then Paul took Babe away, and the logs could be delivered in St. Louis.

Those are just a few samples of all the smart dodges Paul used to get North Dakota logged off by the date he'd set in the contract. After all the timber was off, though, the Swedish Ambassador objected to the stumps. "Can't farm on land as full of stumps as that," he said. So Paul took a big maul and went all over the state, hitting each stump such a whack that it went at least six feet underground. That's why you see so few stumps in North Dakota, even today.

Well, the King of Sweden couldn't have been more pleased than he finally was with the way Paul did that job. He paid Paul the full agreed price and seven dollars bonus.

The Swedes came into North Dakota in droves, and are there to this day. Paul made ready for his trip to the Far West. But that'll have to be put into a later chapter—the one after those telling about Pecos Bill and John Henry, if you don't mind.

13

Pecos Bill, King of Texas Cowboys

ALONG ABOUT THE TIME PAUL BUNYAN WAS DEVELOPING lumbering to a high point up north, down in Texas Pecos Bill was doing likewise for the cowboy business. Since it would be confusing, though, to tell about Paul's work as a lumberman and Bill's work as a cowboy at one and the same time, the writer of this history has wisely decided to use two chapters—one for each of these great subjects.

Nobody knows the name of Bill's father. In Texas, back in the days when he went there, it wasn't healthy to go up and ask a stranger his name, as many a tenderfoot learned to his sorrow. But Bill's mother called him the Ole Man beginning when he was a young twirp of half past seventy, and he called her the Ole Woman, more or less in revenge. So everybody else used those names for them.

So far as is known, there wasn't anything out of the ordinary about this family. They had the usual things people took to Texas in those days—a rifle, a chopping-ax, and an iron hog-rendering kettle. And they had seven boys and six girls, all of them either sons or daughters.

They got into Texas, it's said, about the time Sam Houston and the other Texans were putting the final licks on the Republic of Texas, so she could let the Union join her. This made it possible for Bill to be born in Texas, and from the start he did his best to live up to that great honor.

There was the time, for instance, when, in the middle of a sunny day, all of a sudden the whole place was as dark as the inside of a cotton-picking Negro's pocket. This was just after Bill's family had got a little way into Texas, and the family was still camping out. The Ole Woman had put Bill down on a bearskin on the ground, where he was lying and trying his best to swallow his left foot.

The hum this black cloud made soon showed what it was—a stampeding herd of Texas Gallinippers—swarming down so thick that shortly little Bill was plumb out of sight. Even when the Ole Man fired his rifle into the blackness, a faint ray of light came through a tube-like hole only for a split-second, then the hole closed, leaving the world as dark as it had been before.

"Ole Man," says the Ole Woman, "that newest baby—Bill, I think his name is—is likely to get carried plumb away unless you do something."

The only thing the Ole Man could think to do was push his way through the Gallinippers to the wagon, get the hog-rendering kettle, stumble over to where Bill was lying, turn the kettle upside down, and cover the little fellow up with it. At the last minute, figuring Bill might get bored, he shoved the chopping-ax under the edge for the baby to play with.

Baffled like that by a mere iron kettle, the Texas Gallinippers started to take steps—or swoops, rather—in short order. One of the smartest of them cleared the way several feet above the kettle bottom, took aim, and dived down on the thing with all the speed of a dive-bomber. He hit the kettle with a metallic ping, and rammed his bill clean through the iron.

Then another one did likewise, and another, and another—until the sound of Gallinippers banging against the kettle and sinking their bills into it was like the patter of rain on a tin roof. But there was another noise that at first puzzled the Ole Man and the

Ole Woman—a bang, inside the kettle, following each one of the pings.

"By grannies," says the Ole Man, finally, "I know what's happening. Each time one of those fellows lands, little Bill is taking the chopping-ax and bradding the bill with it."

The Ole Man and the Ole Woman were laughing like hyenas when they saw the kettle, in the murk, slowly beginning to rise. "I'll swan," says the Ole Woman, "those Gallinippers are carrying off that great big kettle."

They did, too, easy as lifting an eyelash. And before long they were disappearing to the West, lugging that big piece of ironware.

"Look!" the Ole Man said. "Those other fool Gallinippers think Bill's still underneath it."

Sure enough, it looked that way. After that kettle the things all flew, so that shortly the family was in the Texas sunshine again, with the skies all clear. But Bill was lying on the bearskin, just as calm as a cow, having a try at swallowing that ax-handle. "Goo," he said, "goo, goo!"

"I'm sure sorry to lose that kettle," the Ole Woman said. "But when a baby's as smart as Bill there is, it's worth while to keep him."

She took extra good care of Bill after that—fed him on panther's milk, weaned him when he was two weeks old, and gave him a bowie knife to cut his teeth on. He grew stronger, and when the first norther came along, and the flames in the fireplace froze stiff as crooked icicles, Bill chewed them up and swallowed them without harm. Soon as they unfroze, they couldn't seem to do more than give him a warm feeling in the stomach that made him giggle a bit.

A few months later, one of the older children ran up to the Ole Man in the field one morning, and said, "There's a panther just went into the cabin where Bill is, and Bill's alone with that varmint!"

"Well," says the Ole Man, "that fool panther doesn't need to expect any help from me!" He didn't feel any different, either, when he stopped plowing at noon, went into the cabin, and found

Bill (who was a year old now) cooking up some panther steaks for the family.

A while later, when the Ole Man found wagon tracks within five miles of the cabin, he decided that the district was getting too crowded, and decided to move away. It was while they were on this trip that Bill jounced out of the wagon just after the family had forded the Pecos River.

By bad luck, he was asleep at the time, so he didn't wake up until hours after he'd taken the spill. And the Ole Man and the Ole Woman were so busy moving the family and all that it wasn't until three days later, counting the children, they found Bill was missing.

"How sad," the Ole Woman said, "our little Bill out there among all those wild animals and poisonous rattlesnakes and such."

"The varmints and rattlers," the Ole Man said, "will have to fend for themselves. We didn't go to lose him."

What Bill had done, meanwhile, was toddle around on his little dimpled feet and find himself a pack of coyotes to be friendly with. After he'd licked them all to persuade them that he was the boss, he started to teach them everything he knew and to learn everything they knew.

He and these varmints taught one another so much that by the time Bill was grown up, the coyotes were smarter than foxes, and Bill was smarter than anybody else his age—except in some ways. For example, he was the only human being who ever learned to palaver in all animal lingoes before reaching the age of ten; and no other human *ever* learned to follow trails, to run, or to foresee weather the way Bill could. Still and all, Bill thought he was a coyote, and he hadn't done any human talking since he'd been lost at the age of two.

That's why he had such an all-fired hot argument with the cowboy that came on him one day when Bill, in his birthday clothes, was loping around out in the sagebrush and making coyote noises.

This cowboy spent a whole day getting Bill not to fear him. Then he spent another day teaching him to talk again, and curing him of some of his baby ways of saying things. Then he spent three days making Bill see that he was a human being instead of a coyote. This was a ferocious argument. The cowboy would put out one argument after another, and Bill would bat each down, until finally the cowboy said:

"Well, if you're a coyote, where's your bushy tail?"

After Bill had looked around and had found this article missing, the cowboy said, "That's a stunner, huh? Here's another. Come over with me and take a squint into the creek with me." When they were bending over their reflections in the water, the cowboy said, "Now, don't you look like me, only less handsome and more whiskery?"

Bill admitted this, gulped, and said, "All right, drat it to dratted drat! I'm a human man then. We'll call me Pecos Bill, because I'm from the Pecos River country—been a coyote there most of my days. And I'll run with my own human pack, if I can slow down enough. First thing I have to do, I suppose, is start looking like you ugly critters. So tell me, how do I get myself bald all over the face, and how do I grow me hair like you've got all over most of you— red and blue and brown like that?"

The cowboy howled with laughter, and pressed hard on his ribs with his hands, as if he was trying to keep them from falling off. "You get the hair off your face by shaving," he said. "And that red and blue and brown stuff isn't *hair*: it's *clothes*. We put clothes on—don't grow 'em. I'll bring you a razor to shave with, and I'll bring you some clothes tomorrow. Then I'll take you to the ranch, and maybe you can join the outfit."

So the next day the cowboy (name of Bowleg Gerber) brought Bill a razor and the biggest suit he could find. Then he showed Bill how to shave and how to get into his clothes. Bowleg brought a horse, too, and a quirt, but he found his friend didn't need them. "Got me an animal of my own, standing still over there," says Bill, pointing out a giant panther that he'd fought to a standstill. "And this is what I'll use for a quirt."

"Good heavens!" says Bowleg, for he saw that Pecos Bill had tamed a huge rattlesnake, that just lay limp and smiling in Bill's big brown paw.

Well, when the two of them rode into camp, Bill's mount and his quirt, as well as his size and his looks in general, made the men

sit up straight and blink. Bill jumped off his panther, cracked his rattlesnake quirt, wiped his wet brow with a handful of prickly pear cactus, and walked over to the fire.

There he asked the question Bowleg had told him to ask. "Who," he said, "is the boss of this here outfit, huh?"

A big cowboy going on seven feet high cleared his throat and answered him back in a low voice, "I—I—*was*, until *you* turned up. What're your orders, sir?"

Anybody else but Pecos Bill probably would have been surprised by this, and puzzled as to what to do. But Bill had been boss of the coyotes so long that he expected exactly this sort of thing to happen. And he'd learned from the coyotes, too, that a varmint was loco if he stuck out his neck too far, without knowing what might happen to what was on the end of the neck.

So Bill just said, "Ahem! You can be vice-boss now, if you want to. You go ahead and run things the way you were until I get the lay of the land and figure out whether we need to make any changes."

Well, what Pecos Bill found in the cowboy business was very much like the sort of thing Paul Bunyan had found, at the start, in the lumber business. Everything was in its infancy, and more messed up than a baby that has dumped a bowl of strained spinach over its head.

Leading his friend, Bowleg Gerber, to the side, Bill said, "What's this pack doing?"

"They're cowboys," Bowleg told him. "They stay out here in this shack near the water. Wandering around in the country hereabouts are a good many head of cattle. Every morning, each of these fellows takes a rope, puts a loop at the end, and lays the loop on the ground. He puts some bait in the loop—maybe a hunk of salt, or some sweet-smelling hay, or a cowslip. Then he takes the other end of the rope and hides behind a tree or cactus with it. Then he waits."

"So far," Pecos Bill said, "the whole show sounds as if it'd bore a body plumb to death. Never, in all my days as a coyote, did I fiddle around in such a dull way."

"The exciting point comes next," Bowleg said. "After while, a cow or a bull comes along to get a drink of water. Before or after drinking, the critter may see the bait. If the critter steps up to get the bait, the cowboy waits until its feet are in the noose, then gives the rope a quick jerk. If the animal isn't scared too soon— doesn't jump away—the cowboy catches its legs in the noose."

"I still think it's a very tame and boresome business," says Pecos Bill. "What's more, there are more 'if's' in it than we coyotes ever had in anything we did. What happens, though, if this fellow has the good luck to catch the critter?"

"We got us a barn over there," Bowleg said, "and we put the critter into the barn. When we've got enough animals so there's one for each cowboy to lead, each of us ties a rope to his particular critter. Then each one leads his animal to market, riding on a horse, you see. We call that a *cattle pull*, because we drag the critters."

"Heavens to Betsy!" Pecos Bill said. "All that boresomeness and all that trouble, and you just market one critter apiece? We've got to get this business more coyote-like and on a bigger scale."

Having this kind of an understanding of the way things were

done and this kind of a hunch they could be done better, Bill started working out improvements. He went riding around on his panther for a while, but found that scared the cows too much. So he went out afoot one day, and ran down the biggest wild horse he could find cavorting around in those parts, broke the animal, and started to ride it. Bill didn't know it, but this in itself was a great thing to do. Before this the cowboys hadn't thought of catching a wild pony and taming it—always bought their horses. After he'd been fed on dynamite for a few days, the horse was good enough to suit his master.

Riding this horse, which he'd named Widow Maker, Pecos Bill went out among the herds of cattle on the plains, watched their ways, and figured out how to handle them. One very important thing he did was take a great long rawhide rope out and do some practicing with it. When he came back about a week later, he had most of the points about the cattle business all worked out.

Pieface Thomason, the vice-boss of the outfit, was hiding behind some mesquite, watching a cow, when Pecos rode up. The noose was all laid out on the ground, baited with a pretty bowl of corn-meal mush, and this cow was sort of stepping up slowly, drooling a little, to have herself a bite. Pieface was watching and watching, all ready to jerk the noose at just the right minute.

When Pecos Bill came thundering in on his brand new broncho, the cow got scared and started to gallumph away.

Pieface came bustling out from behind the mesquite, roaring at Bill. "Look what you went and did!" he yelled. "I've been lying in wait for that danged cow for two hours, and now you've come clumping up and scared her!"

"That's all right," says Pecos. "You can be sure when an old-time coyote makes a noise, it's because he wants to. I'll catch her for you, Pieface."

Spurring Widow Maker (for by that time he'd invented spurs), he went after the cow, swinging his rope around his head.

At the right minute, he let the noose fly through the air. It settled down over the cow's neck. Just at that instant, Bill's broncho braced. The end of the rope had been given a double turn around the saddle-bow. When the cow started to run again, the rope tightened, and first thing the cow knew, she'd flopped onto one horn on the ground.

Pieface was watching open-mouthed and goggly-eyed. "How under the sun did you do that?" he wanted to know.

"Little gadget I worked up," Bill said. "I call her a lariat. Keeps you from spending all that boresome time waiting for critters."

"Can you do that right along?"

"Sure. Call in the men in the outfit."

When the hands had come in, Bill galloped around on his broncho, showing them how to lasso one critter after another, while they all went "Oh!" and "Ah!" like a bunch of kids at a fireworks display. When, to end up his show, he tossed his rope up in the air and pulled down a buzzard that happened to be flying by, they all cheered as loud and as long as they could.

"There's another little thing or two I've worked out that I'd like to show you," Pecos said, riding up to the men. "You've got about twenty cows in that barn, haven't you? Well, turn them loose."

"Pecos," Bowleg Gerber said, "you're the boss, and I don't aim to argue with you. But I'd just like to mention—so you can think about it—that it's taken us six weeks to catch those critters."

"Don't worry," Bill told him. "I've invented a dodge to keep them from getting away."

When the beasts were let out, Bill just watched them go scampering every which way. The cowboys did the same, looking sort of mournful, but keeping their mouths shut and not complaining. When all the cattle were out of sight, Pecos Bill went riding away after them, and got out of sight himself in a jiffy.

After a while, though, to the surprise of all the cowboys, they saw a cloud of dust in the distance, off in the direction where their boss and the cattle had gone out of sight. Then the cattle came loping along in the middle of the cloud of dust, with Bill and Widow Maker busying themselves around the fringes.

"Hey," Pieface said, "I've been counting. Twenty-one went out, but Bill brought in a hundred and three!"

193

Pecos Bill left the cattle drinking at the river and came over to the cowboys. "Now," he said, "I'll tell you about some of the things this old coyote has worked up to fix up the cowboy business. You'll want to remember the names for these new dodges of mine, so pay attention and keep the words in your mind. Now— when I went out on the range and collected those cattle, I *rounded them up,* see?"

"Rounded them up," the cowboys said, all together, like children learning to talk a foreign language.

"When I brought them here, I *herded them.*"

"We hearded them, too," says Bowleg. "'They made a thundering noise, stomping along that way. But watch your grammar, Bill."

"I'm not talking bad grammer," Bill told him. "I H-E-R-D-E-D herded them."

"H-E-R-D-E-D herded them," the cowboys said in chorus.

"Now," says Pecos Bill, "we'll *brand them.*"

Shortly he had a fire started, and the branding-irons (which he'd just invented) were heating on the fire. After a time, when a steer galloped by the fire, Bill reached out, grabbed its tail, and gave it a quick pull to one side. The animal, thrown off balance, crashed over on its head and part of its shoulder.

"That," says Bill, cool as a cucumber, sitting on the brute to hold him down, "is called *tailing.* You can throw a brute that way, or you can *rope* it, either one that suits you. Now I take this poker-like dingus, with the block of type on the end. It's got hot—cherry red—in the fire, see? Now I *brand* the brute with the iron."

"Brand the brute," the cowboys said after him, while he put the hot iron against the hide of the steer.

"Whoa!" yells one of the cowboys, name of the Kid. "You're burning the critter's hide! It'll make a mark there!"

Pecos let the steer go, dusted off his hands, and walked over to where the cowhands were sitting and taking everything in.

"That's what I meant to do," he said, "burn the hide and leave a mark. The brand tells that that critter belongs to this ranch. Matter of fact, it's the name of the ranch—the IXL—that I branded on

194

there. I thought up the name yesterday, when I was figuring out things in general."

"But what do you want a mark on the hide for?" Bowleg wanted to find out.

"I've figured out cow-punching," says Pecos Bill, "according to the great and wonderful way of thinking out things I learned when I was a coyote. I'll tell you how the whole thing works, men, and I think you'll go for it. We'll brand all our cattle like that, so people will know they belong to us, you see. So we won't have to keep them in the barn all the time after this. We'll let our cattle wander around out there on the range, pretty much as they're a mind to, most of the months of the year. Of course, we'll go out and look around regularly, to see they're getting along all right—not eating loco weed, say, or getting into some other sort of trouble. If a cyclone's coming along, for instance, we'll get the critters out of the way. (Not having as much sense as coyotes, of course, they have to be shown what to do.) If it's winter, the line riders and the outriders will see to it that the critters go where they can paw their way to grass, keep sheltered from northers and so forth."

"Sounds like hard work," the Kid said.

"It will be," Pecos Bill told him. "It'll be work in the spring, too, when we round up the animals and see they're all branded. And it'll be work other times, when we have a beef roundup, to get together the animals that're going to market."

"How'll we get them to market?" Pieface asked Bill.

"We'll have *cattle drives*," Pecos Bill said. "After we herd the brutes together, we'll drive them to market, you see. That'll be a lot more according to cow nature than those fool cattle pulls you've had up to this time, and it'll take care of more cattle, too. For a drive like that we'll have a trail boss, his segundo, or right hand man—that'll be you, Pieface, in this outfit, a cook, and one puncher to every two hundred and fifty cattle. Along the side of the herd, we'll have a line of punchers riding, to keep the brutes in order. At the end of this here column, we'll have the tail riders, the remuda and the men in charge of her, and the chuck-wagon.

Figure we ought to make about fifteen miles a day, if we start at sunup and halt at night."

"Sounds all right," says Pieface. "That halting at night stuff sounds very, very good to me. We eat and sleep then, huh?"

"We eat, sure, and sleep a good share of the night. But I figure we'll have to work in shifts—two to four hours apiece, say, to see that the brutes are quiet and peaceful. They'll eat a big meal, you know, soon as we stop, then they'll go to sleep. About midnight, they'll wake up and feed again, then they'll sleep till sunup. That's the way it'll be except on moonlight nights, when the fool animals will eat all night, instead of howling at the moon the way coyotes do. I used to watch them when I was a coyote, and I know that's the way they'll behave."

"Did your life as a coyote," Bowleg wanted to know, "give you any idea what we can do out there on the lone prairie when we're riding alone and lonesome at night?"

"Well," says Bill, "I recalled the high old times I used to have howling at the moon when I was a coyote. So I asked the cattle whether they wouldn't go for a similar kind of entertainment, when I was talking over things with them, you know. They said they didn't like howling, exactly, but songs had a most soothing effect on them. So riding out there at night, we could sing, to keep them cool and to keep ourselves awake. I've made up some songs to sing. Here's one, for instance:

> *A cowboy's life is a dreary, dreary life,*
> *Some think it's free from care;*
> *Rounding up the cattle from morning till night,*
> *In the middle of the prairie so bare.*

CHORUS

> *Half-past four, the noisy cook will roar,*
> *"Whoop-a-whoop-a-hey!"*
> *Slowly you will rise with sleepy-feeling eyes,*
> *The sweet, dreamy night passed away.*

When spring sets in, great trouble does begin,
The weather is so fierce and cold;
Clothes are wet and frozen to our necks,
And the cattle we can scarcely hold.

The cowboy's life is a dreary, dreary life,
From dawn to the setting of the sun,
And even then his work is mighty tough,
For there's night herding to be done.

The wolves and the owls with terrifying howls
Will disturb our midnight dream,
As we lie in our slickers on a wet sticky night,
Way over on the Pecos stream.

All the cowboys agreed that this was a most beautiful song. And when Pecos Bill sang them some of his other little ditties—things like "Bury Me Not" and "Sam Bass" and "Get Along Little Doggies," they thought very highly of them, and learned them, too. Bill, you see, already had made up about half the songs to be sung to cattle. Later, he made up most of the other half. You'll find that most professors think that cowboy songs were put together by somebody named Mr. Anonymous, but all the cowpunchers know that Pecos Bill knocked together almost all of the best of them.

"Well," the Kid said, "I can get the idea of the way it all works, and it amazes me that one man could figure out all those improvements. Only one weakness in it, far as I can see. We'll work about ten times harder than we used to work, and we'll have at least twelve times as many hardships. Seems to me that maybe some of us will sort of tend to drift out of the cowboy business, now it's going to be so all-fired tough."

"The weaklings, they'll drop out, sure enough," Pecos Bill said. "We'll be glad to see them go, too. When I was a coyote, I never did like to have a coyote that was a sniveler join the pack. Matter of fact, I made some of this work tougher than I had to, just to make sure we'd weed out the cry-babies. But I figured that with

197

all these hardships to overcome, the cowpunchers would develop in time into a bunch of rootin'-tootin' heroes. It'd be enough of a challenge, you see, so we'd have a line of work a man could be proud to do. And that'd bring high pay, naturally—thirty dollars a month *and* keep. Another thing, after those hard times on the range, with piles of pay saved up, a cowboy at the end of a cattle drive could have a wonderful time for himself spending all his money. It'll be a fine life, you see, if you have the good luck to live through it."

"It's the life for me," says Bowleg Gerber, and most of the other cowboys said the same. Then they gave six cheers for Pecos Bill (instead of the usual three, since cowboys were always generous). And then they set to work.

That's the way, then, Pecos Bill started up the cowboy business, worked out every part and parcel of it, so to speak, except for a few little improvements he worked out later—things like the six-shooter, for instance. And when word about the IXL outfit and the way it did things got around, everybody else copied Bill's methods. Before long, there were as many cattle on the Texas plains as there'd once been buffalo. And for all Texas was a big state—the biggest in the world, it had more heroes to the square mile than you'd offhand expect.

The IXL was the best outfit there was, naturally, since it had Pecos Bill as a boss. Anybody that was anybody would try to sign up with the IXL, and usually he'd land there, too. Bowleg and Pie-face stuck with Bill, and others just as good joined up with the outfit. Only one to leave was the Kid, who found some easier work—went into the outlaw game, robbed banks and mail trains and suchlike.

Working up cowpunching would seem to be enough for any man to do, but of course Pecos Bill wasn't satisfied. He went on to do things in the cowboy line no one else on earth could do, then or later—came to be the greatest cowboy in all the states of the world, including the Scandinavian.

It's downright hard to pick out the things he did that were most notable, but I suppose that the windies they tell around the campfires most often in Texas are the one about the way he busted the cyclone and the one about the way he courted Sweet Sue.

This cyclone-busting stunt, we happen to know, took place the Year of the Great Drought. Fact is, the Great Drought was what made it happen. The sun beat down on the prairie and dried it until it was about the texture, say, of a bride's biscuits after she's forgotten to use milk in them. The dust began to fly then, getting into everybody's hair, so that when a body brushed his hair, it felt as if he was rubbing the top of his head with sandpaper. And the cattle's tongues lolled out until a body was fearful they might step on them.

Being tenderhearted the way he was, Pecos was very much touched by all this. He went riding around on Widow Maker, heaving heartrending sighs and pondering and pondering—but he didn't get a ghost of an idea until he sighted this cyclone. Like a lightning flash strikes most people—Bill was too fast to get hit by one—an idea came to him. He couldn't make use of this particular cyclone, because it was a baby; but it gave him an idea about using one that had got its full growth.

Next thing he did was go galloping all over the state of Texas, and a few of the neighboring states, on Widow Maker.

Up on the northern edge of Oklahoma, Bill came upon a promising set of weather conditions. The skies were black for a while, and then they started to turn sort of greenish. There was thunder, and then there was a big long purring moan, and all the Okies started to head for storm cellars, hollering as they went, "Here comes a cyclone!"

Pecos Bill watched the big black funnel, with lightning trimmings on its fringes, come whirling up at forty-two and a half miles an hour. When it was the proper distance away, Bill readied his big lariat, by now a thing he'd put together that was only two hundred miles shorter than the equator. He twirled it around his head, let go, and lassoed that fierce cyclone right around the neck.

The cyclone whirled around more fiercely than ever, and of course soon it had wound a large share of that lariat around its neck, mostly at a point just above its Adam's apple. Bill held on until he was pulled right up close to the black twister.

Then, just at the right instant, he leaped a-straddle.

The funnel of wind gave a snort that sounded more or less like a mountain choking to death. Thereafter, it started to use all the tricks bucking bronchos have ever figured out to use when a roughrider is trying to gentle them—only on a much larger scale. Bill quirted a plenty, shoved in the steel, and slapped the brute on the ears with his sombrero, giving a coyote yell of a size to make any state that was less tough than Oklahoma split right down the middle.

Soon the outraged cyclone was high-flying, sun-fishing, pin-wheeling, rearing back, side-throwing, high-diving—doing everything of the sort a broncho had ever invented. But, though Pecos Bill did have a few minutes of what you might call discomfort, he was bound and determined to ride it out. So he rode that bucking cyclone all over Oklahoma, New Mexico and parts of Texas.

When it began to pant and groan, showing it was desperate, Bill edged this cyclone over to the counties in Texas that had been hit hardest by the Great Drought. Then the cyclone did exactly what Pecos had figured it would do when it got licked—rained out from under him.

It did this just in the nick of time to save thousands of cattle from thirsting to death.

Pecos Bill wasn't hurt any, of course. He simply slid down to the ground on a streak of lightning. And when Widow Maker turned up in a couple of days, Bill could go back to work again, in the ordinary way.

A good many of Pecos Bill's friends think that even more wonderful, in some ways, than this cyclone-busting stunt was Bill's taming of Sweet Sue.

Bill had felt kindly toward other girls, now and then, before he met Sue, but never before had he fallen hard enough for one to start calling her his "pretty little coyote." What really got him, doubtless, was seeing Sue one day galloping around on a whale in the Gulf, just off Corpus Christi. He'd seen other Texas girls riding

200

whales, of course, but this was the first one that, from the way she was giggling, appeared to be enjoying herself.

Bill made up to Sweet Sue, courting her with all the thoughtful little favors and all the sugary talk he could think up. He'd call her his little coyote, the way I've said, for instance, and on a moonlight night, he'd stand under her window and howl musical animal howls at the moon.

Soon, naturally, he'd won her. And he was content, except for one thing. "Only trouble with Sweet Sue," he said, "is that the girl seems to think she doesn't have to do what I tell her. Now I've been a leader of a coyote pack or of an outfit of cowhands ever since I can remember, and I'm afraid I'll have to gentle her. I'll have to straighten her out in that one little way, somehow or other, if we're to get along."

He did, too, shortly after the wedding.

"Don't *ever* ride Widow Maker," he'd told Sue, day after day, up to and including the day of the wedding.

But being willful the way she was, Sweet Sue could hardly wait to disobey her lord and master. No sooner was the wedding over than she pranced out, in that lovely wedding gown of hers with the big steel and whalebone bustle, and climbed on Widow Maker. "I'll show Bill who wears the chaps in this family," she said.

Bill had known Sweet Sue would disobey him, and beforehand,

he'd told Widow Maker exactly what to do. And Widow Maker did exactly as he'd been told:

He bucked so hard that, before she knew it, Sweet Sue was flying high in the air—up, up and up—until finally she went looping over the lower prong of the crescent of the new moon, more or less like the cow in the nursery rime.

Then, when Sweet Sue came down—as she did after a time—she lit on her bustle.

And this bustle bounced her as high as Widow Maker had bucked her before. Up she went and looped over the moon. Then, reaching the earth, again she lit on her bustle, and again she did a prodigious bounce.

This went on until it got monotonous. Also, Sue was tired, bedraggled, provoked and hungry.

"Oh, Bill," she finally yelled, when she got within hollering range on one of the trips down. "Bill, I'm fagged out, my hair's all mussed, and I'm bored, and I'm hungry. Can't you save me from all this agony?"

"Guess not," says Bill, slicing himself a slice of Texas watermelon and waving it at her. "Maybe I'll have to shoot you to put you out of your misery, the way we do a horse that's broken its leg. Oh, my pretty little coyote, if you'd only minded me!"

"If I get saved," says Sue (for she was close enough not to yell now), "if I get saved, I'll never disobey you again."

"Sure?" Bill asked her.

"Yes—uh!—I'm sure." The "uh" was when she lit and bounced, and she said the "I'm sure" while she was sailing toward the moon again.

She hadn't got far before Bill put down his slice of watermelon, flipped up his lariat, and brought her down. She bounced around for a little while, but Bill held onto the rope, and soon she stopped.

And it's a pleasure to tell you that she kept her promise, and Sweet Sue and Pecos Bill lived happily ever after.

14
John Henry
and the Machine in
West Virginia

PAUL BUNYAN, IN THE FIRST PART OF HIS GREAT LIFE, AND Pecos Bill, all the time he was a cowboy, didn't have to worry too much about machines. Machines had been on the job, of course, ever since Mike Fink had fought the steamboat, rough-and-tumble; but none of the heroes was very much bothered by them. Even after the Civil War, some heroes could use their strong arms and bodies to win fame, more or less ignoring machines and such.

Just the same, along in there after the Civil War, what with all the science and invention you'd find all over the place, there were more and more machines, and it was harder to do anything without bumping up against them. So now, finally, there had to be a showdown between a hero and a machine.

John Henry was the hero that had the showdown.

From his birth, it was clear that John Henry's life would be out of the ordinary. The day before, there was a rainbow, and a coal black preacher rode by the Henry cabin on a gray mule. The night was black, with a round red moon and no stars. Near by a cock crowed, a hound bayed, and somewhere in the forest panthers screamed. A great black cloud came from the southwest to cover the moon, and rain and forked lightning darted out of the cloud.

And the thunder made a hammer of itself that pounded the earth
till the trees quivered.

Then John Henry was born.

And the cloud went away, the moon shone white and bright, the stars came out, and the nightbirds started their singing. But in the moonlight, a coal black preacher rode by the cabin again, and he was riding on a gray mule.

First thing John Henry knew, someone was saying, "He weigh thirty-three pound!" Next thing he knew, someone else was saying, "My, my, see them great big shoulders!"

"Course I weigh thirty-three pounds," says John Henry. "Course I got big shoulders. And I got me a voice that's deep and strong. And I got me a cravin' in my soul. What's more, I's hungry."

"My, my," John Henry's pappy said. "John Henry's talkin' already. What you aim to eat, son? Want a little old milk, son?"

"Milk's for babies," John Henry answered him back, "and already I's a natural boy, and soon I'll be a natural man. And I's hollow as an old dry well, sure as you born. So bring me seven hawg jowls and three kettle full of blackeyed peas. Bring me seven ham bones and three pot full of giant cabbage sloshed around in gravy. Bring me a bait of turnip greens that's higher than my woolly head, and a like amount of ash cake to soak in the pot-licker."

"Lawd, Lawd," says John Henry's mammy. "Sound like we got a bragful son on our weary hands. Pappy, maybe if we start right now and learn him his eyes is bigger than his stomach, it'll start him on a good life."

So, with the help of the neighbors, they got all those mountains of food together. And there wasn't room for all the food in the fireplace room, so they had to set it forth on seven tables in the yard.

When John Henry's pappy looked at all that food, he grinned from ear to ear. Then he went to that newborn son of his, and he said, "It's all there, son, set forth on seven tables. If you can eat it, it's steamin' in the moonlight."

John Henry walked to the tables, and he started to eat. The food began to fly, and everybody that watched him grinned to see the way he prized his food. Of course, they expected that he'd stop after the first or second table.

But soon every table was clean as a hound dog's tooth and John Henry was untying his napkin from around his neck.

"My, my," his pappy said. "He done et up all that food."

"Course I did," says John Henry. "I told you I was hungry."

"We thought you was just a bragful son," his mammy said.

"No," John Henry told her, "I's not bragful and I's not humble. I's a natural boy, and what I says, I means. And now I's goin' to sleep for nine hours."

Nine hours after he went to sleep—nine hours on the dot—John Henry woke up. "I got me a cravin' in my soul, and I's hungry," he said. "Bring me thirteen possums with sweet taters piled treetop high around them. Bring me ninety-nine slices of fried razorback ham and the red gravy. Bring me three gallons of hominy grits to put the gravy onto. And bring me thirty-three buttermilk biscuits and tree-sweetnin' for them, for to finish off with."

Knowing, by now, that the boy meant business, they brought what he asked, and served it forth on nine tables. He ate it, easy as could be, untied his napkin from around his neck, and went back to bed.

And it went like that for quite a few months, while John Henry grew and grew. By good luck, that was back in the slave days before the war, so Ole Massa had to furnish all that food.

But John Henry grew fast, and his strength grew likewise.

He wasn't many weeks old when he got hold of a piece of steel and his pappy's five pound hammer when the family was at meeting one fine Sunday morning.

When the family was a good piece from the cabin—"Lawd, Lawd," says John Henry's mammy. "Hear that hammer ringin'. It sound like the meetin' house bells when they's tollin' for a buryin'."

When the family came to the house, they found John Henry had gone out with that piece of steel and that hammer. He'd found every big stone he could find, and he'd used the steel and the five pound hammer to break the big stones. He was working away on the biggest stone of the lot now, hammering the steel and singing in time:

> *If I die* (WHAM!)
> *A railroad man,* (WHAM!)
> *Go bury me* (WHAM!)
> *Under the sand,* (WHAM!)
> *With a pick and shovel* (WHAM!)
> *At my head and feet,* (WHAM!)
> *And a twenty pound hammer* (WHAM!)
> *In my hand.* (WHAM!)

With the last wham, the rock broke in two, just as clean as if it'd been sawed, and John Henry stood up grinning, his white teeth shining in his dark face.

"Hello, folkses," says he. "Look like I's found what I want to do—swing a hammer and make the steel ring like a bell. Never been so happy in all my born days, and I's seven weeks old come Thursday. Seem like when I swings this old hammer, I don't have a cravin' in my soul—don't have a cravin' any more."

"My, my," his pappy said. "Look like our son was goin' to be a steel-drivin' man."

While he was saying this, though, there was the clump of hoofs on the red clay road that ran past the quarters. And the smile on John Henry's face faded, and he frowned a little. And the next thing John Henry said was:

"This hammer be the death of me." (He said it kind of puzzled-like, looking fair-to-middling dazed.)

"Lawd, Lawd," his mammy said. "Run out, one of you chillun, and see what that was that was ridin' by."

So one of the little children—all eight of them were smaller than John Henry by now—ran out and looked down the red clay road. When this little girl came back, she said, "It was nothin' but a coal black preacher ridin' on an old gray mule."

"Lawd save us all," mammy said, "that's a bad, bad sign."

After that John Henry slept with his hammer every night, giving it a smacking big kiss before he went to sleep. And many of his childhood days he spent breaking big stones with his hammer and his steel. Not only would he break up stones; some of them he'd

drive with his hammer. He could kill animals by driving the stones
—a whirring partridge or a leaping rabbit, or even a whizzing deer.
He didn't kill much game, though—just what he and the family
needed for the pot. Because his heart was big in proportion to his
size, and he was mighty big.

After a while, though, John Henry got so big and so strong,
that when he lifted the hammer with all his strength and whammed
it down, he broke it. There wasn't any other hammer handy, and
he wouldn't take that old hammer to his bed. But there'd be dark
black nights when he'd wake up to find himself reaching for that
old hammer and full of woe because he couldn't find it.

By the time he was fifteen, John Henry was bigger than any
full grown black man on the plantation. It was still slave days,
then, so Ole Massa had him go to the fields. The fields were snow
white with cotton, and it was cotton picking time in the fields.

When the overseer looked at him, the overseer said: "You're big
and strong beyond your years, John Henry, and maybe we can
make a cotton-picker out of you, sure enough."

John Henry said, in his big deep voice: "Course I's big and
strong beyond my years. But you don't need to *make* a cotton-
picker out of me, cause I already *is* one. Bring me three sacks, big
sacks—one for each shoulder and one for the middle of my back,
and stand out of the way, cause I can pick more cotton—clean
cotton, too, without any bolls and stalks in it—than any nine
black men there is. Three bales a day is what I can pick, sure as
you born."

"Oh! Oh!" says the overseer. "I see what you are, John Henry.
You're bragful and you're uppity, high steppin' and proud. All
right, you black folks, bring him the three sacks, big sacks, and
stand out of the way. And be ready to laugh till your sides ache,
cause John Henry's talked beyond his powers."

Every one of all those cotton pickers got to a place where he
could see and where he had plenty of scope to laugh hearty. But
they soon saw John Henry had a natural-born cotton-picker's
ways. He bent his back and kept it bent, in order that he might
not tire. He passed his bent fingers over the bolls, cupped his hands

208

to catch the cotton as it fell, and moved his hands all the time towards the sacks on his shoulders. What's more, the way a good cotton-picker does, he sang while he worked:

Ole Massa told the slaves,
Pick a bale of cotton,
Ole Massa told the slaves,
Pick a bale a day.

    A-pick a bale, a-pick a bale, a-pick a bale of cotton
    A-pick a bale, a-pick a bale, a-pick a bale a day.

Ole Eli from Shilo
Can pick a bale of cotton,
Ole Eli from Shilo
Can pick a bale a day.

I believe to my soul
I pick three bales of cotton,
I believe to my soul
I pick three bales a day.

    A-pick three bales, a-pick three bales, pick three
        bales of cotton,
    A-pick three bales, a-pick three bales, pick three
        bales a day.

When John Henry first sang that about picking three bales, the slaves laughed deep—"Yugh, yugh, yugh," that way, slapped their knees, and said: "Sakes alive! Ain't he a bragful black man?" For nobody except old Eli from Shilo had ever been known to pick as much as a bale a day, and that'd been his best day, too.

But when the copper sun was setting, and they weighed John Henry's cotton, there was forty-five hundred pounds—a good three bales, and it was clean cotton, too, without any stalks or bolls in it. The slaves' eyes got round as saucers, and the overseer said, "Well, John Henry, I thought you were bragful, and I thought you were uppity, and I thought you'd talked beyond and above your powers. But I see you picked what you promised."

"Course I did," says John Henry. "I's not bragful, I's not uppity, and I's not humble. I's a natural man and a natural-born cotton picker, and what I says, I means."

For quite a time, John Henry was a cotton-picker on the plantation. Then, for quite a time, he was a tobacco-stripper. He was just as good with tobacco as with cotton, better than any other slave on all the plantations. For he was a natural man and a natural-born tobacco-stripper.

In the fields, John Henry sang, he cracked jokes, and he worked hard. John Henry got religion, and he was baptized in Goodman Creek by Parson Day. John Henry married Polly Ann. She had shining black hair as wavy as the ocean, eyes that glowed like stars, teeth like pearls, a dimple on her cheek that came and went like a ripple on a bayou, slender little hands and dancing feet. He loved her more than tongue could tell, and she loved him likewise.

But instead of being as happy as a mocking bird, John Henry had a craving in his soul. At night, he'd sit in front of the cabin, with Polly Ann's head on his weary shoulder, and he'd sing songs like this one:

> *I knows moonlight, I knows starlight,*
> *Lay this body down;*
> *I walks in the moonlight, I walks in the starlight,*
> *To lay this body down.*

> *I walks in the churchyard, I walks through the churchyard,*
> *To lay this body down;*
> *I'll lie in the grass and stretch out my weary arms,*
> *Lay this body down.*

Down the row of the slaves' cabins, John Henry's mammy could hear him sing. "Lawd, Lawd," she said to his pappy, "that boy's got him a cravin' in his weary soul, and his home ain't here."

That was the way it was when the Civil War ended, and all the slaves were free. When John Henry heard he was free, he went to the overseer, and told the overseer this: "Now I's free, I thinks I's goin' to roam. I got me a cravin' in my weary soul, and my home's some place else. So, good-bye, Mr. Overseer, good-bye to you."

Polly Ann and John Henry started to roam, and they roamed far and wide, sure enough. They'd be one place for a while, then they'd be another, but always, in the end, it'd be the same. John Henry would say what he could do, and then he would do it; for he was a natural man that meant what he said. At work, he'd joke and sing his songs—coonjine, and he was a good worker. He was a roustabout for a while, a deckman on a steamboat for a while, a cornpicker for a while.

But always, sooner or later, he'd move along, because he had that craving that I mentioned a while back in his soul.

John Henry and his loving Polly Ann were walking one day in West Virginia, looking for a place to call their home. It'd been a bad night the night before, with a great black cloud from the southwest covering up a copper moon, with forked lightning and rain coming out of the cloud, and with thunder making the ground shake as if a great big hammer had whammed it hard.

This day, though, was a fine day, with a rainbow in the sky, the trees all a brand new green, and the songbirds in the shiny leaves just singing fit to kill. Polly Ann had a pretty red ribbon in her shining black hair, the dress she wore was blue, and she danced along in her little red shoes, happy as a singing lark. But John Henry, he was the one that was doing the singing. He sang a happy song that went like this:

> *I done walk till my feet's gone to rollin',*
> *Just like a wheel, Lawd, just like a wheel;*
> *But I got a feelin' my troubles is over.*
> *That's how I feel, Lawd, that's how I feel.*
>
> *Got me a rainbow shine in the heaven—*
> *Ain't gonna rain, Lawd, ain't gonna rain.*
> *So I got a feelin' my troubles is over;*
> *I's found my home, Lawd, free from all pain.*

"You sure sounds happy, John Henry," says Polly Ann. "I hope it's like you say it in the song—that we've found our home. For I's powerful tired of this life of roamin', John Henry, powerful tired."

"I got me a hunch that's more than a hunch," John Henry said. "I knows. We've had plenty of signs of this, too, Polly Ann. Look what year it is—1872. Add one and eight, and you gets nine. Add seven and two, and you gets nine, likewise. My lucky number is nine, Polly Ann. They's nine letters in my natural-born name. I weighed thirty-three pounds, on the dot, when I was born, and three times three is nine. This is bound to be my lucky year, sure as you born. Listen!"

What they heard when they listened was the ring of hammers on steel off in the distance, and the songs of black men working.

"That's finest music I ever heard," John Henry told his Polly Ann. "It minds me of the time when I's a little bitty boy and I played with my pappy's hammer. I been huntin' a hammer all this livelong time, and now I knows it."

When they got to the place where the hammers were ringing, it was a mountain. And the men that were hammering and singing were at work building the Big Bend Tunnel for the C. & O. Railroad.

This wasn't much of a railroad, so far as size went. But it was an important one, just the same. For one thing, it's just about the only railroad that will get into this history. For another thing, it stood for something mighty big that was happening in America along about this time: people were building a whole mess of railroads—the Union Pacific, the Santa Fe, the Southern Pacific, the Northern Pacific and the Great Northern, to name just the biggest of them. Finally, it was going to be on this railroad that a hero, namely, John Henry, would have it out with a machine.

Captain Tommy was the boss of the men that were working in the Big Bend Tunnel, down there in West Virginia. These men had the job of driving long rods of steel deep into the rock. When the holes were deep enough, and the men had gone far enough away, other men would put nitroglycerin or mica powder or dualin into the holes and blow away the rock, huge hunks at a time.

"You look big and strong," says Captain Tommy, when John Henry braced him for a job, "and maybe we can make a steel drivin' man out of you, sure enough."

John Henry answered him back, in his thunder voice, "Course I's big and strong—bigger and stronger than any black man a-workin' in the Big Bend Tunnel. But you don't need to *make* a steel drivin' man out of me, cause I already *is* one. Bring me a twelve pound hammer, and get me a shaker, and stand out of my way, cause I can drive more steel than any nine men at work in this here tunnel."

"Oh! Oh!" says Captain Tommy. "Sounds to me as if this man that came to me and asked me for work might be just bragful and uppity. Here, you, Li'l Bill, come and shake for this big-mouthed black man. And the rest of you stand back and be ready to laugh till you bust, because here's somebody that talks mighty big, and if his say-so is bigger than his do-so, we'll laugh him out of camp."

The shaker held the steel, and John Henry got himself organized to swing the hammer. Chiefly, to get organized, he got a feel of rhythm in his legs, in his stomach, in his chest, in his shoulders, in his arms and in his head. Also, he started to sing, in time with the rhythm, and he brought down the hammer in time with the tune. He sang:

> *Oh, my hammer, (WHAM!)*
> *Hammer ring, (WHAM!)*
> *While I sing, Lawd, (WHAM!)*
> *Hear me sing! (WHAM!)*

(The whams came in on the rest of the song, the way they did on this verse, but I'll leave them out, because all those whams may be tiresome.)

> *Ain't no hammer,*
> *Rings like mine,*
> *Rings like gold, Lawd,*
> *Ain't it fine?*

213

Rings like silver,
Peal on peal,
Into the rock, Lawd,
Drive the steel.

If'n I dies, Lawd,
I command,
Bury the hammer
In my hand.

When John Henry first sang about his hammer ringing better than any other, the steel drivers laughed "Yugh, yugh, yugh," and hit their knees with the palms of their hands. "Ain't never heard such bragful singin' in all our born days!" they said. But when they watched the way John Henry's hot hammer swung in a rainbow arc around his shoulder, and when they saw the way Li'l Bill, the shaker, had to work to loosen and turn the steel after each ringing wham of the hammer, they stopped laughing and their eyes grew round as dinner plates.

Finally, Captain Tommy said, "Stop for a while, John Henry, while I see the work you've done." Then when Captain Tommy had looked, he said, "Well, well, John Henry, looks like your do-so is as good as your say-so, and you aren't just bragful and uppity, the way I thought you were. You drove steel as good as you promised—more than any nine men at work in the Big Bend Tunnel."

"Course he did," says Polly Ann, grinning with her pearl white teeth. "He's not bragful and he's not uppity. He's a natural-born steel-drivin' man, and what he say, he mean. Praise the Lawd, we's done found our home."

"You work for me," Captain Tommy told John Henry, "and I'll give you four dollars a day and the rent of a company house and enough vittles for you and Polly Ann. I like the way you make that hammer ring and the way the steel goes down."

"Thanks politely, Captain Tommy," John Henry answered him back. "I be proud to work for you, but I wants to ask one little favor. When you goes to town, I'd like to have you get me two twenty pound hammers so I can make 'em ring and drive the steel."

"Anyone else asked for two twenty pound hammers, I'd laugh right square in his face," Captain Tommy said. "But I've seen what you can do with a swinging hammer, so I'll get you what you want. Now pitch in and let me hear that steel ring, because you're working for me from now on."

So John Henry was working for Captain Tommy, and his loving Polly Ann was keeping house in one of the company houses.

It was hard work in the tunnel, of course. The smoke from the blackstrap lamps and the dust from the hard red shale were so thick that a tall man working in the tunnel couldn't see his own feet without stooping almost double. The thick air was hot, and the men stripped to their waists before working.

But John Henry was the best steel driving man in the world. He could sink a hole down or he could sink it sideways, in soft rock or hard—it made no difference. When he worked with two twenty pound hammers, one in each hand, it sounded as if the Big Bend Tunnel was caving in, the ring of the steel was so loud.

And John Henry and his sweet Polly Ann were as happy as singing birds, for their roaming days were over, and they felt they'd found a home.

Everything was going fine until a man came along and tried to peddle his steam drill to Captain Tommy. This man had pictures of the steam drill in a book, and he had a wagging tongue in his head. "This steam drill of mine," he said, "'will out-drill any twenty men. It doesn't have to rest or eat, either, so it'll save you lots of money."

"Hm, maybe," Captain Tommy said, "*maybe*. But I've got one steel driving man here that's the finest in the world, and I'm mighty fond of big John Henry. So I'll tell you what I think we might do. We might have a race between the steam drill and this man of mine. If the steam drill wins, I'll buy it. But if John Henry wins, you give me the steam drill and five hundred dollars."

"I heard about John Henry, all right, and I know he's good," the man said. "But I know a man is nothing but a man. So I'll have that race, the way you say."

"Fine," says Captain Tommy, "except for one thing: I've got to ask John Henry, but I know pretty well what he'll say." So he went to John Henry, and asked him if he'd race that drill for a favor and a hundred dollars to boot.

John Henry said, "Course I'll race it, and course I'll beat it. For I's a natural-born steel-drivin' man that can beat any nine men or any of the traps that ever drove steel. I don't want any old machine to take my place at the happiest work I's ever found. So before I let that steam drill beat me, I'll die with my hammer in my hand."

The day of the race, country folks and all the steel driving gangs in the whole section came to see whether John Henry meant what he said. The race was to be outside the mouth of the tunnel— out there by the blacksmith shops where the steels were sharpened and the hammers were fixed—a place where everybody could see. The steam drill, with a boiler about twenty feet long to make the steam, was on the right hand corner, and the spot where John Henry was to drive was on the left. The crowd was sprinkled all around the edges of the quarry.

At the time the race was to start, the blacksmiths had sharpened piles of drills, the steam drill had its steam up, and the carriers were ready with pads on their shoulders to carry the sharpened steels from the shop and the dull ones back to be sharpened. When there was one minute to go, the steam drill whistled, and John Henry lifted one of his twenty pound hammers. Then Captain Tommy dropped his hat, and the race started.

Says John Henry to Li'l Bill, the shaker, "Boy, you'd better pray. Cause if I miss this piece of steel, tomorrow be your buryin' day, sure as you born."

Then the steam drill was chugging and John Henry was swinging and singing—singing "Oh, My Hammer," "Water Boy, Where Is You Hidin'," "If I Die a Railroad Man" and other hammer songs he could keep time to. The steel rang like silver, the carriers trotted to and from the blacksmith shops, and the crowd watched with all its might and main.

It wasn't long after the start that John Henry took the lead.

The steam drill salesman wasn't worried, though—or if he was his talk didn't show it. "That man's a mighty man," he said. "But when he hits the hard rock, he'll weaken." Then when John Henry hit the hard rock, and kept driving fast as ever, the salesman said, "He can't keep it up."

John Henry did keep it up, though, swinging those two hammers and driving down the steel, stopping only once an hour, maybe, to take a drink of water from the dipper Polly Ann had carried in her slender little hands. Six hours—seven hours—eight hours of that nine hour race, he made his hammer ring like gold. And though Li'l Bill got plumb played out and a new shaker had to take his place, all through the eighth hour John Henry was going strong as ever, with the rhythm in every muscle and joint helping him wham the steel.

It wasn't until the ninth hour that John Henry showed any signs of getting tired. Then, when Captain Tommy came up to ask him how things were going, he answered him back, "This rock is so hard and this steel is so tough, I feel my muscles givin' way. But," he went on to say, "before I let that machine beat me, I'll die with my hammer in my hand."

After that, the crowd that was watching could see signs that John Henry was a weary man—very, very tired and weary.

And John Henry wasn't singing any more. All you could hear was the ring of the hammer on the steel and the chug-chug of the steam drill.

When Captain Tommy, at the end of the ninth hour, looked at his watch and yelled, "The race is over," and when the drills stopped going down, everything was as still as a graveyard. Captain Tommy was looking at the holes. Then, when Captain Tommy said, "John Henry won—three holes ahead of the steam drill," everybody cheered—everybody, that is, excepting the salesman and the steam drill crew—and John Henry.

When the crowd looked at John Henry, they saw the great man was lying on the ground, and his loving Polly Ann was holding his head. John Henry was moaning, and he sort of mumbled, "Before I let that steam drill beat me, I'll die with my hammer in my hand." (Sure enough, he had *two* hammers in his big black hands)

Then he said, "Give me a cool drink of water fore I die."

Polly Ann was crying when she gave him the water.

Then John Henry kissed his hammer and he kissed his loving Polly Ann. She had to stoop down so he could kiss her. Then he lay very still, and Polly Ann cried harder than ever—sounded mighty loud in that quiet quarry.

Just at that minute, there was the sound of hoofs, and a coal black preacher came riding up on a gray mule. "You got troubles, sister?" he said to Polly Ann. "Can I help you?"

"Only way you can help," she answered him back, "is to read the buryin' service for my lovin' John Henry. Cause his home ain't here no more."

So the coal black preacher read the burying services. They buried John Henry on a hillside—with a hammer in each hand, a rod of steel across his breast, and a pick and shovel at his head and feet. And a great black cloud came out of the southwest to cover the copper sun.

15
Paul Bunyan, Scientific Industrialist in the Oilfields

JOHN HENRY BEAT THE MACHINE, ALL RIGHT, WHEN HE HAD the showdown with it. But since it killed him to do it, most heroes after that didn't seem to take to the notion of fighting it out with machines. What they did, instead, was use them.

And I suppose that was the beginning of modern times, as much as anything was. Modern times are partly heroes and other people using science of the kind Febold Feboldson and Jim Bridger invented, and quantity production of the kind Paul Bunyan and Pecos Bill invented—and machines. You can see this if you look around, and see how many people use science, quantity production, and machines—people you like and respect, too. You also can see this if you consider what this chapter and the next one have to say.

Paul Bunyan's life divided up into at least two parts, and this chapter's about Part Two. What separated these two divisions was the difference between the things he did. In the first, he didn't do much except log, and that period was the one when he worked up quantity production, in horse sense ways, more than it ever had been worked up before. In the second period, he applied science to industry, and brought on even bigger quantity production.

In other words, as he finally found out from Jim Hill, Paul

turned into what you might perhaps call a scientific industrialist.

This second period started a while after Paul had finished logging off North Dakota. Paul was doing some logging in northern Minnesota in the Year of the Worst Winter.

This winter was so cold that every night the smoke coming out of the chimneys went and froze in a column half a mile high, so every morning somebody would have to climb up on the roof and chop it down. It got so that on the ground around every house there were these frozen columns of smoke, pointing every which way, like the rays of the sun.

It was so cold that some of the men worked out a new way of letting the folks back home know how things were going. They'd just talk, the words would freeze, then they'd collect them, bundle them up in heavy brown paper, and ship them home. When the family thawed the packages out, they got all the news—usually news to the effect that it was still middling cold up in the woods.

The thing that really got Paul was what the cold did to his coffee. One morning, he set a pot of hot coffee on the back of the stove. When he went to pour it, he found the stuff was frozen stiff. What was worse, it had frozen so fast that it was too hot to handle.

"This won't do," says Paul. "There ought to be a climate somewhere that isn't as unhandy as this one."

As usual, he plunged into doing something right away. Stopping only to put on snowshoes that would get him through that deep Minnesota snow, he started hiking westward, headed up to Oregon and Washington, where the climate was better and where he did some lumbering and some farming.

The lumbering carried out to a logical end all the ways of lumbering Paul had figured out before, and tacked a little science onto them. Take the way he logged that big island in the middle of the Inland Sea (later known as the Inland Empire), then figured out, by science, mind you, where there was a downgrade clear over to the Pacific, and then dug the Columbia River so he could float the logs.

Or take the way he handled the hotcake problem in his biggest camp out there. In place of the old hotcake griddle, he took and built him a four block stove, made so slick that it didn't need greasing and slanted in such a way that the hotcakes would both cook and flip over a couple of times while they were sliding off.

Serving men at tables the size he had there was another problem. But Paul solved it by inventing motorcycles, so that waiters could dash around faster than they could even on roller skates. And to get the orders in from the end of the hall, Paul invented telephones that connected up with the cook shack.

However, aside from the way he made use of science, this lumbering on the Pacific Coast doesn't seem very interesting, because it was too much along the line of Paul's earlier work. The use of science in a big way, though, was rather new. And it led to great things in farming and oil operating.

Paul hadn't paid much heed to farming before he got out near the coast. But when he'd got lumbering down perfect, and he was looking around for some new interest, it happened that he got a push in the direction of farming.

Out in Washington, Paul got another of these letters with a tangle of ribbons and wax around it, so he sent right off for Swede Ole. "Here," he told him, "is another letter from our pal the King of Sweden. Tell me what it says."

When Ole, as excited as before, ciphered out the letter, "It says," he told Paul, "that there still are too many Swedes in Sweden, even after so many have gone to North Dakota. The King wants you to find another big parcel of rich land, so he can send some Swedes over to work it."

"Hm," says Paul. "I don't want to go back East, and that Inland Empire is powerfully dry. Looks to me as if I'd have to figure a scientific way to get water back onto that soil, and then see whether it's rich or not."

That was how Paul happened to invent irrigation, a very scientific way to get water onto dry land. It happened that Teddy Roosevelt, who was president at that time, was all for developing what he called "the natural resources" of the country, and he was glad to chip in some money to help set up the watering system. (By natural resources, I understand, Teddy meant land and woods and water and such, but in politics, you have to use high-toned words.)

What Paul did, as you can see for yourself if you go out to that part of the country (preferably by way of the Black Hills and Yellowstone Park)—what Paul did was figure out the lay of the land, then take a pick and drag it, gently but firmly, through the right places. The result was a sort of network of ditches, to carry water where it hadn't been going recently. He fixed up some gates and such, too, in order that water could be turned on and off, according to what was needed.

Having got the water meandering around to make the soil moist, Paul figured he'd test the land out with pop corn. So he picked up a good healthy looking kernel, walked out to a likely looking place that had been irrigated lately, and dug a hole about a foot deep with his middle finger. He couldn't use his forefinger or thumb, naturally, because he was holding the corn between them.

Well, Paul had no more started back to camp to get Ole to act as a witness, than there was a sort of sputtering up of brown dirt, and a cornstalk came skyhooting through. In no time at all, the corn was up to Paul's knee. And by the time he got back with Ole, the cornstalk had grown so much that the top was buried in a cloud.

"Ole!" says Paul. "Climb up to the top of that baby and chop the top off so she won't grow any more!"

Ole started shinning up the stalk at a great rate. But the thing kept shooting up, and in a minute or so Ole, too, was out of sight in that cloud. It was a handsome cloud with cottony bumps and scallopy edges, but Ole said afterwards that being inside of it wasn't different from being inside of any old cloud. "Nothing but fog inside it," he said.

"When you chop the top off, throw her down," Paul yelled.

Ole's voice came booming down. "The top's above me," he said. "I can't get *to* the thing." Ole's big voice had something like the effect of thunder, and the cloud rained away from around him. But this new moisture made the stalk grow even faster.

"This won't do!" Paul yelled. "Come down, and we'll handle her some other way!"

"Can't come down, either," Ole yelled in a minute. "Every time I go down one yard, this thing shoots up three, and I'm losing ground. I'm getting hungry, too."

Paul yelled for Babe, right then. And while he was waiting for Babe to come along, he used his shotgun to shoot up a few crullers which he hoped—for the time being, at any rate—would keep Ole from starving to death.

When Babe came along, Paul hurried with the beast over to Jim Hill's railroad, the Great Northern, which (by good luck) wasn't far away. Paul loaded Babe up with a pile of steel rails, then hurried back to the cornstalk with them.

"I'll see if I can't choke off the moisture in this cornstalk," Paul said. And with that he started tying those rails together and then knotting them around the cornstalk.

It worked, too.

Soon the ears of corn away up near the top stopped getting moisture and started to dry out. Then the hot sun hit them hard, and shortly the corn began to pop, making considerable noise, too.

After a while, this popped corn came drifting down like so many snowballs. Babe, who'd lived through so much fierce weather, didn't do any more than shiver a little. But a big herd of cattle grazing near by decided they were in a world-beating blizzard and promptly froze to death.

Meanwhile, growing in spite of those knotted steel rails the way it had, the cornstalk had been bitten into by the things, and had cut itself off of itself. Now it started to tumble, slow but sure. Ole rode it down to the ground, just like a logger standing on a log in white water, then at the right time he jumped off lightly and headed back for Paul, following along the cornstalk.

When Ole got there, the owner of the cattle herd, who'd hurried over, was talking up right sassy to Paul. "Look what you did to my cattle, just when they were fat for market!" he yelled. "You'll have to pay for them."

"Course I will," Paul said. And he settled for the cattle, right on the spot, for Paul was always fair and square, regardless of cost.

"Hello, Ole," says Paul. "Glad to see you back. Just bought me a herd of frozen cattle."

"Goodness gracious!" Ole said. "And with our camp so far from where the cattle are, if we ship them they're likely to spoil."

"That won't do," Paul said. "We'll have to figure a way to use the critters. Teddy Roosevelt wouldn't like it if we wasted all those natural resources. Let me think."

After thinking a while, Paul snapped his fingers. "I've got it!" he said. "If the popcorn froze them, the popcorn can keep them frozen."

With that, he strolled over to the railroad and called on the head man, Jim Hill. Jim rented him a raft of box cars. Then, with the help of Babe, Paul stuffed those box cars with animals *and* popcorn. And that way, the meat kept fine until it had been delivered at Paul's camp.

So, without knowing it at the time, Paul had gone and invented refrigerator cars.

Paul had Ole write out in Swedish about the way that corn had grown and then had him go on to say that the soil in the Inland Empire was rich enough to suit anybody, whether he was a Swede or not. Then Paul fixed the letter up with the usual hay wire and stuff, and sent it off to the King. Result was, quite a number of Swedes went out and settled in that part of the country.

An even larger number, though, decided that planting stuff in that kind of soil was too dad-blamed dangerous. And those that came there, as a rule, didn't plant much corn, somehow—grew mostly apples and wheat instead.

It wasn't until Jim Hill wrote a letter to Paul about the refrigerator cars some months later, that Paul got onto the fact that he was well started on the second period of his life.

"Those refrigerator cars you invented," Jim wrote, "stand to make us more money than any invention since Pullman cars. We're packing them with ice, and shipping fruit and meat and such all over the place. You, sir, are a great scientific industrialist."

After Paul had looked up a couple of words in the dictionary, he came swaggering around to Mrs. Bunyan, his chest all swollen out. "By crackey," he told her, "know what I am these days? I'm a scientific industrialist—a scientific industrialist! I seem to have changed over to that from lumbering without scarcely noticing. That draining of the Inland Sea, that gravity-working cookstove, those cook-shanty telephones, those irrigation ditches, not to mention refrigerator cars—all of them show my genius along that line."

"I can think of something even earlier," Mrs. Bunyan said, "back before you met me—back in 1859."

"Log booms and peavys!" Paul said. "Did my genius show up as far back as that? How?"

"Well," Mrs. Bunyan said, "I remember you told me that this fellow named Edwin Laurentine (Crazy) Drake got you to help him back there in Pennsylvania, and you hauled off and invented oil wells."

"So I did," says Paul. "It had slipped my mind. Do you know, I think maybe now that the lumbering business is practically perfect, I might make use of scientific industrialism in the oil business. Might do it down in Oklahoma and Texas maybe."

"Any oil there?"

"Yes," Paul said. "I guess as a matter of fact they've found some already, but I know there's a lot more. I remember the time that my reversible dog and I followed this trail of big tracks—biggest tracks I ever saw, and some of them in solid rocks, too—and they led straight to Oklahoma. We found out after we'd got there that we'd got onto those tracks a little too late. They were dinosaur tracks, you see, and the poor varmint had died something like a million years ago. They say that oil comes from brutes like that getting covered up with coal and rocks and the like, and having the oil squeezed out of them. And I recall now that I got a sniff that smelled pretty much like that oil well I invented for Crazy Drake."

"My stars!" Mrs. Bunyan said. "To think you'd remember a little fact like that all these years! Well, you run along, Paul, and industrify your oil wells. Leave Babe here, and he and I'll run the camp."

No sooner said than done—not much sooner, at least, the way Paul did things. Before you knew it, Paul was over in Oklahoma, getting the oil business all rigged up with scientific industrialism.

First thing Paul did was change the whole system of finding oil. The oil hunters before had used pretty much the same way that people had used to find water. They'd go wandering around with a forked stick, and then where the stick bent toward the ground, they'd say the oil was. Only change they made was to use willow sticks instead of the hazelwood that had been used for water-finding. But they had a batting average of only .122, which wasn't a very good one, of course.

What Paul did was follow dinosaur tracks and sniff for oil, mostly. But sometimes he used his knowledge of geology, picked up here and there in his travels afoot all over the United States. These ways couldn't be used very well by other people—offhand, anyhow, because nobody else had Paul's talents for tracking down dinosaurs and sniffing, and no one else had covered the country, afoot, as well as Paul had.

So other oil hunters, as a rule, had to go to geology schools to learn how to use Paul's system from books.

After he'd found oil, Paul set up a rig, which was the name he'd invented for an oil derrick. This was four straight uprights held together by a mess of cross-ties and braces. At rig-building, Paul outdid any other rig-builder there ever was. He could pull, run, and sight a rig—finish it up completely—in one day, though as a rule it took a crew of three men as many as three days to do a similar job.

Oh, he was a great rig-builder, Paul was, and he could do everything by himself and single-handed, in record time. There'd be these big reels—bull wheels—that the drilling cable would be wound on, and he'd build one of them in the astonishing time of half a day. Or he could hang a walking-beam in just half the usual time, by himself.

When it came to starting the hole, he invented a name for it, "spudding in," and then he went ahead and spudded in, in ways no one else could. For instance, he could take a long narrow spade called a sharp-shooter, and dig down faster than anyone else could with a drill. Or he could drive a sixteen pound hammer he had into the ground until he got the hole nicely started.

When the hole had been started, Paul could do the drilling **any** number of ways, though mostly he used only three. One was to **use** an engine to lift and lower the drill, the way everybody else did. A second was to work the drill himself by hand. He used the second way when he was in a hurry, and the drilling was easy—soft digging, as he called it. The third way was for Paul just to take **the** drill and fling it into the ground, sort of like spearing a fish. For some time, he'd use this third way for tough digging—in hard rock.

But when he banged a drill into the ground with all his strength once, she went clear through to China, and the oil all came spouting out and got a bunch of pagodas and tea orchards all greasy.

So after that, Paul either used Method 1 or Method 2, and if **he** used Method 3, he did it with his left hand.

Well, Paul was busy in the oil business for some time—still is, some people say. I've read somewhere that he brought in all the biggest wells in Oklahoma, Arizona, Colorado, Texas and parts of California, using scientific industrialism on the lot of them, too. And it does stand to reason that to get all those wells started would take even a great man like Paul more than a little while.

But there was one well, just like there was one logging job, that somehow was better remembered than any of the rest. This was in East Texas, I think, not too far from the border of Oklahoma.

This job didn't start out well, it happens, because Paul had a cold. That meant that though he did what he could with geology, and though he sniffed the oil smell, he couldn't do more than guess exactly where the well should be sunk. So the first hole he put down mortified Paul half to death—because it was a dry hole, the first and last one he ever sank. A sixteen inch hole it was, and Paul drilled and drilled without hitting anything but dust.

There was a fellow that was with Paul at the time—not to help him, you understand—so much as to keep him company; for Paul naturally didn't need much help. This fellow finally told Paul they might as well give her up.

"Id's a dry hole, sure as shoodid," says Paul, talking that way because he still had the cold. "Bud we've pud a lod of dime od her, and we'd lose all our work if we stopped dow. That won'd do."

Then he thought and thought, and finally dug out a newspaper he had, and read part of it. That part of the paper said some rancher out on the plains wanted to buy some post holes—ten thousand of the things three feet long apiece. "We'll ged them for him," says Paul.

Babe happened to be down there at the time, paying a visit, so Paul made use of the animal—hitched a chain around this duster hole, then hooked Babe up to pull.

Babe hadn't worked for Paul in a coon's age, and when Paul said, "Giddap," Babe had a happy grin from ear to ear, and almost busted himself, he pulled so hard. It was sort of touching.

It was sort of unfortunate, too, in a way, because Babe pulled so hard and scrabbled around with his hoofs so much, that instead of pulling the whole hole up easy and smooth, he busted her off after he'd tugged only fifteen thousand feet out of the ground.

You'd think that would sink Paul, the way it would most other men, but it didn't—not Paul. He figured, you see—and rightly, too—that there wasn't any need of having post holes sixteen inches across. So he did some scientific industrialism, meaning (in this case) mathematics.

Then he quartered that hole, sawed it all into three foot lengths, and had exactly the number of post holes needed. Made a good profit on the deal, too.

Paul waited until his cold was gone, then went sniffing around. What he smelled made him certain that, if he did it right, he had a chance to bring in just about the biggest well that ever had gushed.

First thing he did was move his derrick over the right place. This he had to do by hand, since Babe had trotted back to Washington to help Mrs. Bunyan. Then he built onto it, until he had a hinge arrangement similar to the one he'd used on the bunkhouse, to let the sun and moon go by. Some yarnspinners claim that he got the thing so high he could move up to heaven while he did his work, but it's been proved that the thing really was seven feet too short for this to be possible. He did get a mighty tall derrick built, just the same.

This derrick was so big, and the well was so deep, that for once Paul had to have some help. After drilling started, a derrick man wouldn't be able to get down more than once a month—usually on pay day: he just lived up there in the derrick.

The hole was proportionate—about seventy-five inches across, and ten miles deep. Drilling a hole that size was a terrible problem— so far as making the drill go was concerned. No engine that'd been built up to that time, as a matter of fact, *could* work a drill of the size needed. Of course, Paul could work the thing by hand; but that was most tiresome and boring.

"This won't do," he finally said, after working the drill by hand for three straight days. "I'll have to think up a little scientific industrialism."

He did exactly that. What he did was use rubber tools. He'd set the drill bouncing, and then he could snooze, or think up scientific stuff, or do anything he had a mind to, until he had to change the bit. And he had so much speed at the bit changing job that he could just wait until the bit bounced out of the hole and then get the new one in before it bounced back again.

When this well came in, it was a creation gusher. Oil shot so high that Paul had to hurry and put a roof up there, to keep the whole sky from getting greasy.

I don't recall, just now, how many million gallons came out of that well, but I do recall one interesting detail about three million gallons of it. These particular gallons came up in some unusually cold weather, and just froze stiff. Well, this didn't faze Paul a single minute. What he did was take his ax, the one with the rope handle, and chop the oil up into big cubes. Then he loaded the cubes on flat cars, and shipped them that way. Since the rate for flat cars at the time was about half as high as the rate for oil cars, this stunt doubled his profits.

But of course, using scientific industrialism the way he did and bringing in all the wells he did, Paul didn't need to worry much about not making *enough* money. Soon, as a matter of fact, he had to start putting aside an hour or two each day to worry about making *too much*.

World War II, though, saw the end of that trouble, if reports are right. When that war started, they say, Paul invented high income taxes, corporation taxes and such, and stopped worrying. Only one that had to worry much was Johnny Inkslinger, who used up a range of mountains figuring out on them how much Paul had to pay.

All Paul worried about was using scientific industrialism to keep the oil supply from getting depleted, so to speak. And from what you know of Paul, you can be sure he didn't have to worry much about that.

16
Joe Magarac, Pittsburgh Steel Man

THE STORY OF PAUL BUNYAN SHOWS HOW A HERO, IN MODERN times, could use scientific industrialism to do great things in industry. This chapter about Joe Magarac will show how a hero, also in modern times, could do great things in manufacturing. That way, this history, which is about as thorough as any book its size could be, will polish off the two great new lines of business of our time—industry and manufacturing.

There are more fool stories about the way Joe Magarac was born than you can shake a stick at, more, as a matter of fact, than there are about the birth of any hero who's turned up in this history so far. There's no doubt *where* he was born: it was some place in the iron and coal country, probably in Pennsylvania. All of the following theories, though, have been offered as to *how* he was born:

1. He was born down in the center of an iron ore mountain—a hematite mountain, so they say—several thousand years ago (three or four, nobody knows which). And because that mountain was more or less on top of him, the poor man had to lie there until a miner came on him one day and told him they needed help in the steel mills. Then he traveled to Pittsburgh in an ore car.

2. He didn't just travel in the ore car; he was born in the thing.

Then, before he could say "Boo," he was run through Bessemer furnaces and then open-hearth furnaces, until he came out as A-1 steel.

3. He wasn't born in an ore car at all, but in a coal mine—at Nanty Glo, not far from Johnstown. (Those that claim this say they could prove it by sticking a pin into Joe and showing there was coal dust in his veins instead of blood. Only time anyone used a pin that way, though, the pin bent double before it had a chance to stick him.) Well, these people claim that he rode to Pittsburgh in a coal car.

4. He didn't just ride in the coal car; he was born in the thing. Then, when a breaker who was sorting out the bad pieces from the good came upon him, the breaker pulled him out and talked him into being a helper.

To sum this up, Joe was either born in a mine (iron or coal) or in a car (coal or iron ore)—so far as anybody has been able to figure out definitely.

However he was born, he did turn up, in time, in Pittsburgh, a great center of the steel making business.

Pittsburgh had changed plenty since Mike Fink had been born there. When Mike was born, the place was a huddle of a few cabins, sawmills, limekilns and stores, with a stockade to keep the Indians from dropping around and scalping the settlers. But going into Pittsburgh in Joe's day, along about the time of World War I, or a little before, first you'd see a dark smudge against the sky, then you'd ride along a boulevard by the slums, and then you'd find yourself on streets lined by skyscrapers so high that their top stories were lost up there in the murky sky.

If you went out to the steel mill district, you'd ride on a street car across an oily river. After a while, you'd come to a place where there were a good many old two-story brick houses without front porches or front yards—with their front doors opening right onto the sidewalks.

This would be Hunkietown, so called because the Hungarian steel workers lived there, in the rows and rows of brick houses.

A day the people of Hunkietown never will forget was the day

233

when Steve Mestrovic had the contest to see who'd marry his daughter Mary. The week before, he'd sent out news to the newspapers about this contest, and now a whole crowd of men had come around to try to win the girl's hand.

Mary Mestrovic was a prize worth trying for. Her eyes were as blue as the flames of a blowtorch; her cheeks were as red as a hunk of red-hot iron, and her hair was the color of melted steel. All the boys in Hunkietown that weren't engaged or married had been calling Saturday nights at the Mestrovic house since Mary had reached the age of fourteen. And she was eighteen now, an age when her father thought it was proper for her to marry.

"The man that wins my Mary," says Steve, "will have to be, of course, a steel man. More than that and in addition on top of it, he will have to be the strongest steel man there is."

Besides the contest, there was to be a party, with as much stuff to eat and drink as you'd ordinarily have at a Hunkie wedding. What with that as an attraction, and the contest as another attraction, a crowd turned up that was a regular whopper. Among those that came that Sunday were steel workers from everywhere, from Homestead, for instance, and Monessen and Duquesne and just about everywhere along the river. They were great strong square men, with muscles stretching tight their Sunday clothes.

Steve Mestrovic climbed on a chair and spoke so everybody could hear. "I am not a speech maker," he said. "But I wish to tell you what this contest is like. From the mill, I have brought to the house three dolly bars, and each one is bigger than the other. One of these, it weighs three hundred and fifty pounds; another, it weighs five hundred pounds; and another, it weighs so much as the other two put together. You can tell which one it weighs the most by seeing which is the biggest. Now, we start with the little one; and the man that is the best lifter is to win my beautiful Mary. I thank you."

So the contest started, and everybody in the contest lifted the little bar over his head without so much as a grunt—everybody, that is, except a couple of fellows from Homestead. They explained the fact that they couldn't lift the bar by saying they hadn't had time to eat any breakfast. But everybody laughed at them anyhow.

Steve climbed up on a chair again, told everybody he wasn't a speech maker again, and made a speech again. "Everybody has lifted the little dolly bar with the utmost of ease," he said, "everybody, I mean, except those two loafers from Homestead, and the men and women that aren't trying to win my Mary's hand in wedded marriage, though they are still most welcome to the party. The next dolly bar is still heavier, so next you try to lift it. I thank you."

The way the men's faces got red when the men tried, and the way they grunted, made clear that the second bar, just as Steve had said, was a heavier one. Only three men, for all the wrestling and grunting that went on, managed to hoist it above their heads. Pete Pussick and Eli Stanoski and a fellow from Johnstown were the three that made it.

"Well," says Steve, back on top of the chair again, "you can see how it goes, and you can see with your own eyes that there aren't so many left to try to lift that biggest and heaviest bar of all. Now this contest is fair and square and on the upright, and I wish the best man to win without prejudice or anything. But I wish to say one little thing. The little thing I wish to say is that I hope either Pete or Eli does it and the fellow from Johnstown doesn't do it. Because the mills in Johnstown, they are coffee mills when you compare them to our mills, as who would? They make only two hundred tons of steel a day, which we here would scorn to do. Now go ahead, and may the best man win, so long as he isn't from Johnstown."

While everybody watched, Eli took hold, grunted, and started to come up with his body, lifting the bar. Of a sudden, though, his body stopped, because he'd come to the end of his arms, and the bar didn't budge any more than if Eli had been trying to lift the world.

Then it was Pete's turn. Pete rolled up his sleeves, rubbed his hands together, and took hold. Then he started up, and this time at any rate, the bar did start to come up too. Of a sudden, though, when it was about an inch and three-quarters up in the air, it started down. And when it hit the floor, the walls of the house sort of trembled and shook, as if an earthquake had come along.

"Ho! Ho!" the fellow from Johnstown yelled. "I show you now what mills are like coffee grinders. You don't know Johnstown, I see. In Johnstown, the steel men are so strong that each man can take hold of his belt, lift, and hold himself out at arm's length. In Johnstown the steel men are so tough that they tear down the mills each night and each day put them up again, just to keep their muscles working. In Johnstown, we take the engines off the ore trains and pull the ore trains ourselves. In Johnstown—"

"You are not in Johnstown now," Steve broke in, "so what you have to tell us about that coffee mill place is without interest to us. You are now in front of that dolly bar. And we will be most grateful to you if instead of trying to talk that dolly bar off the floor, you try to lift it off, which I hope you cannot."

"I will lift it," the Johnstown man said. And he stooped to lift the dolly bar.

Then he lifted a little, and his face got red, as red as the skies above the steel mills at night.

He lifted some more, and his mouth got white, as white as the limestone that's used in making steel.

He lifted some more, and the sweat dripped off his forehead and off his cheeks, like the sweat of three men that're tending open hearth furnaces on a hot day.

But the dolly bar didn't budge.

"Oh, Tuckett!" he said, letting go. And he stood up, swabbed his face, and looked fiercely at everybody, as if he was daring anybody even to snicker. Some of the men took their bandannas out, and held them up to their mouths, and their shoulders shook— but they made coughing noises instead of laughing ones.

The Johnstown fellow half closed his eyes, and looked at them very carefully. His look said that he dared anybody to take his bandanna away from his mouth and laugh out loud.

And then somebody in the back of the crowd *did* laugh— "HO-O-O! HO-O-O!"

(The laugh sounded like somebody that had stuck his head into a big empty iron barrel and was laughing and echoing in there.)

236

"Who was that that laughed?" the Johnstown man asked, quick as a blast in a blast furnace, and fairly close to as loud. "I call you up here, if you dare to come!"

The crowd parted. Then there was some clicking, as if a machine was running with an electric current. Then the crowd saw that the clicks were coming from a great huge fellow that was striding up to the Johnstown man. This fellow was so big that he had to walk with his head bent so he wouldn't bump it on the ceiling. His wrists were as big as another man's waist, and the rest of him, from the top of his pate to his toes, was in proportion.

"I don't care how big you are!" the Johnstown man yelled. Then he started a haymaker down at his shoestrings, and brought his fist up to hit the man on the chest, which was high as he could reach.

There was a "Ping!" like the sort that you'd hear if your fist hit the top of an oil car that had been covered with canvas, and that echoing "HO-O-O! HO-O-O!" laugh again. Then the Johnstown man was dancing around, shaking his fingers and saying, "They're busted! They're busted!"

This big fellow took the Johnstown man in one hand, and the biggest dolly bar in the other, and lifted them over his head as easy as a giant would lift a butterfly and a fountain pen. He stooped down about three feet, but both of them hit the ceiling, just the same. (The dolly bar knocked a bit of plaster off, and Steve Mestrovic shows the place to people to this day.)

Then the big man put the Johnstown man, who was still shaking his fingers, down on the floor. Then he took the biggest dolly bar and bent it until it was in the shape of a figure eight, and he eased it down to the floor.

After he'd watched what the big man did with the dolly bar, the Johnstown fellow sort of oozed out of the crowd, like running steel, and disappeared.

When it was as plain as an ingot mold on a flat car that the big man had won the contest, Steve came bustling up to him. "You win," he said, shaking the big man's hand. "You win fairly and squarely and on the upright. All I hope is that you are a man of Pittsburgh, where the mills they are bigger than coffee grinders. Your name, what is it?"

"My name," the stranger said, "is Joe Magarac."

"Joe Magarac!" says Mary Mestrovic, in a voice that showed she was horrified. "Why, in Hungarian, 'magarac' means 'jackass!'"

"Sure," Joe said. "Jackass, that's me—my name and my nature. I eat like a jackass and work like a jackass, so they call me Joe Magarac."

The crowd laughed, and Steve frowned. "Mrs. Magarac!" he said. "What a name for my beautiful girl to have—what a name

238

to exchange to from a fine name like Mary Mestrovic! I hope you are not a steel man, Joe Magarac. Because if you are not, then you cannot have my girl's hand in wedded marriage, in line with the rules of the contest."

"Oh, I'm a steel man all right," Joe said. "Look!" With that, he unbuttoned his shirt, so everybody could have a look at his chest.

A ray of sunlight hit his chest, and it sparkled.

Then Mary Mestrovic screamed, and somebody said, "He's a steel man all right—made out of solid steel!"

Steve Mestrovic's face puckered up, and it was plain that he was puzzled. "You are *made* of steel," he said. "That I agree. But in the sense I used the word, a steel man is only a man that works in a steel mill—helps make the steel, you see, in the open hearth furnace. Do you do that, Joe Magarac?"

"Sure," says Joe. "I been living in the ore pile by the blast furnace ever since I came here. I work all day and all night without stopping. Sure, I work with the steel."

"Well," says Steve, "it looks as if you met the needs of the contest, and I am pleased to hear that you work in Pittsburgh anyhow. I am most sorry, however, about your name."

Mary started to cry. "I don't want to m-m-marry a m-m-man that w-w-works all the time," she blubbered.

"Wait!" says Joe. "What's this m-m-marry stuff? I never heard of it before."

When they told him that marriage meant staying home at night or in the daytime, depending which shift you were on—"Oh," says Joe. "I didn't want that. I want to work all the time, except when I eat like a jackass. Can't I get out of it?"

Steve and Mary both spoke up at once to say of course he could, and somebody in the crowd said that anybody that worked all the time certainly was a jackass.

So Pete Pussick, who'd done better in the contest than anybody else except Joe Magarac, won Mary's hand, and not long afterward they were married. They tried to get Joe to be best man (since he was the best man, anyhow)—but he said he didn't want to stop work for foolishness of that sort. At the wedding supper, Steve made seven speeches, each of which sounded very good to him.

By the time the wedding came along, Joe was as happy as he could be. For one thing, he'd arranged for board at Mrs. Horkey's boarding house, the best in Hunkietown—and she made five meals a day for him, each about the size of a jackass's meal. For another thing, he'd been put to work at number seven furnace at the open hearth—and he worked there all day and all night, stopping only to eat.

Joe made steel his own way, of course.

First he'd collect the charge—scrap steel, scrap iron, coke, lime-stone, melted pig iron or blown Bessemer steel. Others used cars to carry the charge to the furnace, and others used the charging machine to dump it into the furnace, but not Joe. He just lugged in all this stuff by the armful, and then chucked it into the door.

You know how it is outside the furnaces in one of those Pitts-burgh steel mills. The air is all choked up with heat, and most people find it tolerably warm. But Joe Magarac would go and sit right in the door of the furnace, sticking his hands in now and then, to see if the heat was right or to scoop out some brew to see if the mixture was right—for all the world like a cook tasting soup. If the mixture didn't have the right proportions, he'd heave in whatever was needed—a little coke, or limestone, or whatever would make it right for the best steel.

Finally he'd say, "The mixture's right, and the heat's just right—thirty-two hundred degrees. Guess it's time to pour out."

Then he'd go down to the back of the long row of furnaces, and get in back of number seven. At a time like that, other workers would pick at the clay and sand in the vent hole very carefully and they'd take off the last thin layer with a blow torch.

Not Joe, though. Joe'd put the ladle in place—which was quite a job in itself, since the ladle was a giant bucket that would take twenty-four tons of melted steel without stretching. Then he'd put the slag catcher in place. And then, he'd take his forefinger and tap the vent hole. Then the moulten steel would come pour-ing out in a white rush.

When the ladle was full, others had to use cranes to pick up the ladles and dump the liquid steel into the ingot molds. Not Joe, though. Joe would cup his hands, dip up the stuff, and throw it into the molds himself.

And when the stuff was cooled enough, instead of taking it over to the rolling mill, the way others did, Joe would take the stuff in his hands and squeeze it, hard and slow.

It would come rolling out between his fingers in the prettiest rails you ever laid eyes on.

Well, you can imagine that a fellow that worked like that in the steel mills was pretty much of a sensation. The big boss was so proud that he had a big sign painted and nailed outside the mill. What it said was:

THIS IS THE HOME OF JOE MAGARAC

Bosses from all over the country—from Youngstown and Johnstown and even Gary—came to Joe and tried to hire him at wages that were terrific. But, "Not on your life I work for you," says Joe. "Your furnaces, they look like cookstove in Mrs. Horkey's boarding house. Your finishing mill rolls, they look like toothpicks. Besides, if I went to another mill, I'd miss work, and I work like a jackass, you know—all the time."

The men were downright proud to have Joe work with them. A good many were so interested in the way Joe made steel that they'd stay on after they'd finished their shifts just to watch him. And quite a few fellows from other places heard about him, got jealous, came around, and had contests with him.

Joe Magarac always won, though, naturally. Best race he ever had was with a fellow from Gary, who raced Joe for three days and was only three thousand tons behind him at the end. That was mighty close for a race with Joe Magarac.

When times were good, back there in the days of World War I,

242

Joe was most useful, and hardly a week would go by without some government official turning up and trying to pin a medal on Joe, and bending the pin. But after a while, hard times came, and the workers were working only part time, and then some weren't working at all.

When this happened, a committee made up of Steve Mestrovic and Steve's son-in-law, Pete Pussick, and a fellow from Johnstown came around to see Joe.

Steve cleared his throat and made a little speech. "Look," he said, "I'm not much of a speech maker, but I can tell you how things are, and you can for yourself decide what you are to do. The point is that you work so much that you keep other men from working. It isn't fair. You ought to work just eight hours or maybe four hours, like the rest of us, that have families to feed."

"You're right," Joe answered him back. "Even a jackass can see that when there's not work enough to go around, the right thing is to divide up. But I'm not happy unless I work all the time, except when I eat like a jackass. What can I do?"

"Well," Steve said, "before you started to work, you lay around somewhere, didn't you? It has been told to me, see, that you lay in a mine or a car or some such place. Maybe perhaps you might do that once more again until the times they get better."

"Good idea," says Joe. "Come to think of it, I haven't got around to doing any sleeping for fifteen or twenty years. It is high time, therefore, that I did."

So he went out and slept and slept in some secluded place or other, nobody knew where.

And since nobody thought to wake him up when things got better again, I suppose he's still there.

17
"We've Still Got Heroes"

It was in Washington, D. C., either in 1942 or 1943—at any rate after the United States had got into World War II. Washington had changed astonishingly since Long Tom Jefferson had started being president there, even since Davy Crockett had sailed in to see old Andy Jackson in the White House. Either Long Tom or Davy would have been flabbergasted if he'd been popped down into this wartime Washington, it had changed so much.

For one thing, there'd been so many new buildings put there that there wasn't room for many more. But wherever there was any room, new buildings were being started and finished with banging rivet machines and with buzzing saws. Alongside almost all the old buildings, yellow holes were yawning—waiting for new ones to be set up on them.

And a good many buildings were having to go out to the edge of town to find room for themselves to get built on.

People, too, were having a terrible time finding room for themselves either in the capital or around the edges. Thousands of them were getting up before sunrise to race one another to hotel rooms, apartments or houses that they'd heard they might be able to get.

But ninety-two times in ninety-three, they were disappointed.

Well, this particular morning, there was this army officer with stars or some such things on his shoulders that had a house but he had troubles just the same. He was standing in the doorway, looking as if he'd eaten something that was sour. His wife and the children, little Johnny and little Janey, were standing there looking the same.

The officer kissed the lot of them, then, looking sad but brave, he marched down the walk towards his car.

"Farewell, farewell!" yells his wife, looking proud but sad.

"Farewell!" he yelled right back at her. Then he climbed into his car and drove away.

"Is daddy going across the ocean this time?" Johnny asked his mother.

"No, dear," she said. "But he's going on another of those dangerous missions—to the Pentagon Building."

"He goes there every day," little Janey said, calming down a bit.

"But you can't tell—ever—whether he'll be able to find his way out and come back home," her mother said. Then she began to cry.

In one of the big crowded hotels, at about the same time, a little man got out of bed, dressed, and walked down the hall. After waiting in line for the elevator, he went to the hotel dining room. There, after waiting in line for a table, he waited at the table for breakfast.

After breakfast, he went into the lobby, stepped over the people sleeping on the floor, and joined up with the queue that was waiting to see the desk clerk. When, after half an hour, the man had worked up to the front, the desk clerk looked up at him.

He saw a fellow maybe five feet tall, twisting his brown derby hat in his gnarled fingers. The little man had a shiny bald pate, a bulging forehead, thick eyebrows, thick spectacles, a button nose and a bushy mustache. He wore an old-fashioned wing collar, a Prince Albert coat, baggy pants and old-fashioned boots.

"Go away! We won't have any rooms until a year from Easter," the clerk said—before the man had had a chance to speak to him.

"I beg your pardon," the little man said. "I didn't want to bother you about a room. I've got one, I think. Let's see. Yes, here's the key." And he dangled one of those keys with tabs on that they have in hotels.

"What *do* you want to bother me about then?" the clerk snarled at him.

"Ahum!" the little man cleared his throat. "I wanted to find out about going to a building. Wait, I've got it down here. Yes, yes, the Pentagon Building. I'm sorry."

"I'm sorry, too," the clerk said, and he even *looked* sorry. "It's dangerous going to that building. Even if you don't get tangled up in all the gold braid and red tape lying around there, you'll probably get lost. A hundred and seven and a half people, on an average, get lost there every day, some of them for good."

"Oh, dear," the man said, twisting his derby harder than ever. "But the men in the Army get along all right in there, don't they?"

"Sure," says the clerk. "But then you see they have supplies. Any of them that goes in there takes supplies with him—a sleeping bag, food and water for a week, clothes for a week, iron rations, two extra pairs of shoes, a scout knife and roller skates or a scooter. They're set for trouble, you see. Do you have to go there?"

"I'm sorry. I do. It's to help— Let me see. Oh, I remember now. It's to help my country win the war, you see. Can you assist me in any way?"

"Oh, we'll do the usual thing. We'll make a note that you've gone out there, and if you don't get back within a week, we'll send out a searching party. But maybe I ought to warn you that the last two parties we sent out never came back."

"Thank you kindly," the little man said, and he left the desk and went out in front of the hotel and waited in line for a taxicab.

When, finally, he got one, he said to the driver: "Wait till I get my notes out. Yes, yes, here they are. Pentagon Building, please. I'm sorry."

"I'm sorry, too, mister," says the driver. "Understand, I can't guarantee to get you out there. All I can do is try."

"My gracious, driver! Is it even hard to *get* there?"

"I'll say. There's the traffic jams, for one thing, that make it hard to get out to the bridge. Then even when you get across the river, there's such a tangle of roads that you never can be sure where you're likely to end up. But I'll do my best."

They started driving along the wide streets. On the sidewalks, by this time, there were millions of government workers milling around on their way to be disassembled, converted, loaned, decentralized, transferred, distributed or liquidated. There also were thousands of business men with brief cases, looking for contracts, priorities, Congressmen, taxicabs or hotel rooms.

The streets were full of traffic snarls, too. Partly the snarls were caused by automobiles and such, partly by the strange way the streets were laid out—with a good many blocks shaped like triangles instead of squares. A good share of the trouble was caused, of course, by the huge trucks carrying great loads of red tape, thousands of them, that had to dash around day and night to keep all the government offices supplied.

The driver managed to keep his car moving and, at the same time, to tell his passenger about the Pentagon Building. "It's the biggest office building, so far as we know, in the universe," he said. "It's got sixteen and a half miles of halls and corridors, at least. And if you get a pass to get in, mister, for the love of Mike, hang onto it the way you would a ticket to heaven."

"Why?" the little man wanted to know.

"Because you need it to get out. And if you don't have it when you want to get out, you'll be stranded in there for at least three weeks."

"Deary me," the passenger said.

By that time, they'd crossed the Potomac, and the driver told him, "There she is, mister."

The runt saw a white building that was such a whopper it

247

scared him even to look at it. What's more, it wasn't shaped like any building he'd ever seen before: it was more in the nature of a circular building.

But soon he was being just as horrified by the roadways the driver was driving on. They were cloverleaf-under-and-over-roadways that squirmed and twisted around so much that one minute he'd headed for the building and the next he'd be headed back for Washington. It made the passenger a little seasick to swoop around so much.

Finally, though, the driver was saying, "Hurrah! Made it this time!"

Then the little man stumbled out of the cab, paid the fare, and went into the Pentagon. He found himself in a reception room, waiting in line to show a receptionist his letter. Finally, she wrote out a pass and assigned a guide to him.

Then he was following this guide through a snarl of corridors, doing his best to keep out of the way of the messengers that were dashing around on bicycles. And eventually, he was standing by the desk of the Army officer with stars or some such stuff on his shoulders that had been telling the family good-by at the doorway of his house the selfsame morning.

"What is it?" says the officer.

The little man cleared his throat. "I beg your pardon," he said, tugging at his walrus mustache. "But I was talking to Congressman Speaklots a while back about— Wait a minute: I've got some notes here about it. Oh, yes, yes, it was about a plan I'd worked out. He thought it was a good plan, and he told me to come and see you. Ahum! (Pardon me.) And he got me priorities and suchlike, and wrote a letter so I could see you."

"Wonderful!" says the officer. "Have a chair. We want all the plans we can lay hands on, of course, so we can write memos about them. Now, what's the nature of this plan?"

"I'm sorry," the man answered him back, smoothing down a hair or two on the top of his shiny head and easing himself into the chair. "It's a little plan I worked out to— Wait until I look it up in my notes. Oh, here! I call it the 'Win-the-War-Plan,' so I gather it's a plan to win the war."

"Dandy!" the officer said, reaching for a pencil. "Sounds like just the sort of plan we can use just now. Besides, we haven't had a win-the-war plan for the last three days. Now, you just tell me all about it."

"Ahum, er—maybe I'd better tell you my name first. My name is—" He stopped for a minute, looking scared. "Why, I'll swan, I've forgotten it!"

"You might look at your pass," the officer told him. "They usually put it on a pass."

"Of course, here it is—'Professor Lotus C. Blur,' that's what it is, I remember now. I'm a professor of American history at some college or other. I think it's an agricultural college, either in the South or the Middlewest. Or maybe it's a high school. Got a note somewhere, but I suppose you don't care much."

"All I really care about, Professor Blur, are the details of this wonderful plan of yours."

"Yes, yes, of course. I'll tell you about it with the help of some notes, if you don't mind. I'm afraid I'm a mite forgetful." So he started in, using some notes he'd had the good luck to find in his pocket.

"You see," he said, "America has always been a country that had a mess of snarling, snorting, rock-ribbed hardships. We had them from the start, oodles of them, and hardships made heroes. So America, in its time, has had more than its share of heroes."

The officer, taking notes, didn't look up, but said, "I know. Go right ahead, Professor Blur."

"Thank you. If you know history, you know we had a great clipper ship man—Captain Stormalong. We had Davy Crockett, Mose the Fireman, Paul Bunyan, and Pecos Bill, just to name a few."

"Of course, I know about all of them, and about Febold Feboldson and Joe Magarac, too."

"Good, Mr. Officer, very good. Now some of these heroes died. That's a known fact. Johnny Appleseed, for instance, he died, tending an orchard in the cold; and John Henry, he died, having the race with the steam drill. But listen—" the little man leaned forward, and his spectacles were gleaming. "Some of them *didn't* die. Take Joe Magarac. He's lying around somewhere, waiting for somebody to wake him up and start him working in the steel mills. And Paul Bunyan. After he went abroad to tote supplies and build camps for the U. S. Army in World War I, he went back to the oil fields. And Febold Feboldson, he's out in California, managing the weather."

"How about the rest, though?"

"Well, it's never been set down that they're not still alive. I've looked it up in documents and things. There's Old Stormalong, and Mike Fink, and—"

"Oh, come, come, Professor," says the officer. "Maybe you didn't find a record of their death, but look how long ago they were famous. Now Old Stormalong, for instance, he helped Paul Jones in the Revolution. Mike Fink was a keelboatman in Jefferson's time. And so on. Now, you know very well that mighty few men can live much more than a hundred years, as a rule, anyhow."

"Yes, yes, of course I grant that," the runt said. "But I know I've got a point about that here in my notes somewhere. Oh, here it is. Even so, a good many of them doubtless had sons or grandsons or great grandsons, that're still alive. And you can be sure *they* will be heroes, with great forebears like that."

"Very well, Professor, I'll grant that. So what?"

"Well, that leads up to my proposal. I propose that you get me an appropriation and priorities and things like that, and that I go out around the country and look everywhere that's likely until I've found every hero, his son, his grandson or his great-grandson, and that then we put them to work."

The officer dropped his pencil. "For heavens' sakes, why?" he asked the man.

"Let's see. Somewhere in my notes I've got an answer to that interesting question. Yes, yes, here it is. It's because we'll win the war that way! You see, every one of those ripsnorting heroes could be helpful in his own fashion. Take Captain Stormalong, for instance. Remember what a close squeeze it was for him to get his ship through the English Channel? Well, we could have Old Stormy or his son or his grandson or his great-grandson take that super-ship, the *Albatross,* and cram her right into the Channel. Then we could chop off the siderails and the mast and such and just use the deck as a bridge for the invasion."

The officer was looking at him with round eyes. "Never heard anything like it," he said. "Go on!"

"Here, look, I typed out this part. You can look at it if you want to." And the professor handed the officer a typewritten page that went as follows:

WAR JOBS FOR HEROES

MIKE FINK, SON, GRANDSON OR GREAT-GRANDSON—Great trapper. Could be sent to Africa or some place where there's plenty of game, trap many animals, and keep up the supply of meat.

DAVY CROCKETT, SON, GRANDSON OR GREAT-GRANDSON—Wonderful soldier, etc. Could lead our armies or help Mike hunt wild game.

MOSE HUMPHREYS, SON OR GRANDSON—Courageous fireman. Could be used to put out fires and save people in London or other places after bombings.

WINDWAGON SMITH, SON OR GRANDSON—Brilliant inventor. Could invent and manufacture windmobiles for use all over the country—save gasoline and rubber.

PECOS BILL OR SON—Stupendous cowboy. Could 1) raise tremendous herds of cattle, remedy beef shortage, 2) lasso any divisions, battalions or things of the enemy needed, capture them that way.

FEBOLD FEBOLDSON—Prodigious controller of weather. Could 1) fix up weather so U. S. crops will be bumpers, 2) control weather so it would be the best possible for invasions and air operations.

JOE MAGARAC—Marvelous maker of steel. Could do away with manpower shortage in steel industry.

PAUL BUNYAN—Super-scientific industrialist. Could 1) supply needed oil, 2) set up feeding systems for whole army and civilian population, 3) fix up living conditions in Washington by building big bunkhouses, 4) drill a hole to the underside of the earth to be used for purposes of invasion.

"I didn't write them all down," says Professor Blur. "Those are just a sample."

"It's a very fine sample," the officer said. "In some ways, this is one of the most interesting documents I've seen since the Atlantic Charter was issued. If you'll let me keep it, I'll be able to present your plan to the proper authorities. We're very grateful for your interesting plan, and you can expect action on it one way or another (or maybe both ways), some time or another in the future. Good day, sir."

But the professor just sat there, twisting his brown derby and clearing his little throat. "I'm sorry," he said, "but I think it'd be helpful if you could tell me whether the plan is likely to go through. You see, if I take that trip—let me see—yes, yes, looking for heroes, I'll have to get a leave of absence. That'll take time, you know."

The officer got up and walked over to the window. He stood there, looking out at the Potomac and the capitol building beyond, thinking. Finally he came back and sat down.

"Of course, it'd be good if I could let you know," he said. "I can understand that. And I'm sorry I can't give you a yes or no answer, right off. The reason is this: By and large, we're running this war pretty well, in my opinion, but you can't tell whether a scheme like yours will come through or not. One does, every now and then, even when it's as bad as yours is. But I'd guess that your scheme won't have much chance."

"Deary me!" the little man said. "I take it you don't like my Plan-to-Win-the-War. Could you tell me why?"

"Well," says the officer, "I'll tell you. Let me give you one instance to start off with. You say Paul Bunyan is a great scientific industrialist and, in a way, he is. But out on the Pacific Coast there's a fellow, this war, that runs some shipyards, and you never saw the way ships get built out there. Why, just the other day, they had a famous Senator out there to launch a ship. So they took the Senator up onto a platform and they gave him a champagne bottle that you break on a ship, you know, when you launch the thing. He looked out from the platform to see the ship, and he didn't see a thing under the sun in front of him.

" 'Hey,' says the Senator, 'where's the ship?'

" 'Don't worry,' they told him. 'Just start your swing. And when the bottle swoops to the right place, the ship'll be there, waiting to be launched.' "

"Whew!" Professor Lotus C. Blur said, tugging at his mustache.

"That's scientific industrialism times three! But why do you tell me about this?"

"Because," the officer answered him back, "I want you to know how it is all over the home front. It's not only that way in ship-building; it's that way all over the place—in farming, manufacturing, mining—all over the place. Or take the battle front."

"I suppose I might as well," says the little professor.

"Take the Navy. They've got ships that make Captain Storm-along's *Albatross* look like a fishing dory. Take one of those big battleships. Maybe a ship like that isn't as wide as the *Albatross*, but it's higher by about thirty-nine decks. And as to that bridge across the Channel—well, we've got enough ships and men to build a bridge of ships, and without the help of Stormalong or any of his descendants."

"Sounds as if we had a pretty good Navy."

"You bet. The rest of the services are the same. Think of what the air force flying from England has to put up with. The enemy keeps banging at them with anti-aircraft guns and fighter planes, and that's bad enough. But on top of that, there are gremlins, you know."

"No, I don't, Mr. Officer. What under the heavens are gremlins?"

"They're little critters, something like goblins, but modernized and streamlined, so to speak. Now, these little rascals have taken a fancy to airplanes, and they ride them whenever they can, even on raids or over battlefields. And on these trips, they like nothing better than to be-devil the pilots. They stop up carburetors. They make noises like knocking motors, and they jam up guns. When a pilot has been flying through clouds for a while, a gremlin will whisper, 'Hey, you fathead, you're flying upside down!' And when the pilot turns the plane over and really flies upside down, the gremlin laughs and laughs—to himself. Oh, they're trouble-makers, gremlins are."

"I should say," the little fellow said. "Do they cause a lot of accidents?"

"Not many, any more," says the officer. "You see, our aviators

are very well outfitted with hardships, and they shortly turn into the best brand of heroes. Gremlins can't stop them, any more than the enemy can. And it's that way with the Army, too, and with the Marines. There was this hill that the enemy was trying to take on one of those Pacific Islands. 'Listen, men,' the enemy general said to his Army, 'there's just one Marine left up there on top of the hill. Now if the Army charges up there, shooting all the way, you can get him easily. Go ahead, and I'll stay behind so you can have all the glory.'

"So the Army marched up the hill, shooting and banging, and soon the general couldn't see them for the trees and vines and such. After while, though, the shooting stopped and he heard pounding feet coming in his direction. Then, in a minute or two, the whole Army came skyhooting down the hill. They were running as if an army of ghosts was chasing them.

" 'What's the matter?' the general yelled.

" 'You lied to us,' the Army answered him back. "There are *two* Marines up there!' "

"I can see that the people at home and the fighting forces are wonderful," says the professor. "But what does that have to do with—er—with—er—whatever we've been talking about?"

"I'll tell you," says the officer. "You say hardships make heroes and, of course, I agree with you. Now, I'd like to know whether we haven't got as big a pile of hardships as we ever did have—right now and today. And the way we always have, we've still got heroes to match those hardships and to whop 'em, too. You don't have to go scooting around the country, looking here and there to find a bunch of old heroes or their sons or their grandsons or their great-grandsons. You'll bump smack into heroes anywhere you go.

"And it'll always be that way, is my guess, Professor Blur. After this war, we won't have the same old kind of hardships, sure; but we'll have a creation mess of brand new ones—corkers, too—that'll raise up heroes if anything will, I'll tell you. No, we're doing all right, and I think we'll continue to, without using your plan."

"I beg your pardon," the little man said. "I'm sorry." And he scooted out of the door sort of running.

"Hey!" the officer yelled after him, hightailing it for the door. "You forgot your pass! You forgot to get a guide!"

But at the door, he couldn't see hide nor bald head of the man anywhere in the corridor.

"Well," says the officer to himself, coming back to his desk, "if hardships make heroes, Professor Blur's going to be a ripsnorter before he gets out of the Pentagon Building!"

Afterword

AFTER HE'D BEEN A SENSATIONALLY POPULAR HUMOROUS WRITER for forty years, Mark Twain noticed a startling fact: During that period, of a hundred American humorists who'd been conspicuous favorites, every single one except Mark Twain had vanished. So his work alone had managed, as he put it, to "live forever." "By forever," he explained, "I mean thirty years." The calculation makes clear that *Tall Tale America,* published in 1944, in print until 1982 and now being reissued, is immortal. Its awesome venerability encouraged me to hope that some readers may care to learn how this immemorial work came into being, how it fared, and what I believe its nature is.

Anyone familiar with my biography who reads Mark Twain's article, "How to Tell a Story," will notice another uncanny resemblance between the great humorist and me. "I claim to know how a story ought to be told," he wrote, "for I have been almost daily in the company of the most expert story-tellers for many years." So, like me, he came to appreciate "the high and delicate art" of well-told stories by listening to experts, and when he wrote, he too tried to benefit by their example.

My storytellers, like Twain's, included family members, coworkers, and friends. My Uncle John Merritt told the first tall tale I remember hearing to a family audience around a campfire beside Idaho's Lake Coeur d'Alene one evening when I was eleven. One of many he'd tell, it was an Americanization of Münchausen's yarn in which the baron, his ride across country halted by a blizzard, tied his mount to a stump protruding from the deep snow, slept through a thaw, and awoke to find the horse dangling from a weathercock on a steeple high above him. A dozen years later as a Spokane newspaper reporter, during long waits for jury decisions, election counts, or other developing events, I heard many well-told anecdotes, some of them true, about celebrities and eccentrics. And on visits to Pipestone, Montana, as we sat on cousin Roy Alley's porch with its fine view of the Rockies, my wife and I listened long into many nights as Roy reminisced about the shenanigans of Montana miners, politicians, and copper kings.

Eventually, having left the Far West and settled in Chicago, for twenty-five years I belonged to a very informal group of men who lunched in a Loop restaurant Saturdays and swapped gossip, badinage, and (usually soiled) stories. Some members were known beyond Chicago, notably Pat Covici, discoverer, publisher, and lifelong editor of John Steinbeck, and Roark Bradford, whose Biblical stories in black dialect became a Pulitzer Prize drama and whose legendary *John Henry* was a bestseller and, dramatized, a Broadway play. Others, though less famous, told stories with comparable skill.[1] John Drury, in *Dining in Chicago,* called us "Chicago's Algonquin Round Table," and while nobody called the more widely publicized Manhattan quipsters[2] "New York's Saturday Lunch Group," one of us who was twice their guest informed us that we were louder and funnier. Also, at the University of Chicago, where I taught regularly, and at other universities where I was a visiting teacher, I heard some superb academic raconteurs recycle oral stories.[3]

Since the years 1930-44 were great ones for the rediscovery, reassessment, and reprinting of vernacular stories of the past, I also read and pondered many such stories. Franklin Meine pioneered in the movement by publishing *Tall Tales of the Southwest* in 1930, as did Constance Rourke with her *American Humor* a year later, and other scholars and critics soon followed.[4] I did a great deal of reading of many of their primary sources—America's rural and frontier humor of the nineteenth and twentieth centuries. I wrote at some length in a talk-like style about two legendary American heroes—Mike Fink in 1933 and Davy Crockett in 1940. Impartial friends at whose jokes I'd laughed listened in turn to mine and did likewise, and when my students noticed in class that I thought I was being amusing, they usually responded appropriately. Books and articles had been written about individual tall tale heroes who'd lived from colonial times to the mid-1940's.[5] They'd played roles in the development of our country. They differed amusingly from the legendary figures of the Old World such as Cuchulain, King David, Hercules, Til Eulenspiegel, Arthur and his knights, and Baron Münchausen. I decided to write a playful tall tale history of our country in which these legendary American characters, rather than political leaders, generals, thinkers, and tycoons, were the "heroes"—and to write it in a vernacular style.

I wrote the book in about six months, reading chapters as I finished them to my wife and teenage daughter for their unbiased applause. Since I'd recently read about the lives and deeds of my leading characters and could think up appropriate additions when they were needed, I didn't have to do much new research concerning them. But I had to do a great deal of research about different historical periods, and even more to collect details about the tricks of the trades in which these toilers engaged—navigating, exploring, peddling, trapping, logging, planting, cowpunching, steeldriving, and so forth. Such details, I figured, were vital ingredients in yarns whose most amusing (and American) contrasts would, I hoped, be between soaring fantasy and earthbound actuality. And though I didn't want anyone to catch me making technical errors, I constantly enjoyed remembering that, as a man whose fingers are all thumbs, I'd have been fired minutes after I tried to perform any of my heroes' workaday chores. My revisions, as I remember them, were to clarify meanings, chuck in more facts, and make the style more like talk.

In several ways, the reception that *Tall Tale America* received and its subsequent fortunes surprised me—the readers it attracted, some criticism of it, and arguments about the kind of a book it is.

I'd written my mock history with a specific audience in mind—young readers—and an editor of books for children had seen it by installment as I wrote it. The publisher decided that it would appeal not only to juvenile readers but also to adults, and he so advertised it and marketed it. Book reviewers agreed. A wartime committee of journalists, publishers, and critics voted for the issuance of a paperback Armed Services Edition, and a hundred and forty thousand copies of the 5¼" by 3¾" paperback reprint were sent out to men and women in uniform scattered around the globe. A number of recipients pleased me by writing letters from near and far-off places saying that at a time when they'd urgently needed to be diverted, *Tall Tale America* had done the job. One letter that I particularly prized came from a former colleague, Paul Douglas, then a major in the Marines, thanking me for the amusement and relaxation his reading of the book had provided the night before he'd taken part in the invasion of Iwo Jima, February 19, 1945.

The popularity of the book, though naturally it gratified me, exceeded my fondest expectations. The original publisher issued at intervals twenty-six printings. Looking for reasons, I found some evidence that juvenile audiences—fresh new ones that, thank the Lord, came along every few years—were partly responsible. A separate Cadmus textbook edition sold seventeen thousand copies. Decade after decade new young readers sent me letters, practically all of them complimentary, though a few helpfully cited instances when in their opinion some so-called facts I'd set down appeared to be questionable.[6] Teachers wrote too, one of them to cheer me with the news that of all the books in the library of his high school, *Tall Tale America* was the one most often stolen.

From the start, adults as well as young readers were hospitable to the book. Some probably were influenced by an early reviewer who announced that the final chapter made explicit "the relevancy [it had] to the contemporary scene": "This book ends in a burst of tribute to American deeds and courage that leaves the reader in a mellow and proud spirit." Well, it is possible, as some critics claim, that an author is the last to know what his book's theme is, but I found this startling. Although I saw no reason to say so since I've never been unfavorable to patriotism provided it's my brand, truly I hadn't meant to freight my "history" with such a burst. What I'd done in the final chapter didn't differ from what I'd been doing throughout the book—setting down the talk and the tall tales going the rounds in conversations and in print during various periods. Naturally, these, during any war period, include boasts about violent conflicts and triumphs. But here as elsewhere I didn't leave out swipes at current foibles that were being kidded: District of Columbia architectural atrocities, scrambles for favors and for housing, bureaucratic foulups, greed, gobbledegook, waste, and (as always) academic theoreticians.[7]

Looking back through the mists of time after I reread this reviewer and others, I was impressed by the frequency with which they commended the book for doing something that was unusually popular in the 1930s and 1940s—telling humorous stories in the vernacular. That reviewer whom I just quoted, for instance, grouped me with "Baron Munchausen and his ilk" who "lie for the joy that they get from it and the fun they give by it," and who are skillful "in telling stories that belie belief." Another called the book "a cracker barrel version of our national history" which managed to catch "the intonations of oral narrative."

As far back as 1918, a portent of far greater successes to come had been furnished by the very ingratiating Frank Bacon, coauthor and star of *Lightnin'*. This comedy, an immediate hit, had one of the longest unbroken runs in American theatrical history not only on Broadway but on stages scattered across the country. In it for more than a decade, Bacon as Lightnin' Bill Jones delighted theatergoers with his hilarious renderings of inventive tall tales. After more than six decades, I still relish the memory of Lightnin's account of the way he drove a herd of bees all the way across the plains and never lost a bee.

Beginning about 1930 and on into the 1940s, two technical developments enabled other yarnspinners to captivate doting audiences many times larger than the total of those Bacon had entertained during a lifetime—sound for motion pictures and network radio broadcasting. Anyone who didn't live through this period can't imagine how addicted we, the huge besotted populace, were to "the talkies" and—even more—the weekly or even nightly radio programs delivered into practically every living room.

Both media were very cordial to oral storytellers. So several who'd developed skills in burlesque, vaudeville, and stage revues became fantastically popular performers on screens, on airwaves, or (as a rule) on both.

W. C. Fields, for instance, after years of vaudeville and revue stints as a comic juggler, turned actor in 1923 and found himself in a role he'd repeat in movies and radio shows for twenty-three years. It was that of a hard-drinking, pompous, lecherous, yarnspinning confidence man. His bland deadpan expression, martini-soaked drawl, and nervous gestures fortunately are immortalized in movies he himself wrote. Hear him in *The Bank Dick* (1940) rescuing a fly which a pal starts to swat:

> Don't hurt that fly—that's Old Tom . . . followed me out here from the show. . . . He used to drive the chariot races in the flea circus. . . . One afternoon in a small town outside of Hoosic Falls, when I was ignominiously dragged off to the local bastille and placed in durance vile at the behest of a blackguard regarding the loss of his silver timepiece, . . . Old Tom . . . stuck his left hind leg into the Governor's inkwell, dragged it above the dotted line, forging the Governor's signature. The Governor's secretary, . . . picked up the document, gave it to a messenger and sent it to the warden who released me with profound apologies. I love that fly.

After years in burlesque, Jack Pearl was a sensation on Ed Sullivan's star-creating radio show, and from 1932 to 1937 had his own series of high-rated network shows. His role was that of an updated Baron Münchausen, teller of whoppers in German dialect. Ed Wynn, discovered in *The Follies*, became the Fire Chief on a top-rated network show (1932-44) who convulsed audiences as he giggled, lisped, punned, and smart-cracked his way through shaggy-dog stories and synopses of novels, operas, and fairy tales. Frederick Chase Taylor as Colonel Stoopnagle in the same years got laugh after laugh by telling long yarns full of puns, portmanteau words, coinages, and especially spoonerisms.

Finally, an Elysium and an El Dorado for storytellers was a sensationally popular network show that had a run of fifteen years long (1935-50) under one satisfied sponsor, *Fibber McGee and Molly.* Year after year its scriptwriter, Don Quinn, populated it with yarnspinners, its chief attraction. Chief of the group (all fugitives from vaudeville) was Jim Jordan as Fibber himself, who every Tuesday evening told monstrous untrue tales about his careers as seadiver Mudbank, wrestling champion Mad Mauler, "pugilistic pixie of pedigreed paperweight pugs" Murder McGee, stratosphere pilot, broncobuster, hunter, fisher, and so forth,[8] although quite obviously he was a champion bungler. And other loquacious tellers of windies joined this star in unwinding yarns—Mayor Trivia, whose lies were stuffed with spoonerisms; Dr. Gamble, a pseudo-intellectual; Throckmorton Gildersleeve ("the Great Gildersleeve," a blowhard supreme); and Old Timer, who rashly tried to correct or to top the peerless McGee. Jordan's wife, Marian, as Molly, played superbly the vital role of skeptic-in-residence. Constantly she deflated the windbags surrounding her, and her putdown of Fibber, " 'Tain't funny, McGee!" became a national catchphrase, good for a laugh whenever quoted from Maine to California.[9]

Some readers, thanks to a growing interest in American folklore, probably were led to read *Tall Tale America* by early reviewers who called it "a folklore history" and its characters "folk-tale heroes." In time quite a few United States folklore bibliographies included the book. In Germany, Heinz Ohff, the translator of two editions published as *Das Grosse Lügengarn von Trappern, Schelmen, und anderen Amerikanern,* in an Afterword called the characters "folk heroes," New World counterparts of Eulenspiegel, Pinocchio, Snow White, Münchhausen, and other figures in Old World folk tales. Advertisements of the translation said that "here speaks the America of folk humor and folk heroes." In 1963, when a large committee of leading librarians, publishers, and scholars in every part of the United States compiled a list of the country's books that should be included in the White House library, this was one of the three books called "American folklore."[10]

Well, were these tall tales folk tales? The subtitle, "A Legendary History of Our Humorous Heroes," didn't say, and I didn't mind.

I wrote for the fun of it—mine and that of lucky readers—and frankly, like Rhett Butler, I didn't give a damn. But in time some leading scholars of American folklore attacked the book for not being something I'd never happened to claim it was—folklore.

The chief leveler of this attack, Richard M. Dorson, was a man I'd become acquainted with quite early in his career—when he was in his twenties and recently had been converted to scholarship by his Harvard professors. He and a friend were traveling by car across the United States, arguing along the way about the precise route they'd take. Should they visit important historic scenes and scenic wonders, or should they, as Dick preferred, call on some scholars of folklore? I was teaching at the University of Texas that summer, and the two agreed to follow a route that would lead, not necessarily in that order, to the Grand Canyon, folklorist par excellence Frank Dobie, and me. In subsequent years, Dick came to be one of the great all-time students of American folklore. Because I'd done some work in the field that he respected and some he didn't, we had discussions by letter and in person during which we exchanged compliments, arguments, and insults over the decades until his untimely death in 1981.

Dick's complaints about *Tall Tale America* were that several of its heroes and their deeds hadn't had their origins in oral storytelling sessions but in the writings of journalists and fiction writers, and that I had been too inventive in telling about all of the heroes. I agreed with his first claim and held I'd been just inventive enough. And I held that it didn't follow that the book should be condemned. Although he never told me that my arguments had worn him down, I rather thought that some of them—along with scholarly discoveries made about lore concerning a figure he'd believed was untarnished, Davy Crockett—perhaps had an impact. At any rate, he wrote in *America in Legend* (1973) a statement about the *Crockett Almanack* stories that I felt tended to reconcile his views and mine about *Tall Tale America*:

> After [Davy's] death in action, the oral and written traditions about him multiplied in the series of Crockett almanacks (1835-1856), . . . and in humorous songs. . . . [In this] phase of Crockett's folkloric history, popular literature [was] written

about him, rather than folk anecdotes told by him, or told by others about him. A shift takes place from oral tradition to popular culture. . . . The almanack yarns constitute a sub-literature rather than folklore. But they represent a transition, not a sharp break.

In addition, I've been heartened by some of the things that I learned as I studied the peregrinations of tall tales, jokes, and anecdotes. Gershon Legman summarized what for me was a crucial discovery when he said "jestbooks . . . which derive mainly from one another, and seldom from coeval folk sources—are not so much being alimented by folk sources as constituting, themselves, a main source of the jokes in oral transition . . . from one mouth to another, one book to another, one land to another." My happy conclusion is that even if the tall tales that make up this book aren't folklore, inevitably, in time, they will be.

W. B., 1986

NOTES

1. Others in the group: Vincent Starrett, *Chicago Tribune Books* columnist who published several highly respected critical books; Franklin J. Meine, pioneer historian of American humor and editor of the *Peoples Encyclopedia* and other valuable reference works; Kurt M. Stein, the author of several books of humorous poems in "die schönste lengevitch" that H. L. Mencken and others praised for their German-American dialect; Douglas C. McMurtie, one of the most informative, still, of the historians of American printing; Lew Sarrett, author of six books of poetry and a Northwestern University professor; and Richard Atwater, columnist on the *Chicago Post* and translator of *The Secret History of Procopius*.

2. "The Vicious Circle" that lunched in the Hotel Algonquin included Heywood Broun, Robert Benchley, Dorothy Parker, Edna Ferber, Ring Lardner, Harpo Marx, F. P. Adams, Tallulah Bankhead, George S. Kaufman, Robert E. Sherwood, and Alexander Woollcott.

3. I know that in the most popular jokes, even when they're not (like my Professor Lotus C. Blur) unworldly and moonstruck, such fellows are pretentious asses. Perhaps because they were mellowed by their study of history and humanized by immersions in folklore, these colleagues were great storytellers: Bernard DeVoto of Harvard; Frank Dobie and Mody Boatright of the University of Texas; George Hastings of the University of Arkansas; Tom Peete Cross, John Kunstman, Napier Wilt, and Archer Taylor of the University of Chicago.

4. Bernard DeVoto, *Mark Twain's America* (1934); Max Eastman, *The Enjoyment of Laughter* (1936); A. P. Hudson, *Humor of the Old Deep South* (1936); Thomas D. Clark, *The Rampaging Frontier* (1939); and James Masterson, *Tall Tales of Arkansaw* (1943). The selections in B. A. Botkin's bestselling *Treasury of American Folklore* (1944) indicated the emphasis during the preceding decades: at least half recorded oral performances—boasts, hoaxes, tall tales, monologues, and anecdotes.

5. These are listed in "Proof (A Bibliographical Note)," pp. 267-272.

6. Every now and then, young readers would write to ask how I could, as I put it, "make improvements" on "a good many things in this history" that had been told me "by fine honest Americans," and how I could "truthen up" facts. I gave them elaborate metaphysical explanations which I'm not sure that they—or even I—completely understood. If my claims made sense, I suppose that those technical facts about heroes' occupations and background historical facts deserve some credit. Also, I like to believe that I truthened up my history by satirizing some vulnerable aspects of American life; for example, the way some entrepreneurs interlace smug piety and sharp practices; the crassness and cruelty of some hair-trigger toughs; Johnny Appleseed's self-righteousness and sentimentality; undemocratic practices; super efficiency combined with inhumanity and pretentiousness.

7. In 1980, I again disagreed with some remarks about that final chapter. The writer, in a valuable article about the early *Crockett Almanacks*, said that in that chapter, the author "in effect enlisted Crockett—along with the likes of Mike Fink, Pecos Bill, John Henry, Paul Bunyan, and Joe Magarac—in the war effort." It was a clownish professor, Lotus C. Blur, who made the feckless proposal and who was ridiculed for making it.

8. Arthur Frank Wertheim notices a kinship in *Radio Comedy* (New York: Oxford University Press, 1979), pp. 220-21: "Fibber McGee descended from a long line of yarnspinners. . . . Often the protagonists became American folklore heroes, as did Davy Crockett and Mike Fink . . . The early campfire stories and Fibber's radio whoppers were a hundred years apart, but both were aural forms of humorous entertainment."

9. So did Jack Pearl's—"Baron Münchausen's"—putdown of his straight man's every expression of doubt, "Vos you dere, Sharlie?"

10. The idea in 1963 was that instead of Westerns, James Bond thrillers, political rhetoric, scandalous biographies, or nothing, the denizens of the White House would enjoy reading great novels, histories, treatises, or folklore collections. A few years later, the Blair House Library Foundation, making a similar though smaller selection of important American books, gave mine alone the job of acquainting important foreign visitors to Blair House with "American folklore."

Proof (A Bibliographical Note)

IT'S POSSIBLE that at one point or another in reading this history the gentle reader may have been a little doubtful about its truth. The next few pages, though, will settle all doubts by showing that this book must be true, since it is based on the best sources I could find.

A good many things in this history are things that fine honest Americans have told me. And whenever I showed a smidgeon of doubt (by saying, for instance, "Wow! *That's* a whopper!"), these upstanding men and women swore that everything they had said was absolutely true. Other things came out of books or stories that are set down in print and that, therefore, can hardly be doubted. And on top of all this, I've made improvements of my own all along the way—fixed up fact after fact to make it truer than it ever was before.

Just to sample some of my sources, the reader, if he has a mind to, can look at the works I am listing below. The reader will get an idea, that way, about how careful I've been to use only the most likely facts I could find and how I've truthened up even those facts. He'll also have a fine time for himself learning a number of high grade facts I didn't have room for.

In CHAPTER I, most of the facts about CHRISTOPHER COLUMBUS came from Samuel Eliot Morrison, *Admiral of the Ocean Sea* (Boston: Little, Brown, 1942), 2 vols., a book chock-full of facts about the discoverer of America. Henry H. Hart, *Venetian Adventurer* (Stanford University Press, 1942) gave me details about MARCO POLO and his maps. The part of the chapter about explorers' reports came from old travel books and plays written in the time of Shakespeare. And I found out about PONCE DE LEON and his dog BEREZILLO in William Henry Johnson, *Pioneer Spaniards in North America* (Boston: Little, Brown, 1903).

Before I wrote CHAPTER II, I learned all about MILES STANDISH by reading a long and truthful poem by Henry Wadsworth Longfellow, a Harvard professor—"The Courtship of Miles Standish," *Poetical Works* (Boston: Houghton Mifflin, 1904), II, 305-371. JOHN SMITH told about himself in *Works,* ed. Edward Arber, published in 1884. To find out about ALFRED BULLTOP STORMALONG, I read a little pamphlet by Charles Edward Brown, *Old Stormalong Yarns* (Madison, Wis.: C. E. Brown, 1933), the first and best biography of this hero. Facts about sailing ships and krakens may be checked in Howard I. Chapelle, *The History of American Sailing Ships* (New York: W. W. Norton & Co., 1935) and Hendrik Willem Van Loon, *Ships* (New York: Simon & Schuster, 1935). The biography of Stormy's pal, PAUL JONES, which told of naval battles and of Paul's job in the Russian Navy was Valentine Thompson, *Knight of the Seas* (New York: Liveright, 1939).

JONATHAN SLICK and his home Down East, told about in CHAPTER III, came from many humorous books of the 1830's, 40's and 50's, chiefly those by Seba Smith which told about a Yankee named Jack Downing and his family. THE SOUTHERNERS and THE PENNSYLVANIA DUTCH were told about in a number of travel books of the same period. Modern books which I found helpful were Shields McIlwaine, *The Southern Poor-White* (Norman: University of Oklahoma Press, 1939), and Jane Louise Mesick, *The English Traveller in America* (New York: Columbia University Press, 1922). None of the latest writers about DANIEL BOONE seems to have found out the most interesting facts about him; for these, I read early newspaper stories and biographies like Edward S. Ellis, *The Life and Times of Col. Daniel Boone* (Philadelphia:

Porter & Coates, 1884) and Timothy Flint, *The First White Man of the West* (Cincinnati: Appelgate & Co., 1854).

CHAPTERS IV and V (MIKE FINK) are based on stories and books listed by Walter Blair and Franklin J. Meine in their *Mike Fink* (New York: Holt, 1933), pp. 273-283. The best of these are Morgan Neville, "The Last of the Boatmen," *Western Souvenir* (Cincinnati: N. & G. Guilford, 1829); "Crockett Beat at a Shooting Match," *Crockett Almanac* (Nashville: Ben Harding, 1840); and J. M. Field, "Mike Fink, the Last of the Boatmen," *St. Louis Reveille*, June 14 and June 21, 1847. Two very fine books about the kind of work Mike did are Leland D. Baldwin, *The Keelboat Age in Western Waters* (Pittsburgh: The University of Pittsburgh Press, 1941) and Edwin L. Sabin, *Kit Carson Days* (New York: The Pioneer Press, 1935), 2 vols.

CHAPTERS VI and VII, about DAVY CROCKETT took some of their best words and all of their most interesting facts from the *Crockett Almanacs*, published in a number of cities between 1835 and 1856, and from newspaper stories published between 1828 and 1837. The almanacs are rather hard to get, but Richard M. Dorson has published a fine collection of the stories from them in *Davy Crockett, American Comic Legend* (New York: Rockland Editions, 1939). A biography that makes very good reading is Constance Rourke, *Davy Crockett* (New York: Harcourt Brace, 1934).

CHAPTER VIII is about JOHNNY APPLESEED, whose story has been told by many writers. The biographies of him I liked best and used most were W. D. Haley, "Johnny Appleseed: A Pioneer Hero," *Harper's Magazine*, XLIII, 830-836 (1871); Harlan Hatcher, *The Buckeye Country* (New York: H. C. Kinsey & Company, 1940), pp. 166-173; Henry A. Pershing, *Johnny Appleseed and His Time* (Strasburg, Va.: Shenandoah Publishing House, 1930), and Dixon Wecter, *The Hero in America* (New York: Charles Scribner's Sons, 1941), pp. 193-199.

The truth of what is said about MOSE in CHAPTER IX can be tested in Herbert Asbury's two books, *The Gangs of New York* (New York: Alfred A. Knopf, 1928), pp. 32-37, and *Ye Olde*

Fire Laddies (New York: Alfred A. Knopf, 1930), and in B. A. Baker, *A Glance at New York* (New York: S. French, 1848); Abram C. Dayton, *Last Days of Knickerbocker Life in New York* (New York: George W. Harlan, 1882); Richard M. Dorson, "Mose the Far-Famed and World-Renowned," *American Literature*, XV, 288-300 (November, 1943); Alvin Harlow, *Old Bowery Days* (New York: Appleton, 1931); E. Z. C. Judson, *Mysteries and Miseries of New York* (New York: Berford & Co., 1848); J. Frank Kernan, *Reminiscences of the Old Fire Laddies* (New York, 1885); "Mose Keyser; the Bowery Bully's Trip to the California Goldmines," in *The Clown* (Philadelphia and Baltimore: Fisher and Brother, n.d.); and George W. Sheldon, *The Story of the Volunteer Fire Department of the City of New York* (New York: Harper and Brothers, 1882).

WINDWAGON SMITH, the hero of CHAPTER X, was first told about in print in a newspaper story, "Westport's Dry-Land Navy," *Kansas City Star*, p. 10, August 5, 1906. It was retold, with improvements, by Stanley Vestal in *The Old Santa Fe Trail* (Boston: Houghton Mifflin, 1939), and with still more improvements, by Wilbur L. Schramm, in "Windwagon Smith," *Atlantic*, CLXVIII, 26-35 (July, 1941). I, too, have done my best to improve on the newspaper story.

What CHAPTER XI says about FEBOLD FEBOLDSON is based on some newspaper stories about him and on two pamphlets by Paul R. Beath, *Legends of Febold Feboldson* (Federal Writers' Project in Nebraska, 1937). What it says about JIM BRIDGER is based on the old stories retold by J. Cecil Alter in *James Bridger* (Salt Lake City: Shepard Book Company, 1925), and on yarns oldtimers out in Montana told about Jim in recent years.

CHAPTERS XII and XV—about PAUL BUNYAN—came from only the stories among many about this hero that I like best: John Lee Brooks, "Paul Bunyan, Oil Man" and Acel Garland, "Pipeline Days With Paul Bunyan," both in *Follow de Drinkin' Gou'd* (Austin: Texas Folklore Society, 1928), pp. 45-49, 55-61; Charles E. Brown, *Paul Bunyan Tales* (Madison, Wis.: The Author, 1922); W. B. Laughead, *Paul Bunyan* (Westwood, Cal.: Red River Lumber Co., 1922-38); Wayne Martin, "Paul Bunyan on the Water Pipeline," *Folk-Say* (1929), pp. 50-63; Glen Rounds, *Ol' Paul* (New York: Holiday House, 1936); Esther Shepard, *Paul Bunyan* (New York: Harcourt Brace, 1924); K. B. Stewart and H. A. Watt, "Legends of Paul Bunyan, Lumberman," *Transactions of Wisconsin Academy of Sciences*, XVIII, 639-651 (1916); Ida Virginia Turney, *Paul Bunyan Comes West* (Boston: Houghton Mifflin, 1928).

CHAPTER XIII, about PECOS BILL, was based on windies told by people down in Texas and these retellings: Mody R. Boatright, "The Genius of Pecos Bill," *Southwest Review*, XIV, 419-428 (July, 1929) and *Tall Tales from Texas* (Austin: Texas Folklore Society, 1934); James Cloyd Bowman, *Pecos Bill* (Chicago: Whitman, 1937); J. Frank Dobie, "Giants of the Southwest," *Country Gentleman*, XVI, 11, 71-72 (August, 1926); Edward J. O'Reilly, "The Saga of Pecos Bill," *Century Magazine*, LXXXIV, 827-833 (October, 1923), and Frank Shay, *Here's Audacity* (New York: Macaulay, 1930), pp. 119-159.

CHAPTER XIV took facts about JOHN HENRY from James Cloyd Bowman, *John Henry, the Rambling Black Ulysses* (Chicago: Whitman, 1942); Roark Bradford, *John Henry* (New York: Harper and Brothers, 1931); Louis W. Chappell, *John Henry; a Folklore Study* (Jena, 1933); W. C. Hendricks, ed., "John Henry of the Cape Fear," in *Bundle of Troubles and Other Tarheel Tales* (Durham: Duke University, 1943), pp. 37-51; Guy B. Johnson, *John Henry: Tracking Down a Negro Legend* (Chapel Hill: University of North Carolina Press, 1929).

JOE MAGARAC's story, as it is told in CHAPTER XVI, is mostly based on stories collected by Mr. J. Ernest Wright, to whom I am very grateful. Mr. Richard M. Dorson, who had these stories in typescript, very kindly sent them to me and allowed me to use them. Some facts also came from Carl Carmer, *America Sings* (New York: Alfred A. Knopf, 1942), pp. 118-121, and from Anne Malcolmson, *Yankee Doodle's Cousins* (Boston: Houghton Mifflin, 1941), pp. 29-35.

CHAPTER XVII comes from the talk of Americans in recent

times, and from newspapers, magazine stories and books about our modern life and heroes. For facts about Washington, D. C., the reader may look at "Greatest U. S. Boomtown," *Life*, X, 74-85 (March 10, 1941) and D. Wilhelm, "America's Biggest Boom Town," *American Mercury*, LIII, 338-343 (September, 1941). Articles about the Pentagon Building are "America's Giant Five-by-Five," *Popular Mechanics*, LXXIX, 8-13 (February 22, 1943); R. E. Lauterbach, "Pentagon Puzzle," *Life*, XIV, 11-13 (February 22, 1943) and H. F. Pringle, "My Thirty Days in the Pentagon Building," *Saturday Evening Post*, CCXVI, 26-27 (October 16, 1943). For facts about gremlins, see "It's Them," *Time*, XL, 37 (September 14, 1942); B. E. Browne, "Lore of the Gremlins," *Christian Science Monitor*, September 19, 1942, and Quentin Reynolds, "What Every Pilot Knows," *Colliers*, CX, 30 (October 31, 1942). Some good books of stories about World War II heroes are: Thomas E. Bradford, *Paul Bunyan in the Army* (Portland, Ore.: Binfords and Mort, 1942); *Pocket Book of War Humor*, ed. B. Cerf (New York: Pocket Books, 1942), and *Tall Tales They Tell in the Services*, ed. Sgt. Bill Davidson (New York: Thomas Y. Crowell Company, 1943).